THE POEMS OF RICHARD HENRY STODDARD

COMPLETE EDITION

When I walk by myself alone
It doth me good my songs to render

OLD PLAY

NEW YORK
CHARLES SCRIBNER'S SONS
1880

Trow's
PRINTING AND BOOKBINDING COMPANY,
201–213 *East 12th Street*,
NEW YORK.

PROEM.

Like one who hath been long in cities pent,
Content with their close neighborhoods, wherein
There is no sight nor sound of the bright world
That God made, slope of hills where cattle feed,
Valleys where rivers glisten, shady woods,
And over all the immeasurable sky,
Through which, with pomp of clouds, the Sun and Moon
Go on their way rejoicing, but, instead,
A low-hung vault of vapor, sullen, dense,
That shuts the day and night out, dull brick walls.
Houses with locked, inhospitable doors,
From out whose narrow windows no one looks,
For what is there to see save noisy streets,
Over whose stony pavements heavy drays
Rumble in dust, and, where the long streets end,
And the dark waves begin, the masts of ships,
The only forestry that cities have?
It happens, or is ordered, that this man
Departs from these some day, and finds himself
Flying by rail through urban villages,
Past cosey cottages, gardens, winding roads,
That lead, be sure, to happy country homes;
Or, sailing up a river, or a Sound,
He sees their ruffled billows come and go,
Dashing in ragged foam against the bow,
And weltering swift astern in a long, white wake

That tumbles, and boils, and bubbles, until at last
It breaks in little ripples on the shore,
Green to the water's edge: before he knows
The sight of this bright river, or this Sound,
The everlasting freedom of their ways,
Whether they journey to the parent Sea,
With messages and prophecies from Land,
Or, drawn from out its depths, return in clouds,
And find their secret springs among the hills,
To straightway journey to the Sea again:
The touch of the cool wind that stirs his hair,
And fans his cheek, and wafts him scent of flowers,
Or the salt savor of the yesty brine;
Before he knows the winds and waves efface
Remembrance of the City from his brain,
And make him Man again: and when he comes
Back to the dear old place where he was born,
And where his childhood passed, the burden of years
Slips suddenly from him, and his heart grows light:
There is a springy motion in his step,
As though the blood was lilting in his veins,
And, if his feet could overtake his thoughts,
(They will,) he would be everywhere at once,
For he is child, and boy, and man at once.
Here is the rustic porch in which he sat,
Here are the garden beds, edged round with box,
Down which he played, and plucked forbidden flowers:
Here is the barn, upon whose seedy floor
He stumbled, and in whose dry, dark mow he hid:
There are the orchard trees he used to climb
For russets, winter greenings; this the path,
Through which, at morn, he loitered, book in hand,
And reached the school-house just as the bell was rung:
And this a short cut to the gnarled oak,
Where he discovered the bird's nest, full of eggs,

Which soon were little, downy, cheeping birds:
And this green lane, whose grassy footpath winds
Through rows of slender beeches, white and tall—
What leaps of heart were his that happy night,
When, after strong persuasions long refused,
And promises made, and broken, came the hour
That she relented, and he walked with her,
Under the soft light of the summer moon
For the first time, and stole his clinging arm
Around her waist, and pressed his lips to hers
For the first time—Was it a dream of bliss,
Too sweet, too deep, too heavenly high to last,
Or the sober certainty of waking life,
The sudden flowering of a double Life,
Foretaste of Heaven in this dark, work-day world?
Like this poor, rich, unhappy, happy man,
Who, when his short-lived season of delight
In the old town where he was born, and where
His happiest hours were spent, is gone, returns
Unwillingly to the City where he dwells,
And where the remnant of his days will end,
Am I, for I have been sojourning late
Among the pleasant places of my Past,
The green and quiet neighborhoods of Thought,
In which I wandered in my wayward youth,
With no companion but the constant Muse,
Who sought me when I needed her—ah when
Did I not need her, solitary else?
I have lived over my dead life with her,
And it hath made me happy for a time,
But left me saddened, for I see, too late,
Both what it was, and what it might have been.
These songs of mine, the best that I have sung,
Are not my best, for caged within the lines
Are thousands better (if they would but sing!)

Silent amid the clamor of their mates.
I know they are imperfect, none so well,
Echoes at first, no doubt, of older songs,
(Not knowingly caught, but echoes all the same,)
Fancies where facts were wanting, or hard facts
Which only fancies made endurable;
I grant, before hand, all the faults they have,
Too deeply rooted to be plucked up now,
And leave them to their fate: content to know
That they sustained me in my dreariest days,
That they consoled me in my darkest nights,
And to believe, now I have done with them,
I may do well enough to win at last
The Laurel I have missed so many years.

R. H. S.

CONTENTS.

EARLY POEMS.

THE CASTLE IN THE AIR.

I.

WE have two lives about us,
Two worlds in which we dwell,
Within us, and without us,
Alternate Heaven and Hell;
Without the sombre Real,
Within our heart of hearts the beautiful Ideal.
I stand between the portals of the two,
Fettered, at birth, with many a heavy chain,
Whose links I strive to sunder, but in vain,
So strong the False that holds me from the True:
Only in dreams my spirit wanders o'er
The golden threshold of that world of bliss,
And lives the life which Fate denies in this,
Which may have once been mine, but will be—nevermore!

II.

My Castle stands alone,
In some delicious clime,
Away from Earth and Time,
In Fancy's tropic zone,
Beneath its summer skies,
Where all the life-long year the Summer never dies.
A stately marble pile, whose pillars rise
From deep-set bases fluted to the dome,

With wreathèd friezes crowned, and rare device
Of carven leaves, like ragged rims of foam.
The spacious windows front the rising sun,
And when its splendor smites them, many-paned,
Tri-arched, and richly stained,
A thousand mornings brighten there as one.
Before the Castle lies a shaven lawn,
Sloping and shining in the dews of dawn,
With turfy terraces, and garden bowers,
Where rows of slender urns are full of flowers.
Oaks overarch the winding avenues,
Edged round with evergreens of fadeless bloom,
And pour a flood of intermingling hues
In green and golden gloom.
Far-seen through twinkling leaves,
The fountains spout aloft like silver sheaves,
Shaking in marble basins, pure and cold,
A drainless, beaded shower of diamond grain,
Which winnows off in sun-illumined rain
A cloud of misty gold.
And swans are floating round the ruffled tide,
Through beds of bowing lilies, chaste and white,
Like royal ladies, beauteous in their pride,
Sweeping amid their maids with trains of light.
A herd of dappled deer, with startled looks,
In quiet parks within whose shade they browse,
Drink from the lucid brooks,
Their antlers mirrored with the tangled boughs.
My rivers flow beyond, with guardant ranks
Of silver-liveried poplars on their banks,
Whereat my barges ride,
With gilden pennons blown from side to side.
Then comes a dreamy range of distant bowers,
With rounded hills, and hollow vales between,
And folded lawns in everlasting green;

And, last, a line of palaces and towers
That lessen on till mountains bar the view,
Shooting their jagged peaks sublimely up the blue.

III.

My chambers lie apart,
The Castle's very heart,
And all things rich and rare,
From land, and sea, and air,
Are lavished, as in dreams, with waste profusion there.
The carpeting was woven in Turkish looms,
From softest fleeces of Circassian sheep,
Tufted like springy moss in forests deep,
Illuminate with all their autumn blooms.
The chairs were carven out of cedar trees,
Felled on the lofty peaks of Lebanon,
Veined with the rings of vanished centuries,
And touched with frost and sun.
Suspended, silver-ringed, on rods of gold,
The Tyrian curtains capture and enfold
The summer daylight in the slumbrous room,
In depths of purple gloom.
Hard by are cabinets of curious shells,
From far Pacific beaches, wreathed and curled,
And some like moons in rainbow mists impearled,
With coral boughs from ocean's deepest cells;
Medallions, coins antique,
Found in the dust of cities, Roman, Greek:
Clusters of arms, the spoils of hateful wars,
Sharp scymetars of true Damascus brand,
Short swords, with basket hilts to guard the hand,
Chain-armor, dinted casques with visor-bars,
Stout jousting lances, battle-axes keen,
With crescent edges, shields with studded thorns,

Yew bows, and shafts, and curvèd bugle horns,
With tasselled baldricks of the Lincoln green.
And on the walls in long procession, see
The portraits of my noble ancestry,
Thin-featured, stately dames with powdered locks,
And courtly shepherdesses tending flocks,
Stiff lords in wigs and ruffles white as snow,
Haught peers and princes centuries ago,
And dark Sir Richard, bravest of the line,
With all the grimly scars he won in Palestine.

IV.

My books may lie and mould,
However rare and old;
I cannot read to-day,
Away with books—away!
Full-fed with sweets of sense,
I sink upon my couch in honeyed indolence.
Here are rich salvers heaped with nectarines,
Blue-misted plums, and clusters fresh from vines;
And here are drinking cups, and long-necked flasks
In wicker mail, and bottles broached from casks
In cellars delvèd deep, and winter cold,
Superlative and old.
What more can I desire? What book can be
As dear as Idleness and Luxury?
Brimming with Helicon I dash the cup;
Why should I waste my years in hoarding up
The thoughts of eld? Let dust to dust return;
No more for me—my heart is not an urn.
I will no longer sip from little flasks,
Covered with damp and mould, when Nature yields
A riper growth from later vintage-fields;
Nor peer at Beauty in her mortal masks,

When I at will may have them all withdrawn,
And feast my eyes on her transfigured face:
Nor limp in fetters in a weary race,
When I may fly unbound, like Mercury's fawn.
No more contented with the sweets of old,
Albeit embalmed in nectar, since the trees,
The Eden bowers, the rich Hesperides,
Still droop around my path with living fruits of gold.

V.

O what a life is mine,
A life of ease and mirth,
The natural life of Earth,
Of light, and flowers, and wine—
What more could I demand—what else is so divine?
When eastern skies, the sea, the misty plain,
Illumined slowly, doff their nightly shrouds,
And Heaven's bright archer Morn begins to rain
His golden arrows through the banded clouds,
I rise, and tramp away the jocund hours,
Knee-deep in dewy grass and meadow flowers.
I race my eager grayhound on the hills,
And climb with bounding feet the craggy steeps,
Peak-lifted, gazing down the cloven deeps
Where mighty rivers shrink to thready rills.
The ramparts of the mountains loom around,
Like splintered fragments of a ruined world:
The cliff-bound dashing cataracts downward hurled
In thunderous volumes shake the chasms profound.
The savage eagle with a dauntless eye
Wheels round the sun, the monarch of the sky:
I pluck his eyrie in the ragged wood
Of blasted pines, and when the vulture screams
I track its flight along the solitude,

Like some dark spirit in the world of dreams.
When evening comes I lie in dreamy rest,
Where lifted casements front the flaming west,
And watch the clouds, like banners wide unfurled
Hanging above the threshold of the world.
The flocks are penned, the fields are growing dim,
The moon comes rounding up the welkin's rim,
Glowing through thinnest mist,—an argent shell
Washed from the caves of darkness on a swell.
One after one the stars begin to shine
In drifted beds, like pearls through shallow brine;
And lo, through clouds that part before the chase
Of silent winds a belt of milky white,
The Galaxy, a crested surge of light,
A reef of worlds along the sea of Space.
I hear my sweet musicians far withdrawn
Below my wreathèd lattice, on the lawn,
With harp, and lute, and lyre,
And passionate voices full of tears and fire,
And emulous nightingales with rich disdain
Filling the pauses of the languid strain:
My soul is tranced and bound,
Drifting along the magic sea of sound,
Driven in a bark of bliss from deep to deep,
And piloted at last into the ports of Sleep.

VI.

Nor only this, though this
Might seal a life of bliss,
But something more divine,
For which I used to pine,
The crown of worlds above,
The heart of every heart, the Soul of Being—Love!
I bow obedient to my Lady's sway,

The sovereignty that won my soul of yore:
I linger in her presence night and day,
And feel a heaven around her evermore.
I sit beside her couch in chambers lone,
And oft unbraid and lay her locks apart;
I take her taper fingers in my own,
And press them to my lips with leaps of heart.
Sometimes I kneel to her with cups of wine,
With pleading eyes, beseeching her to taste,
And when she sips thereof I clasp her waist,
And kiss her budding mouth which answers mine
With long-delaying lips, and shake her curls,
And in her coy despite unloose her zone of pearls!
I live for Love, for Love alone, and who
Dare chide me for it? who dare call it folly?
It is a holy thing, if aught is holy,
And true, if Truth is true.
Then let us seize the hours before they fly;
Bright eyes should answer eyes, red lips should meet,
And hearts enlocked to kindred hearts should beat,
Till all that live on earth in love shall live and die.

VII.

My dear and gentle wife,
The Angel of my life,
Who moves its deepest springs,
Has folded up her wings,
And lies in quiet deep,
Like some immortal Dream upon the couch of Sleep.
Nor sound nor stir profanes her bridal room,
Haunted by Sleep and Silence,—happy pair:
The very light itself muffled in gloom
Steals in, and melts into the enamored air
Where Love doth brood and dream, while Passion dies,

Breathing his soul out in a mist of sighs.
Lo, where she lies behind the curtains white,
Pillowed on clouds of down, her golden hair
Braided and wound around her forehead fair,
Like a celestial diadem of light.
Her sweet, voluptuous lips are drawn apart,
As if to grant the kiss so late denied:
Her snowy breast—its covering brushed aside—
Betrays the slow pulsation of her heart.
The rosy hand, that from my fingers slid,
Beneath the sheets is hid,
(Ah, happy sheets, to hide a hand so sweet!)
Nor all concealed amid their folds of snow
The soft perfection of her shape below,
Rounded, and tapering to her little feet.
O Love, if Beauty ever left her sphere,
And sovereign sisters, Art and Poesy,
Moulded in loveliness she slumbers here,
Incarnate, dear, in thee!
It is thy smile that makes the chamber still,
It is thy breath that fills the odorous air;
The light around is borrowed from thy hair,
And all things else are subject to thy will:
And I am so bewildered by this deep
Ambrosial calm, and drowsy atmosphere,
I know not whether I am dreaming here,
Or in the world of Sleep.

VIII.

My eyes are full of tears,
My heart is full of pain,
To wake, as now, again,
And walk, as in my youth, the wilderness of Years.
No more, no more, the autumn winds are loud

In stormy passes, howling to the Night;
Behind a cloud the moon doth veil her light,
And the rain pours from out the hornèd cloud:
And hark, the solemn and mysterious bell,
Swinging its brazen echoes o'er the wave:
Not mortal hands, but spirits ring the knell,
And toll the parting ghost of Midnight to its grave.

——o——

HYMN TO FLORA.

COME, all ye virgins fair, in kirtles white,
Ye debonair and merry-hearted maids,
Who have been out in troops before the light,
And gathered blossoms in the dewy shades.
The shrine is wreathed with leaves, the holy urns
Brimming with morning dew are laid thereby;
The censers swing, the odorous incense burns,
And floats in misty volumes up the sky.
Lay down your garlands, and your baskets trim,
Heaped up with floral offerings to the brim,
And knit your snowy hands, and trip away
With light and nimble feet,
To music soft and sweet,
And celebrate the joyous break of day,
And sing a hymn to Flora, Queen of May.

O Flora! sweetest Flora, Goddess bright,
Impersonation of selectest things,
The soul and spirit of a thousand Springs,
Bodied in all their loveliness and light,
A delicate creation of the mind,
Fashioned in its divinest, daintiest mould,
In the bright Age of Gold,

Before the world was wholly lost and blind,
But saw and entertained with thankful heart
  The gods as guests—O Flora! Goddess dear,
Immaculate, immortal as thou art,
  Thou wert a maiden once, like any here.
Yes, thou didst tend thy flowers with proper care,
And shield them from the sun, and chilly air,
Wetting thy little sandals through and through,
As is the wont of maids, in morning dew,
Roving among the urns, and mossy pots,
About the hedges, and the garden plots,
Straightening and binding up the drooping stalks
That kissed thy sweeping garments in the walks,
Setting thy dibble deep, and sowing seeds,
And careful-handed plucking out the weeds,
Not more divine than we this vernal morn,
  Till Zephyrus saw thee in the dews of May;
  Flying behind the chariot of the Day,
    With love and grief forlorn,
  Sighing amid the wingèd, laughing Hours,
Pining for something bright which haunted him,
Sleeping on beds of flowers in arbors dim,
Breaking his tender heart with love extreme,
  He saw thee on the earth amid thy flowers,
    The Spirit of his Dream.
Entranced with passionate love he called the Air,
  And melting softly in the sunny South,
Twined his invisible fingers in thy hair,
  And, stooping, kissed thee with his odorous mouth,
And chased thee, flying through thy garden shades,
And wooed, as men are wont to woo the maids,
And won at last, and then flew back to Heaven,
Pleading with Jove, till his consent was given,
And thou wert made immortal,—happy day,
The Goddess of the flowers, the Queen of May.

Happier than we, thy flowers are not like ours,
For thou hast asphodels, unfading flowers,
Where thou dost lie, and dream the hours away,
Lulled by the drowsy sound
Of trees around,
And springs that fall in basins full of spray.
Sweet are thy duties there,
In those bright regions of serener air.
Sometimes to wreathe imperial Juno's tresses,
That cluster round her brow like beams of light;
Or Cytherea's, with bosom bare and white,
Melting to meet Adonis's caresses,
When he lies in his death-sleep, stark and cold;
And oft with Hebe and with Ganymede
Stooping in dews, a task by Jove decreed,
Entwining chaplets round their cups of gold;
And round the necks of Dian's spotted fawns,
Like strings of bells, and Leda's linkèd swans,
That float and sing in Heaven's unwrinkled streams,
Like thoughts in poets' dreams.
And when red Mars, victorious from the field,
Throws down his glittering spear and dinted shield,
Thou dost a-sly with flowery fetters bind him,
And tie his arms behind him,
Smoothing with playful hands his furrowed cheek,
Until, beguiled and meek,
He kisses thee, and laughs with joy aloud.
And when Minerva, lost in Wisdom's cloud,
Muses abstracted in profoundest nooks,
Thou dost unclasp her books,
And press the leaves of flowers within their leaves;
And thou dost bind the same in Ceres' sheaves,
And wreathe Apollo's lyre, and Hermes' rod,
And, venturing near the cloud-compelling God,
Sitting with thought-concentred brows alone,

Bestrew the starry footstool of his throne.
Or, drowsing gloomy Pluto, stern and pale,
  With slumberous poppies plucked in Lethe's bowers,
  Thou givest to Proserpine a bunch of flowers,
Such as she dropped in Enna's bloomy vale,
      That solemn morn in May
      When she was stolen away;
And, pressing it to her white lips in fear,
She kisses thee for that remembrance dear,
And then ye weep together. Softened so,
  When Cytherea knelt down, and plead with thee,
And Death was drugged, she let Adonis go;
  And so gave Orpheus Eurydice.
But ere the darkness fades thou dost up-soar,
And walk the Olympian palaces once more.
And when young Hesper folds the morning star,
  And harnesses the wingèd steeds of Light,
And flushed Aurora urges on her car,
  Chasing the sullen shadows of the Night,
Thou dost with Zephyrus fly in pomp behind,
Shaking thy scarf of rainbows on the wind;
And when the Orient is reached at last,
      Thou dost unbar its gate
        Of golden state,
And wait till she and all her train have passed,
And soar again far up the dappled blue,
To wet the laughing Earth with fresher dew,
As now thou dost, in pomp and triumph gay,
      This happy, happy day,
Thy festival, divinest Queen of May.

O Flora! heavenly Flora, hear us now,
  Gathered to worship thee in shady bowers;
Accept the simple gift, the tuneful vow
  We offer thee, that thou hast spared the flowers.

The Spring has been a cold, belated one,
Dark clouds, and showers, and a little sun,
And in the nipping mornings hoary frost;
We hoped, but feared the tender seeds were lost:
But, thanks to thee, they soon began to grow,
  Pushing their slender shoots above the ground,
  In cultured gardens trim; and some were found
Beside the edges of the banks of snow,
      Heedless, and gay, and bold,
Like children laughing o'er a father's mould.
The sward to-day is full, and swells with more;
Earth never was so bounteous before.
Here are red roses throwing back their hoods,
  Like willing maids, to greet the kissing wind;
And here are violets from sombre woods,
  With tears of dew within their lids enshrined;
Lilies like little maids in bridal white,
  Or in their burial-garments, if you will;
  And here is that bold flower, the daffodil,
That peers i' th' front of March; and daisies bright,
The vestals of the morn that love its breeze;
Snowdrops like specks of foam on stormy seas,
And yellow buttercups that gem the fields,
Like studs of richest gold on massive shields;
Anemones, that sprung in golden years,
  (The story goes they were not seen before,)
  Where young Adonis, wounded by the boar,
Bled life away, and Venus rained her tears;
(Look, in their hearts, a small ensanguined spot!)
      Here is forget-me-not;
And prim Narcissus, vain and foolish elf,
Enamored (would you think it?) of himself,
Looking for ever in the brook, his glass;
And drooping Hyacinthus, slain, alas!
By rudest Auster, blowing in the stead

Of Zephyrus, then in Love's bright meshes bound;
Pitching with bright Apollo in his ground,
He blew the discus back, and struck him dead.
Pied wind-flowers, oxlips, and the jessamine,
The sleepy poppy, and the eglantine;
Primroses, Dian's flowers that ope at night,
Also that little sun the marigold,
And fringèd pinks, and water-lilies white,
Like floating naiads from the rivers cold;
Carnations, gilliflowers, and savory rue,
And rosemary that loveth tears for dew,
With other nameless flowers, and pleasant weeds
That grow untended in the marshy meads
Where flags shoot up, and ragged grasses wave
Perennial, when Autumn seeks her grave
Among the withered leaves, and breezes blow,
And Winter weaves a winding-sheet of snow.
Flowers, O, what loveliness there is in flowers!
What food for thoughts and fancies rich and new!
What shall we liken them to,
In this broad world of ours?
Mosaics scattered o'er
Creation's palace-floor;
Or Beauty's dials marking with their leaves
The pomp and flight of golden morns and eves;
Illuminate missals open on the meads,
Bending with rosaries of dewy beads;
Or characters inscribed on Nature's scrolls;
Or sweet thoughts from the heart of Mother Earth;
Or wind-rocked cradles, where the bees in rolls
Of odorous leaves are wont to lie in mirth,
Full-hearted, murmuring the hours away,
Like little children at their summer play;
Or cups and beakers of the butterflies
Brimming with nectar; or a string of bells,

Tolling, unheard, a requiem for the Hours;
Or censers swinging incense to the skies;
Pavilions, tents, and towers,
The little fortresses of insect powers
Who wind their horns within; or magic cells
Where happy fairies dream the time away,
Night elfins slumbering all the summer day,
Sweet nurslings thou art wont to feed with dew
From silver urns, replenished in the blue!
But this is idlesse all, away, away!
White-handed maids, and scatter buds around;
And let the lutes awake, and tabors sound,
And every heart its just devotion pay.
Once more we thank thee, Flora, and once more
Perform our rites as we are wont to do;
O, smile upon us, Goddess fair and true,
And watch the flowers till summer's reign is o'er;
Preserve the seeds we sow in winter-time
From burrowing moles, and blight, and icy rime,
And in their season cause the shoots to rise,
And make the dainty buds unseal their eyes;
And we will pluck the rarest, and entwine
Chaplets, and lay them on thy rural shrine,
And sing our choral hymns, melodious, sweet,
And dance with nimble feet,
And worship thee, as now, serene and gay,
The joy of all the world, the merry Queen of May!

ODE.

PALE in her fading bowers the Summer stands,
Like a new Niobe with claspèd hands,
Silent above the flowers, her children lost,
Slain by the arrows of the early frost.
The clouded Heaven above is pale and gray,
  The misty Earth below is wan and drear,
The baying Winds chase all the leaves away,
  As cruel hounds pursue the trembling deer;
It is a solemn time, the Sunset of the Year.

If I should perish with it none would miss
An idle dreamer in a world like this.
Whate'er our beauty, worth, or loving powers,
  We live, we strive, we die, and are forgot;
We are no more regarded than the flowers,
  Short life, and long, long darkness is our lot.
One bud from off the tree of Life is naught,
One fruit from off the ripening bough of Thought;
The hinds will not lament, in harvest-time,
The bud, the fruit that fell and wasted in its prime.

Away with Action, and Laborious Life,
    They were not made for man,
      In Nature's plan.
For man was made or quiet, not for strife.
The pearl is shaped serenely in its shell
  In the still waters of the ocean deep;
The buried seed begins to pulp and swell
  In Earth's warm bosom in profoundest sleep,
And, sweeter far than all, the bridal rose
Flushes to fulness in a soft repose.

Let others gather honey in the world,
  And hoard it in their cells until they die;
    I am content to lie,
    Sipping, in summer hours,
    My wants from fading flowers,
An Epicurean till my wings are furled!

What happy hours, what happy, happy days
  Were mine when I was young, a careless boy,
  Oblivious of the world, its woe or joy,
I lived for Song, and dreamed of budding bays.
I thought when I was dead, if not before,
  (I hoped before,) to have a noble name,
To leave my eager footprints on the shore,
  To rear my statue in the halls of Fame.
I pondered over Poets dead of old,
  Their memories living in the minds of men;
I knew they were but men of mortal mould,
  They won their crowns, and I might win again.
I drank delicious vintage from their pages,
Flasks of Parnassian nectar, stored for ages;
My soul was flushed within me, maddened, fired,
I leaped impassioned, like a seer inspired.
I lived and would have died for Poesy,
  In youth's divine emotion:
  A stream that sought its Ocean,
    A Time that longed to be
Engulfed and swallowed in Eternity.

O Poesy! my spirit's crownèd Queen,
I would that thou couldst in the flesh be seen,
The shape of light and loveliness thou art
Enshrined within the chambers of my heart.
I would build thee a palace, richer far
  Than princely Aladeen's renowned of old,

With walls and columns all of massy gold,
And every gem incrusting it a star.
Thy coffers should overflow, and mock the Ind,
Whose boasted wealth would dwindle down to naught,
The rich-ored driftings of the streams of Thought,
Washed lucidly from cloven peaks of Mind.
And I would bring to thee the daintiest things
That grow beneath the summer of thy wings;
Wine from the glorious vineyards of the Greek,
Brimming in cups antique;
The luscious fruitage of enchanted trees,
From magic orchard plots with charmèd gates;
And golden apples of the Hesperides,
Stolen by Fancy from the watchful Fates.
And I would hang around thee day and night,
Nor ever heed or know the night from day:
If Time had wings I should not see his flight,
Or feel his shadow in my sunny way.
Forgetful of the world, I'd stand apart,
And gaze on thee unseen, and touch my lute,
A perfect type and image of my heart,
Whose trembling chords will never more be mute;
And Joy and Grief would mingle in my theme,
A swan and shadow floating down the stream.
And when, forgetful of thy heavenly birth,
It pleases thee to walk the common earth,
In brave array I marshal thee around,
With pomp and music sweet,
And spread my shining mantle on the ground,
For fear the dust should soil thy golden-sandalled feet.

Away, away! The days are dim and cold,
The withered flowers are crumbling in the mould;
The Heaven is gray and blank, the Earth is drear,
And fallen leaves are heaped on Summer's bier,

Sweet songs are out of place, however sweet,
When all things else are wrapt in funeral gloom;
True Poets never pipe to dancing feet,
But only elegies around a tomb.
Away with fancy now! The Year demands
A sterner chaplet, and a deeper lay;
A wreath of cypress woven with pious hands,
A dirge for its decay!

——o——

LEONATUS.

The fair boy Leonatus,
The page of Imogen.
It was his duty evermore
To tend the Lady Imogen;
By peep of day he might be seen
Tapping against her chamber door,
To wake the sleepy waiting-maid,
Who rose, and when she had arrayed
The Princess, and the twain had prayed,
(With pearlèd rosaries used of yore,)
They called him, pacing to and fro,
And, cap in hand, and bowing low,
He entered, and began to feed
The singing birds with fruit and seed.

The brave boy Leonatus,
The page of Imogen.
He tripped along the kingly hall,
From room to room, with messages;
He stopped the butler, clutched his keys,
(Albeit he was broad and tall,)
And dragged him down the vaults, where wine

In bins lay beaded and divine,
To pick a flask of vintage fine;
Came up, and clomb the garden wall,
And plucked from out the sunny spots
Peaches and luscious apricots,
And filled his golden salver there,
And hurried to his Lady fair.

The strange boy Leonatus,
The page of Imogen.
Sometimes he used to stand for hours
Within her room, behind her chair;
The soft wind blew his golden hair
Across his eyes, and bees from flowers
Hummed round him, but he did not stir:
He fixed his earnest eyes on her,
A pure and reverent worshipper,
A dreamer building airy towers.
But when she spoke he gave a start,
That sent the warm blood from his heart
To flush his cheeks, and every word
The fountain of his feelings stirred.

The sad boy Leonatus,
The page of Imogen.
He lost all relish and delight
For all things that did please before;
By day he wished the day was o'er,
By night he wished the same of night:
He could not mingle in the crowd,
He loved to be alone, and shroud
His tender thoughts, and sigh aloud,
And cherish in his heart its blight.
At last his health began to fail,
His fresh and glowing cheeks to pale,

And in his eyes the tears unshed
Did hang like dew in violets dead.

The timid Leonatus,
The page of Imogen.
"What ails the boy?" said Imogen.
He stammered, sighed, and answered "Naught."
She shook her head, and then she thought
What all his malady could mean.
It might be love, her maid was fair,
And Leon had a loving air;
She watched them with a jealous care,
And played the spy, but naught was seen.
And then she was aware at first,
That she, not knowing it, had nursed
His memory till it grew a part,
Another heart within her heart!

The dear boy Leonatus,
The page of Imogen.
She loved, but owned it not as yet.
When he was absent she was lone,
She felt a void before unknown,
But Leon filled it when they met.
She called him twenty times a day,
She knew not why, she could not say;
She fretted when he went away,
And lived in sorrow and regret.
Sometimes she frowned with stately mien,
And chid him like a little queen;
And then she soothed him meek and mild,
And grew as trustful as a child.

The neat scribe Leonatus,
The page of Imogen.

She wondered that he did not speak,
  And own his love, if love indeed
  It was that made his spirit bleed;
And she bethought her of a freak
  To test the lad; she bade him write
  A letter that a maiden might,
  A billet to her heart's delight.
He took the pen with fingers weak,
  Unknowing what he did, and wrote,
  And folded up, and sealed the note.
  She wrote the superscription sage,
  "For Leonatus, Lady's Page."

The happy Leonatus,
The page of Imogen.
The page of Imogen no more,
  But now her love, her lord, her life,
  For she became his wedded wife,
As both had hoped and dreamed before.
  He used to sit beside her feet,
  And read romances strange and sweet,
  And when she touched her lute repeat
Impassioned madrigals of yore,
  Uplooking in her face the while,
  Until she stooped with loving smile,
  And pressed her melting mouth to his,
  That answered in a dreamy bliss—
The joyful Leonatus,
The Lord of Imogen.

SPRING.

THE trumpet winds have sounded a retreat,
  Blowing o'er land and sea a sullen strain;
  Usurping March, defeated, flies again,
And lays his trophies at the Winter's feet.
And lo, where April, coming in his turn,
  In changeful motleys, half of light and shade,
  Leads his belated charge, a delicate maid,
    A nymph with dripping urn.

Hail, hail, thrice hail! thou fairest child of Time,
  With all thy retinue of laughing Hours,
Thou paragon from some diviner clime,
  Bright ministrant of its benignest Powers,
Who hath not caught the glancing of thy wing,
And peeped beneath thy mask, delicious Spring?
Sometimes we see thee on the pleasant morns
  Of lingering March, with wreathèd crook of gold,
  Leading the Ram from out his starry fold,
A leash of light around his jagged horns.
Sometimes in April, goading up the skies
The Bull, whose neck Apollo's silvery flies
Settle upon, a many-twinkling swarm;
  And when May-days are warm,
  And drawing to a close,
      And Flora goes
With Zephyrus from his palace in the west,
Thou dost upsnatch the Twins from cradled rest,
    And strain them to thy breast,
And haste to meet the expectant, bright new-comer,
The opulent Queen of Earth, the gay, voluptuous Summer!

Unmuffled now, shorn of thy veil of showers,
Thou tripp'st along the mead with shining hair
Blown back, and scarf out-fluttering on the air,
White-handed, strewing the fresh sward with flowers.
The green hills lift their foreheads far away,
But where thy pathway runs the sod is pressed
By fleecy lambs, behind the budding spray,
And close at hand the marten builds his nest.
The forest waves its plumes, the hedges blow,
The south wind scuds along the meadowy sea
Thick-flecked with daisied foam, and violets grow
Blue-eyed, and cowslips star the bloomy lea.
The snake casts off his skin in mossy nooks,
The long-eared rabbits near their burrows play,
The dormouse wakes, and see, the noisy rooks
Sly foraging about the stacks of hay.

What sights, what sounds, what rustic life and mirth!
Housed all the winter long from bitter cold,
Huddling in chimney-corners, young and old
Come forth and share the gladness of the Earth.
The ploughmen whistle as the furrows trail
Behind their glittering shares, a billowy row;
The milkmaid sings a ditty while her pail
Grows full and frothy, and the cattle low.
The teamster drives his wagon down the lane,
Flattening a broader rut in weeds and sand;
The angler fishes in the shady pool;
And loitering down the road, with cap in hand,
The truant chases butterflies, in vain,
Heedless of bells that call the village lads to school.

Methinks the world is sweeter than of yore,
Sweeter to-day, and more exceeding fair;

There is a presence never felt before,
  The soul of inspiration everywhere.
Incarnate Youth in every idle limb,
  My vernal days, my prime returns anew;
My happy spirit breathes a silent hymn,
    My heart is full of dew.

——o——

AUTUMN.

DIVINEST Autumn! who may paint thee best,
  For ever changeful o'er the changeful globe?
Who guess thy certain crown, thy favorite crest,
  The fashion of thy many-colored robe?
Sometimes we see thee stretched upon the ground,
  In fading woods where acorns patter fast,
Dropping to feed thy tusky boars around,
  Crunching among the leaves the ripened mast;
Sometimes at work where ancient granary-floors
  Are open wide, a thresher stout and hale,
  Whitened with chaff up-wafted from thy flail
While south winds sweep along the dusty floors;
And sometimes fast asleep at noontide hours,
  Pillowed on sheaves, and shaded from the heat,
    With Plenty at thy feet,
Braiding a coronet of oaten straw and flowers.

What time emerging from a low-hung cloud
  The shining chariot of the Sun was driven
Slope to its goal, and Day in reverence bowed
  His burning forehead at the gate of Heaven,
Thy portly presence was to me revealed,
Slow trudging homeward in a stubble-field;
Around thy brow, to shade it from the west,
  A wisp of straw entwisted in a crown;

A golden wheat-sheaf, slipping slowly down,
Hugged tight against thy waist, and on thy breast,
Linked to a belt, an earthen flagon swung;
Over thy shoulder flung
A bundle of great pears,
Bell-shaped and streaky, some rich orchard's pride;
A heavy bunch of grapes on either side,
Across each arm, tugged downward by the load,
Their glossy leaves blown off by wandering airs;
A yellow-rinded melon in thy right
In thy left hand a sickle caught the light,
Keen as the moon which glowed
Along the fields of night:
One moment seen, the shadowy masque was flown,
And I was left, as now, to meditate alone.

Hark, hark, I hear the reapers in a row,
Shouting their harvest ditties blithe and loud,
Cutting the rustled maize, whose crests are bowed,
And soon will be laid low;
And down the pastures, where the horse goes round
His ring of tan, beneath the mossy shed,
And cider-presses work with creaky din,
I see great heaps of apples on the ground,
And hour by hour, a basket on his head,
The ploughman pour them in;
And where the squashes stud the garden vine,
Crook-necked, or globy, golden, wagons wait,
Soon to be urged o'erloaded to the gate
Where drying apples on the stages shine.
And children soon will go at eve and morn
And set their snares for quails with baits of corn;
And when the house-dog snuffs a distant hare
Will overrun the woods with noisy glee;
And when the walnuts ripen, climb a tree,

And shake the branches bare.
And by and by, when northern winds are out,
Great back-log fires will blaze and roar at night,
While chairs draw round, and pleasant tales are told:
And mugs of cider will be passed about,
Until the household, drowsy with delight,
Creep off to bed a-cold!

——o——

THE WITCH'S WHELP.

ALONG the shore the slimy brine-pits yawn,
Covered with thick green scum; the billows rise,
And fill them to the brim with clouded foam,
And then subside, and leave the scum again.
The ribbèd sand is full of hollow gulfs,
Where monsters from the waters come and lie.
Great serpents bask at noon along the rocks,
To me no terror; coil on coil they roll
Back to their holes before my flying feet.
The Dragon of the Sea, my mother's god,
Enormous Setebos, comes here to sleep;
Him I molest not; when he flaps his wing
A whirlwind rises, when he swims the deep
It threatens to engulf the trembling isle.
Sometimes when winds do blow, and clouds are dark,
I seek the blasted wood whose barkless trunks
Are bleached with summer suns; the creaking trees
Stoop down to me, and swing me right and left
Through crashing limbs, but not a jot care I.
The thunder breaks above, and in their lairs
The panthers roar; from out the stormy clouds
Whose hearts are fire sharp lightnings rain around
And split the oaks; not faster lizards run

Before the snake up the slant trunks than I,
Not faster down, sliding with hands and feet.
I stamp upon the ground, and adders rouse,
Sharp-eyed, with poisonous fangs; beneath the leaves
They couch, or under rocks, and roots of trees
Felled by the winds; through briery undergrowth
They slide with hissing tongues, beneath my feet
To writhe, or in my fingers squeezed to death.
There is a wild and solitary pine,
Deep in the meadows; all the island birds
From far and near fly there, and learn new songs.
Something imprisoned in its wrinkled bark
Wails for its freedom; when the bigger light
Burns in mid-heaven, and dew elsewhere is dried,
There it still falls; the quivering leaves are tongues,
And load the air with syllables of woe.
One day I thrust my spear within a cleft
No wider than its point, and something shrieked,
And falling cones did pelt me sharp as hail:
I picked the seeds that grew between their plates,
And strung them round my neck with sea-mew eggs.
Hard by are swamps and marshes, reedy fens
Knee deep in water; monsters wade therein
Thick-set with plated scales; sometimes in troops
They crawl on slippery banks; sometimes they lash
The sluggish waves among themselves at war.
Often I heave great rocks from off the crags,
And crush their bones; often I push my spear
Deep in their drowsy eyes, at which they howl
And chase me inland; then I mount their humps
And prick them back again, unwieldy, slow.
At night the wolves are howling round the place,
And bats sail there athwart the silver light,
Flapping their wings; by day in hollow trees
They hide, and slink into the gloom of dens.

We live, my mother Sycorax and I,
In caves with bloated toads and crested snakes.
She can make charms, and philters, and brew storms,
And call the great Sea Dragon from his deeps.
Nothing of this know I, nor care to know.
Give me the milk of goats in gourds or shells,
The flesh of birds and fish, berries and fruit,
Nor want I more, save all day long to lie,
And hear, as now, the voices of the sea.

HYMN TO THE BEAUTIFUL.

My heart is full of tenderness and tears,
And tears are in my eyes, I know not why,
With all my grief content to live for years,
Or even this hour to die.
My youth is gone, but that I heed not now,
My love is dead, or worse than dead can be,
My friends drop off, like blossoms from a bough,
But nothing troubles me,—
Only the golden flush of sunset lies
Within my heart like fire, like dew within my eyes.

Spirit of Beauty! whatsoe'er thou art,
I see thy skirt afar, and feel thy power;
It is thy presence fills this charmèd hour,
And fills my charmèd heart:
Nor mine alone, but myriads feel thee now,
That know not what they feel, nor why they bow.
Thou canst not be forgot,
For all men worship thee, and know it not;
Nor men alone, but babes with wondrous eyes,
New-comers from the skies.

We hold the keys of Heaven within our hands,
The heirloom of a higher, happier state,
And lie in infancy at Heaven's gate,
Transfigured in the light that streams along the lands.
Around our pillows golden ladders rise,
And up and down the skies,
With wingèd sandals shod,
The angels come and go, the Messengers of God.
Nor, though they fade from us, do they depart—
It is the childly heart:
We walk as heretofore,
Adown their shining ranks, but see them nevermore.
Heaven is not gone, but we are blind with tears,
Groping our way along the downward slope of Years!

From earliest infancy my heart was thine,
With childish feet I trod thy temple aisles;
Not knowing tears, I worshipped thee with smiles,
Or if I wept it was with joy divine.
By day, and night, on land, and sea, and air,
I saw thee everywhere.
A voice of greeting from the wind was sent,
The mists enfolded me with soft white arms,
The birds did sing to lap me in content,
The rivers wove their charms,
And every little daisy in the grass
Did look up in my face, and smile to see me pass.

Not long can Nature satisfy the mind,
Nor outward fancies feed its inner flame;
We feel a growing want we cannot name,
And long for something sweet, but undefined.
The wants of Beauty other wants create,
Which overflow on others, soon or late;

For all that worship thee must ease the heart,
By Love, or Song, or Art.
Divinest Melancholy walks with thee,
And Music with her sister Poesy;
But on thy breast Love lies, immortal child,
Begot of thine own longings, deep and wild;
The more we worship him the more we grow
Into thy perfect image here below;
For here below, as in the spheres above,
All Love is Beauty, and all Beauty—Love!
Not from the things around us do we draw
The love within, within the love is born,
Remembered light of some forgotten morn,
Recovered canons of eternal law.
The painter's picture, the rapt poet's song,
The sculptor's statue, never saw the Day—
Were never in colors, sounds, or shapes of clay,
Whose crowning work still does its spirit wrong.
Hue after hue divinest pictures grow,
Line after line immortal songs arise,
And limb by limb, out-starting stern and slow,
The statue wakes with wonder in its eyes:
And in the Master's mind
Sound after sound is born, and dies like wind,
That echoes through a range of ocean caves,
And straight is gone to weave its spell upon the waves.
The mystery is thine,
For thine the more mysterious human heart,
The Temple of all Wisdom, Beauty's Shrine,
The Oracle of Art!

Earth in thine outer court, and Life a breath.
Why should we fear to die, and leave the Earth?
Not thine alone the lesser key of Birth,
But all the keys of Death.

And all the worlds, with all that they contain
  Of Life, and Death, and Time, are thine alone;
The Universe is girdled with a chain,
    And hung below the Throne
Where Thou dost sit, the Universe to bless,
Thou sovereign Smile of God, Eternal Loveliness!

TO A CELEBRATED SINGER.

OFT have I dreamed of music such as thine,
  The wedded melody of lute and voice,
  Immortal strains that made my soul rejoice,
And woke its inner harmonies divine.
And where Sicilia smooths the ruffled seas,
  And Enna hollows all its purple vales,
  Thrice have I heard the noble nightingales,
All night entranced beneath the bloomy trees.
But music, nightingales, and all that Thought
    Conceives of song are naught
To thy rich voice, which echoes in my brain,
And fills my longing heart with a melodious pain!

A thousand lamps were lit, I saw them not,
  Nor saw the thousands round me like a sea;
All things, all thoughts, all passions were forgot—
    I only thought of thee!
Meanwhile the music rose sublime and strong,
  But sunk beneath thy voice, which rose alone,
  Above its crumbled fragments to thy throne,
    Above the clouds of Song.
Henceforth let Music seal her lips, and be
The silent ministrant of Poesy.
For not the delicate reed that Pan did play

To partial Midas, at the match of old,
Nor yet Apollo's lyre with chords of gold,
That more than won the crown he lost that day,
Nor even the Orphean lute, that half set free
(O, why not all!) the lost Eurydice,
Were fit to join with thee;
Much less our instruments of meaner sound,
That track thee slowly o'er enchanted ground,
Unfit to lift the train thy music leaves,
Or glean around its sheaves.

I strive to disentangle in my mind
Thy many-knotted threads of softest song,
Whose memory haunts me like a voiceless wind
Whose silence does it wrong.
No single tone thereof, no perfect sound,
Lingers, but dim remembrance of the whole,
A sound which was a Soul,
The Soul of Sound diffused, an atmosphere around:
So soft, so sweet, so mellow, rich, and deep,
So like a heavenly soul's ambrosial breath,
It would not wake, but only deepen Sleep
Into diviner Death!
Softer and sweeter than the jealous flute,
Whose soft, sweet voice grew harsh before its own,
It stole in mockery its every tone,
And left it lone and mute.
It flowed like liquid pearl through golden cells,
It jangled like a string of golden bells,
It trembled like a wind in golden strings,
It dropped and rolled away in golden rings:
Then it divided and became a shout,
That Echo chased about,
However wild and fleet,
Until it trod upon its heels with flying feet.

At last it sank and sank from deep to deep,
Below the thinnest word,
And sank till naught was heard
But charmèd Silence sighing in its sleep!

Powerless and mute beneath thy mighty spell,
My heart was lost within itself and thee,
As when a pearl is melted in its shell,
And sunken in the sea.
I sank and sank beneath thy song, but still
I thirsted after more the more I sank,
A flower that drooped with all the dew it drank,
But still upheld its cup for Heaven to fill.
My inmost soul was drunk with melody,
Which thou didst pour around,
To crown the feast of sound,
And lift in light to all, but chief to me,
Whose spirit, uncontrolled,
Drained all the fiery wine, and clutched its cup of gold!

——o——

ARCADIAN IDYL.

WALKING at dew-fall yester-eve I met
The shepherd Lycidas adown the vale.
"What ho, my piping wonder!" I exclaimed,
Seeing his eyes were bent upon the ground,
Counting the pebbles, lost it seemed in thought.
"What cheer, dear Lycid? Why are you so wrapt?
Has Galatea, white-handed maid, been false?
Or have the Muses quite forsaken you?"
"O, no, Theocritus," he said with smiles,
"White-handed Galatea has not been false,
Nor have the Muses yet forsaken me.

You know my friend, the man I love so much,
The Spartan Poet, brave and beautiful,
I have been crooning over to myself
A song about his singing and my own."
"O, let me hear it," I replied with glee,
"Fresh from your brain, with all its fire and faults;
There 's nothing like a poet's first rude draft.
Go on, go on," said I. And he began.

"Great is Apollo with his golden shell,
The gift of Hermes in his infancy,
And great is Hermes' self, light-fingered god:
But greater far than both illustrious Pan,
Who taught the shepherd swains of Thessaly
The cunning and the wonder of his pipe.
Hear me, great Pan! O, let thy spirit breathe
From out these oaten stops, and I will pile
Three square stones, altar-wise, and offer up
A lamb to thee, the firstling of my flock.

We love in others what we lack ourselves,
And would be every thing but what we are.
The vine uplifts its trailing parasites,
And clasps the great arms of the stooping oak,
Till both are wedded with a thousand rings.
I have a friend as different from myself
As Hercules from Hylas, his delight.
True Poets both, but he by far the best.
His songs are full of nobleness and power,
Magnificent as when the Ocean chants
White-haired in echoing caverns; mine are low
As Spring's first airs, and delicate as buds.
He loves the rugged mountains, stern and wild,
Lifting their summits in the blank of dawn
Crested with surging pines, the wild, waste seas

That urge their heavy waves on rocky crags,
And the unmeasured vastness of the sky,
With all its stars, intense, and white, and cold.
But I am soft and gentle as a fawn
That licks the hand that feeds it; or the dove
That nestles in the breast of Cytherea.
My heart is full of sweetness like a rose,
And delicate melodies like vernal bees
Hum to themselves within its folded leaves.
I would be Pleasure's Poet till I died,
And die at last upon her burning heart.
But he, selected for his majesty,
To Wisdom turns, and worships her afar,
Awed by her calm, large eyes, and spacious brow.
And yet, in sooth, his heart is soft enough
With all its strength, enthroned in loveliness
Like Etna looming from its base of flowers.
And he will wed his love ere Summer dies,
While I must live a pensive bachelor,
A state I am not fond of,—no, by Jove.
But never mind it, I will still sing on,
And be the ablest nightingale I can,
And he may be the eagle if he will.
I cannot follow him, I know right well,
None half so well; but I will watch his flight,
And love him, though he leave me for the stars."

Thus sang the shepherd Lycidas to me,
And when the sickle of the Moon was drawn
From out its sheaf of clouds, and Hesper lit
His harvest torch, we parted for the night.

THE SOUTH.

FALL, thickly fall, thou winter snow!
  And keenly blow, thou winter wind!
Only the barren North is yours,
  The South delights a summer mind;
    So fall and blow,
    Both wind and snow,
My Fancy to the South doth go.

Half-way between the frozen zones,
  Where Winter reigns in sullen mirth,
The Summer binds a golden belt
  About the middle of the Earth.
The sky is soft, and blue, and bright,
With purple dyes at morn and night;
And bright and blue the seas which lie
In perfect rest, and glass the sky.
And sunny bays with inland curves
  Round all along the quiet shore;
And stately palms in pillared ranks
Grow down the borders of the banks,
  And juts of land where billows roar.
The spicy woods are full of birds,
  And golden fruits and crimson flowers;
With wreathèd vines on every bough,
  That shed their grapes in purple showers.
The emerald meadows roll their waves,
  And bask in soft and mellow light;
The vales are full of silver mist,
  And all the folded hills are bright.
But far along the welkin's rim
The purple crags and peaks are dim;

And dim the gulfs, and gorges blue,
With all the wooded passes deep;
All steeped in haze, and washed in dew,
And bathed in atmospheres of Sleep.

Sometimes the dusky islanders
Lie all day long beneath the trees,
And watch the white clouds in the sky,
And birds upon the azure seas.
Sometimes they wrestle on the turf,
And chase each other down the sands,
And sometimes climb the bloomy groves,
And pluck the fruit with idle hands.
And dark-eyed maidens braid their hair
With starry shells, and buds, and leaves,
And sing wild songs in dreamy bowers,
And dance on dewy eves,
When daylight melts, and stars are few,
And west winds frame a drowsy tune,
Till all the charmèd waters sleep
Beneath a yellow moon.

Here men may dwell, and mock at toil,
And all the dull, mechanic arts;
No need to till the teeming soil,
With weary hands and aching hearts.
No want can follow folded palms,
For Nature doth supply her alms
With sweets, purveyors cannot bring
To grace the table of a King;
While Summer broods o'er land and sea,
And breathes in all the winds,
Until her presence fills their hearts,
And moulds their happy minds.

TRIUMPHANT MUSIC.

AY, give me music! Flood the air with sound!
  But let it be superb, and brave, and high,
Not such as leaves my wild ambition bound
  In soft delights, but lifts it to the sky.
No sighs, nor tears, but deep, indignant calm,
  And scorn of all but strength, my only need;
  From whence but Music should my strength proceed?
    From some Titanic psalm?
Some thunderous strand of sound, which in its roll
Shall lift to starry heights my fiery soul!

Strike on the noisy drum, and let the fife
  Scream like a tortured soul in pain intense,
But let the trumpet brood above their strife,
  Victorious in its calm magnificence.
Nor fear to wake again the golden lute,
  That runs along my quivering nerves like fire;
  Nor let the silver-chorded lyre be mute,
    But bring the tender lyre,
For sweetness with all strength should wedded be,
But bring the strength, the sweetness dwells in me!

Play on! play on! The strain is fit to feed
  A feast of Gods, in banquet-halls divine;
Not one would taste the cups of Ganymede,
  But only drink this more ambrosial wine!
Play on! play on! The secret Soul of Sound
  Unfolds itself at every cunning turn;
  The trumpet lifts its shield, a stormy round,
    The lute its dewy urn,

But in the lyre, the wild and passionate lyre,
Lies all its might, its madness and desire!

Again! again! And let the rattling drum
  Begin to roll, and let the bugle blow,
Like winter winds, when woods are stark and dumb,
  Shouting above a wilderness of snow.
Pour hail and lightning from the fife and lyre,
  And let the trumpet pile its clouds of doom;
  But I o'ertop them with a darker plume,
      And beat my wings of fire;
Not like a struggling eagle baffled there,
But like a Spirit on a throne of air!

In vain! in vain! We only soar to sink,
  Though Music gives us wings, we sink at last;
The peaks of rapture topple near the brink
  Of Death, or Madness pallid and aghast.
But still play on, you rapt musicians, play!
  But now a softer and serener strain;
  Give me a dying fall, that lives again,
      Again to die away.
Play on! but softly till my breath grows deep,
And Music leaves me in the arms of Sleep!

——o——

A HOUSEHOLD DIRGE.

I'VE lost my little May at last,
  She perished in the spring,
When earliest flowers began to bud,
  And earliest birds to sing.
I laid her in a country grave,
  A green and still retreat,

A marble tablet o'er her head,
And violets at her feet.

I would that she were back again,
In all her childish bloom;
My joy and hope have followed her,
My heart is in her tomb.
I know that she is gone from me,
I know that she is fled,
I miss her everywhere, and yet
I cannot think her dead.

I wake the children up at dawn,
And say a simple prayer,
And draw them round the morning meal,
But one is wanting there.
I see a little chair apart,
A little pinafore,
And Memory fills the vacancy,
As Time will—nevermore!

I sit within my quiet room,
And think and write for hours,
And miss the little maid again
Among the window flowers,
And miss her with her toys beside
My desk in silent play;
And then I turn and look for her—
But she has flown away.

I drop my idle pen, and hark,
And catch the faintest sound:
She must be playing hide-and-seek
In shady nooks around;

She'll come and climb my chair again,
  And peep my shoulder o'er;
I hear a stifled laugh,—but no,
  She cometh nevermore!

I waited only yester-night,
  The evening-service read,
And lingered for my idol's kiss
  Before she went to bed;
Forgetting she had gone before,
  In slumbers soft and sweet,
A monument above her head,
  And violets at her feet.

——o——

How are songs begot and bred?
How do golden measures flow?
From the heart, or from the head?
Happy Poet, let me know.

Tell me first how folded flowers
Bud and bloom in vernal bowers;
How the south wind shapes its tune,
  The harper, he, of June.

None may answer, none may know,
Winds and flowers come and go,
And the selfsame canons bind
Nature and the Poet's mind.

SILENT SONGS.

IF I could ever sing the songs
Within me day and night,
The only fit accompaniment
Would be a lute of light.

A thousand dreamy melodies,
Begot with pleasant pain,
Like incantations float around
The chambers of my brain.

But when I strive to utter one,
It mocks my feeble art,
And leaves me silent, with the thorns
Of Music in my heart!

——o——

THERE 'S a new grave in the old churchyard,
Another mound in the snow,
And a maid whose soul is whiter far
Sleeps in her shroud below.

The winds of March are piping loud,
The snow comes down for hours;
But by and by the April rain
Will bring the sweet May flowers.

The sweet May flowers will deck the mound
Greened in the April rain;
But blight will lie on our memories,
And our tears will fall in vain.

SONG.

WE love in youth, and plight our vows
  To love till life departs;
Forgetful of the flight of time,
  The change of loving hearts.

To-day departs, to-morrow comes,
  Nor finds a weed away;
But no to-morrow finds a man
  The man he was to-day.

Then weep no more when love decays,
  For even hate is vain;
Since every heart that hates to-day,
  To-morrow loves again.

—o—

SONG.

YOU know the old Hidalgo,
  (His box is next to ours,)
Who threw the Prima Donna
  The wreath of orange-flowers:
He owns the half of Aragon,
  With mines beyond the main;
A very ancient nobleman,
  And gentleman of Spain.

They swear that I must wed him,
  In spite of yea or nay,
Though uglier than the Scaramouch,
  The spectre in the play;

But I will sooner die a maid
  Than wear a gilded chain,
For all the ancient noblemen
  And gentlemen of Spain!

——o——

SONG.

THE walls of Cadiz front the shore,
  And shimmer on the sea:
Her merry maids are beautiful,
  But light as light can be.

They drop me billets through the post,
  They meet me in the square,
They even follow me to mass,
  And lift their veils at prayer.

But all their smiles and wanton arts
  Are thrown away on me:
My heart is now an English girl's,
  And she is o'er the sea.

My English love is o'er the sea,
  But ere a month is flown,
The Spanish maids will be as far,
  And she will be my own.

——o——

THE TWO BRIDES.

I SAW two maids at the kirk,
  And both were fair and sweet:
One in her wedding robe,
  And one in her winding-sheet.

The choristers sang the hymn,
  The sacred rites were read,
And one for life to Life,
  And one to Death was wed.

They were borne to their bridal beds,
  In loveliness and bloom;
One in a merry castle,
  And one in a solemn tomb.

One on the morrow woke
  In a world of sin and pain;
But the other was happier far,
  And never awoke again.

——o——

I SYMPATHIZE with all thy grief,
  As though it were my own and more,
  For all my loving days are o'er,
While thine still last, though dark and brief.

If any prayer of mine could save
  The well-belovèd from her fate,
  I would not cease to storm the gate
Of Heaven till Mercy shut her grave.

But prayers on prayers are all in vain,
  The destiny of man is fixed,
  The bitter cups of Death are mixed,
And we must drink, and drink again.

All words are idle: words from me—
  Are doubly so: my soul for years
  Has used no other speech than tears:
But these I freely offer thee.

A SERENADE.

THE moon is muffled in a cloud,
  That folds the lover's star,
But still beneath thy balcony
  I touch my soft guitar.

If thou art waking, Lady dear,
  The fairest in the land,
Unbar thy wreathèd lattice now,
  And wave thy snowy hand.

She hears me not, her spirit lies
  In trances mute and deep;
But Music has a golden key
  That opes the gate of Sleep.

Then let her sleep, and if I fail
  To set her spirit free,
My song will mingle in her dream,
  And she will dream of me.

——o——

THE yellow Moon looks slantly down,
Through seaward mists, upon the town;
And ghost-like there the moonshine falls
Between the dim and shadowy walls.

I see a crowd in every street,
But cannot hear their falling feet;
They float like clouds through shade and light,
And seem a portion of the Night.

The ships have lain for ages fled
Along the waters, dark and dead;
The dying waters wash no more
The long, black line of spectral shore.

There is no life on land or sea,
Save in the quiet Moon and me;
Nor ours is true, but only seems,
Within some dead old World of Dreams.

——o——

ALONG the grassy slope I sit,
And dream of other years;
My heart is full of soft regrets,
My eyes of tender tears.

The wild bees hummed about the spot,
The sheep-bells tinkled far,
Last year when Alice sat with me,
Beneath the evening star.

The same sweet star is o'er me now,
Around the same soft hours,
But Alice moulders in the dust
With all the last year's flowers.

I sit alone, and only hear
The wild bees on the steep,
And distant bells that seem to float
From out the folds of Sleep.

SONGS OF SUMMER.

THE FLIGHT OF YOUTH.

THERE are gains for all our losses,
  There are balms for all our pain:
But when youth, the dream, departs,
It takes something from our hearts,
  And it never comes again.

We are stronger, and are better,
  Under manhood's sterner reign:
Still we feel that something sweet
Followed youth, with flying feet,
  And will never come again.

Something beautiful is vanished,
  And we sigh for it in vain:
We behold it everywhere,
On the earth, and in the air,
  But it never comes again.

——o——

[BRITTANY.]

THY father is a King, my child,
  And thou a Prince by birth;
But he has banished us from court
  To roam about the earth:

But let him be that wrongeth thee,
For all the holy angels see,
  Said patient, pale Custance.
["*Peace, little son, I will do thee no harm.*"
But still the babe lay weeping on her arm.]

From door to door we beg our bread,
  From day to day we pine,
While he doth at his banquet sit,
  And drain the cups of wine:
But let him be, O, let him be,
For God will care for you and me,
  Said patient, pale Custance.
["*Peace, little son, I will do thee no harm.*"
But still the babe lay weeping on her arm.]

—o—

[ANTIQUE.]

A FEW frail summers had touched thee,
  As they touch the fruit;
Not so bright as thy hair the sunshine,
  Not so sweet as thy voice the lute:
Hushed the voice, shorn the hair,—all is over,
  An urn of white ashes remains;
Nothing else save the tears in our eyes,
  And our bitterest, bitterest pains.

We garland the urn with white roses,
  Burn incense and gums on the shrine,
Play old tunes with the saddest of closes,
  Dear tunes that were thine;
But in vain, all in vain,
Thou art gone—we remain!

THE SONG OF THE SYRENS.

LONG have you buffeted the winds,
  And urged the weary oar:
Now you reach our little isle
Furl your sail, and rest awhile,
  On the happy shore.

What is here that you should fear?
What is there so deadly here?
A quiet island in the sea,
  Grass-fringed, and shadowed deep with palms,
  Winds that winnow summer balms,
Flowers in each vale, and fruits on every tree.
We weave slow dances in the shade,
  With lifted arms and floating hair:
Or, when the golden noon is come,
List the wild-bee's drowsy hum,
  Or watch the insects in the air,
  Or kiss each other on the lips,
And softly swoon away in Sleep's divine eclipse.
  What is there to fear in this?
  Where's the danger of a kiss?
  But, if dangerous it be,
It is to maids like us, not to men like thee!

——o——

[ITALY.]

RANGE yourselves, my merry men,
  And wake your sweetest numbers,
My lady will forgive the voice
  That melts her silent slumbers:

For ladies listen with delight
To music in the summer night.

Run your hands across the strings,
  Like the wind through vernal rains,
Softly : not of lovers' fears,
Nor their idle rain of tears—
  Sing serener strains :
Sing the joy, the happy smart,
In a little maiden's heart,
That finds in dreams her lover dear,
And wakes—to find him near!

——o——

THE SEA.

[STORM.]

THROUGH the night, through the night,
  In the saddest unrest,
Wrapt in white, all in white,
  With her babe on her breast,
Walks the mother so pale,
Staring out on the gale,
  Through the night.

Through the night, through the night,
  Where the sea lifts the wreck,
Land in sight, close in sight,
  On the surf-flooded deck,
Stands the father so brave,
Driving on to his grave,
  Through the night.

THE SHADOW OF THE HAND.

[ITALY.]

YOU were very charming, Madam,
  In your silks and satins fine;
And you made your lovers drunken,
  But it was not with your wine.
There were court-gallants in dozens,
  There were princes of the land,
And they would have perished for you,
  As they knelt and kissed your hand.
    For they saw no stain upon it,
    It was such a snowy hand.

But for me, I knew you better,
  And, while you were flaunting there,
I remembered some one lying
  With the blood on his white hair.
He was pleading for you, Madam,
  Where the shriven spirits stand:
But the Book of Life was darkened
  By the Shadow of a Hand.
    It was tracing your perdition,
    For the blood upon your hand!

——o——

THE SPEECH OF LOVE.

YOU ask me, love, to sing of you,
  Dear heart, but what and why?
Songs are but sweet and skilful words,
That tinkle unto certain chords,
  And are but born to die.

Words cannot show my burning love,
  My passion's secret fire :
I try to speak, and make it plain,
About my pleasure, and my pain,
  But song and speech expire.

There is more eloquence in looks,
  More poesy in sighs,
Than ever yet in speech was framed,
Or any song of poets famed,
  Though lit at ladies' eyes.

Then bid me sing of love no more,
  But let me silent be ;
For silence is the speech of love,
The music of the spheres above,
  That suits a soul like thee.

——o——

YOU may drink to your leman in gold,
  In a great golden goblet of wine ;
She's as ripe as the wine, and as bold
As the glare of the gold :
  But this little lady of mine,
  I will not profane her in wine.
I go where the garden so still is,
  (The moon raining through,)
To pluck the white bowls of the lilies,
  And drink her in dew!

THE SEA.

[THE LOVER.]

YOU stooped and picked a red-lipped shell,
  Beside the shining sea :
"This little shell, when I am gone,
  Will whisper still of me."
I kissed your hands, upon the sands,
  For you were kind to me.

I hold the shell against my ear,
  And hear its hollow roar :
It speaks to me about the sea,
  But speaks of you no more.
I pace the sands, and wring my hands,
  For you are kind no more.

——o——

BIRDS.

BIRDS are singing round my window,
  Tunes the sweetest ever heard,
And I hang my cage there daily,
  But I never catch a bird.

So with thoughts my brain is peopled,
  And they sing there all day long :
But they will not fold their pinions
  In the little cage of Song !

THE LOST LAMB.

[TARTARY.]

THE little Tartar maiden
  That tends my master's sheep—
She makes a lamb her pillow,
  When she lies down to sleep.

She parts her gray tent-curtains
  Before the morn is seen,
And drives our flocks together,
  To pastures fresh and green.

My heart goes with the maiden,
  For when I wake I find
No heart within my bosom,
  No happy peace of mind.

I track the lost lamb's footsteps,
  And find it fast asleep,
Beside the little maiden
  Among my master's sheep.

——o——

THE sky is a drinking-cup,
  That was overturned of old,
And it pours in the eyes of men
  Its wine of airy gold.

We drink that wine all day,
  Till the last drop is drained up,
And are lighted off to bed
  By the jewels in the cup!

ON THE PIER.

DOWN at the end of the long, dark street,
  Years, years ago,
I sat with my sweetheart on the pier,
  Watching the river flow.

The moon was climbing the sky that night,
  White as the winter's snow :
We kissed in its light, and swore to be true—
  But that was years ago.

Once more I walk in the dark, old street,
  Wearily to and fro :
But I sit no more on the desolate pier
  Watching the river flow.

——o——

SPRING, they tell me, comes in bloom,
  Flowers already star the lea :
But thou art lying in thy tomb,
  And there is no Spring for me.
      Skies are gay
      Day after day,
   And the snow-drifts melt away :
  But there is no Spring for me,
      Perdita.

Over thee the willows wave,
  And the waning moon doth shine :

But thou art happy in thy grave,
And I would I were in mine.
Heart and brain
Are racked with pain,
For I seek thy grave again:
But I soon shall rest in mine,
Perdita.

———o———

THE gray old Earth goes on
At its ancient pace,
Lifting its thunder-voice
In the choir of space;
And the years as they go
Are singing slow,
Solemn dirges, full of wo.

Tyrants sit upon their thrones,
And will not hear the people's moans,
Nor hear their clanking chains:
Or if they do they add thereto,
And mock, not ease their pains.

But little liberty remains,
There is but little room for thee,
In this wide world, O Liberty!
But where thy foot has once been set
Thou wilt remain, though oft unseen:
And grow like thought, and move like wind,
Upon the troubled sea of Mind,
No longer now serene.
Thy life and strength thou dost retain,
Despite the cell, the rack, the pain,
And all the battles won in vain;

And even now thou see'st the hour
That lays in dust the thrones of Power:
When man shall once again be free,
And Earth renewed, and young like thee,
O Liberty! O Liberty!

———o———

THERE is no sin to hearts that love,
  Whatever men may say;
For they are lifted far above
  The laws of lesser clay.

They are unto themselves a law,
  No other law can bind:
No other wakes a moment's awe,
  For meaner men designed.

Then tell me not 'tis love that parts,
  Nor fear the powers above;
For all the sins of loving hearts
  Are washed away by love.

———o———

THE DIVAN.

[PERSIA.]

A LITTLE maid of Astrakan,
An idol on a silk divan;
She sits so still, and never speaks,
  She holds a cup of mine;
'Tis full of wine, and on her cheeks
  Are stains and smears of wine.

Thou little girl of Astrakan,
I join thee on the silk divan:
There is no need to seek the land,
  The rich bazaars where rubies shine;
For mines are in that little hand,
  And on those little cheeks of thine.

——o——

HERE I lie, a tress of hair,
Kissed by every wandering air,
Wishing you would kiss me too:
Why don't you, oftener than you do?
Through my ringlets ran her fingers,
  Whom you love so fond and true,
And their sweetness lingers, lingers
  In the ringlets still for you.

Only kiss them once, and see
What love lies embalmed in me:
Kiss me now, and it shall seem
As if you kissed her in a dream;
Nay, it shall not seem, but be,
You shall kiss her, sir, and she—
She shall stand before you there,
    Pale and fair,
By only kissing me, a little tress of hair!

——o——

THE sky is thick upon the sea,
  The sea is sown with rain,
And in the passing gusts we hear
  The clanging of the crane.

The cranes are flying to the south,
We cut the northern foam:
The dreary land they leave behind
Must be our future home.

Its barren shores are long and dark,
And gray its autumn sky;
But better these than this gray sea,
If but to land—and die!

——o——

DAY AND NIGHT.

Day is the Child of Time,
And Day must cease to be:
But Night is without a sire,
And can not expire,
One with Eternity.

Day and the angel Life
Circle the worlds of air,
With a speed that looks not back;
For Night is on their track,
Clutching their golden hair.

She comes, she comes again,
In her dark and pitiless flight;
The baby Sleep on her arm reclined,
The skeleton Death behind—
The Shadow that haunts the night!

THE DEAD.

I THINK about the dead by day,
  I dream of them at night :
They seem to stand beside my chair,
Clad in the clothes they used to wear,
  And by my bed in white.

The common-places of their lives,
  The lightest words they said,
Revive in me, and give me pain,
And make me wish them back again,
  Or wish that I were dead.

I would be kinder to them now,
  Were they alive once more ;
Would kiss their cheeks, and kiss their hair,
And love them, like the angels there,
  Upon the silent shore.

——o——

THE SEA.

[MAID.]

BY the rolling waves I roam,
  And look along the sea,
And dream of the day and the gleaming sail
  That bore my love from me.

His bark now sails the Indian seas,
  Far down in the tropic zone :
But his thoughts like swallows fly to me,
  By the northern waves alone.

Nor will he delay, when winds are fair
  To waft him back to me:
But haste, my love, or my grave will be made
  By the sad and moaning sea.

——o——

MANY'S the time I've sighed for summer,
  Many's the summer I've known;
But to-day I cling to the flying spring,
  And fear to have it flown.
    Not that May is gay,
    For the sky is cold and gray,
  And a shadow creeps on the day:
But the laden summer will give me
  What it never gave before,
Or take from me what a thousand
  Summers can give no more.

——o——

A SERENADE.

[FRANCE.]

THERE'S a door in your chamber, lady mine,
  I, the King, have the key:
There's a walk in my garden's deepest shade,
  For you, Sweet, and me.

We are loyal and distant by day,
  When the world is in sight:
But at night we have hearts, and we love,
  And are happy at night.

The lamps have gone out, lady mine,
  All is still, let us rise :
I can track you by the beat of your heart,
  And the light of your eyes.

Through the dusk of the lindens we glide,
  To that alley of ours :
And kiss in the light of the moon,
  And the odor of flowers.

———o———

THE house is dark and dreary,
  And my heart is full of gloom ;
But out of doors, in the summer air,
The sun is warm, the sky is fair,
  And the flowers are still in bloom.

A moment ago in the garden
  I scattered the shining dew :
The wind was soft in the swaying trees,
The morning-glories were full of bees,
  And straight in my face they flew.

Yet I left them unmolested,
  Draining their honey-wine,
And entered the weary house again,
To sit, as now, by a bed of pain,
  With a fevered hand in mine.

[ANTIQUE.]

THE phantom that walks in the sun,
The terror that creeps in the air,
Has entered the Garden of Youth,
And vainly we look for thee there:
Thy spirit has vanished, but where?

I question the wind of the summer,
That blows o'er the land and the sea;
It gives me a moan for my moan,
But no tidings of thee:
Nor answer the stars in the skies,
Pining still for the light of thine eyes.

THE NIGHT BEFORE THE BRIDAL.

THE bridal flower you gave me,
The rose so pure and white,
I press it to my lips, dear,
With tears of soft delight.

Its odor is so heavy
It makes me faint and pine;
It is thy kiss that freights it,
That sweet, sweet love of thine.

To-morrow thou wilt give me,
For a spell of joy and power,
The hand that gave the rose-bud,
And thy heart, a richer flower.

Then this may fade, and wither,
  No longer kissed by me,
For these, my burning kisses,
  Will then be showered on thee.

——o——

DIM grows the sky, and dusk the air,
And shadows settle everywhere,
Save when the embers streak the wall
With flames, that soon in darkness fall.

Pensive I sit, relapsing fast
Into the dead, the silent Past.
The Past returns, the dead are here;
Was that a whisper in my ear?

No, dear one, no, I did not sigh,
Nor does a tear bedim mine eye:
'Twas the officious light you brought,
And something alien to my thought.
But even if my tears do flow,
I weep for pleasure, not for wo,
I weep—because I love you so.

——o——

SUMMER AND AUTUMN.

THE hot mid-summer, the bright mid-summer
  Reigns in its glory now:
The earth is scorched with a golden fire,
There are berries, dead-ripe, on every brier,
  And fruits on every bough.

But the autumn days, so sober and calm,
  Steeped in a dreamy haze,
When the uplands all with harvests shine,
And we drink the wind like a fine cool wine—
  Ah, those are the best of days!

——o——

THE HELMET.

[GERMANY.]

WHERE the standards waved the thickest,
  And the tide of battle rolled,
Furiously he charged the foemen,
  On his snow-white steed so bold;
But he wore no guarding helmet,
  Only his long hair of gold.

"Turn, and fly, thou rash young warrior,
  Or this iron helmet wear."
"Nay, but I am armed already,
  In the brightness of my hair;
For my mother kissed its tresses,
  With the holy lips of prayer."

——o——

ROSES AND THORNS.

THE young child Jesus had a garden,
  Full of roses, rare and red:
And thrice a day he watered them,
  To make a garland for his head.

When they were full-blown in the garden,
He called the Jewish children there,
And each did pluck himself a rose,
Until they stripped the garden bare.

"And now how will you make your garland?
For not a rose your path adorns."
"But you forget," he answered them,
"That you have left me still the thorns."

They took the thorns, and made a garland,
And placed it on his shining head;
And where the roses should have shown
Were little drops of blood instead.

——o——

BENEATH the heavy curtains,
My face against the pane,
I peer into the darkness,
And scan the night in vain.

The vine o'erruns the lattice,
And lies along its roof,
So thick with leaves and clusters
It keeps the moon aloof.

By yonder pear-tree splintered
The feeble radiance falls,
But fails to pierce the branches,
Or touch the sombre walls.

No moon, no starlight gleaming,
The dark encircles me;
And, what is more annoying,
My neighbor cannot see.

She stands beneath her curtains,
  Her face against the pane,
Nor knows that I am watching
  For her to-night again.

——o——

RATTLE the window, Winds,
  Rain, drip on the panes;
There are tears and sighs in our hearts and eyes,
  And a weary weight on our brains.

The gray sea heaves and heaves,
  On the dreary flats of sand;
And the blasted limb of the churchyard yew—
  It shakes like a ghostly hand.

The dead are engulfed beneath it,
  Sunk in the grassy waves:
But we have more dead in our hearts to-day
  Than Earth in all her graves!

——o——

THE VEILED STATUE.

THERE'S a statue in my chamber,
  Carved in other years for me,
From the memory of a lady
  In a land beyond the sea.

In its niche I keep it hidden
  By a veil from common eyes:
But my own behold it ever,
  And its shade upon me lies.

Through the day it stands before me,
  And appals my shrinking sight,
And at night it grows so awful
  That I cannot sleep for fright.

For when falls the ghostly moonlight
  In the silence of the room,
And my spirit faints within me
  As it hearkens for its doom—

'Tis no more the woman's statue,
  But the woman's self I see,
Pallid with her love and sorrow,
  And the death she died for me.

And so strange her spell upon me
  As she bends above my bed,
She becomes the wretched living,
  I the still more wretched dead!

——o——

DEAD LEAVES.

THE day is dead, and in its grave,
  The flowers are fast asleep;
But in this solemn wood alone
  My nightly watch I keep.
The night is dark, the dew descends,
But dew and darkness are my friends.

I stir the dead leaves under foot,
  And breathe the earthy smell;
It is the odor of decay,
  And yet I like it well.
Give others day, and scented flowers,
Give me dead leaves, and midnight hours.

"POEMS OF THE ORIENT."

WE read your little book of Orient lays,
And half believe old superstitions true;
No Saxon like ourselves, an Arab, you,
Stolen in your babyhood by Saxon fays.
That you in fervid songs recall the blaze
Of eastern suns, behold the deep-blue skies,
Lie under rustling palms, breathe winds of spice,
And dream of veiled sultanas, is no praise.
All this is native to you as the air;
You but regain the birthright lost of yore:
The marvel is it now becomes our own.
We wind the turban round our Frankish hair,
Spring on our steeds that paw the desert's floor,
And take the sandy solitude alone.

—o—

THE SEA.

[THE LOVER.]

THOU pallid fisher maiden,
  That standest by the shore,
Why dost thou watch the ocean,
  And hearken to its roar?

It is some Danish sailor,
  That sails the Spanish main:
Nor will thy roses redden
  Till he returns again.

Thou simple fisher maiden,
He cares no more for thee:
He sleeps with the mermaidens,
The witches of the sea.

Thou should'st not watch the ocean,
And hearken to its roar,
When bridal bells are ringing
In little kirks ashore.

Go, dress thee for thy bridal,
A stalwart man like me
Is worth a thousand sailors,
Whose bones are in the sea.

———o———

AT REST.

WITH folded hands the lady lies
In flowing robes of white,
A lamp beside her lonely couch,
A globe of tender light.

With such a light above her head,
A little year ago,
She walked adown the shadowy vale
Where the blood-red roses grow.

A shape or shadow joined her there,
To pluck the royal flower,
But stole the lily from her breast,
Albeit her only dower.

With that all went, her false love first,
  And then her peace of heart:
The hard world frowned, her friends grew cold,
  She hid in tears apart:

And now she lies upon her couch,
  Amid the dying light,
Nor wakes to hear the little voice
  That moans throughout the night!

———o———

WRECKS of clouds of a sombre gray,
  Like the ribbed remains of a mastodon,
Were piled in masses along the west,
  And a streak of red stretched over the sun.

I stood on the deck of the ferry-boat,
  As the summer evening deepened to night;
Where the tides of the river ran darkling past,
  Through lengthening pillars of crinkled light.

The wind blew over the land and the waves
  With its salt sea-breath, and a spicy balm,
And it seemed to cool my throbbing brain,
  And to make my restless spirit calm.

The forest of masts, the dark-hulled ships,
  The twinkling lights, and the sea of men—
I read the riddle of each and all,
  And I knew their inner meaning then.

For while the beautiful moon arose,
  And drifted the boat in her yellow beams,
My soul went down the river of thought,
  That flows in the mystic land of dreams.

No, I will not leave you, Madam,
  In the darkness and the rain;
'Tis for you to be so cruel,
  But for me, I pity pain.
Be my silly love forgotten,
  I forgive you your disdain.

You have goodly halls and houses,
  And your loves of high degree;
I have nothing but my passion,
  You can never think of me,
In your pride as far above me
  As the moon above the sea.

But it seems at last you love me,
  If I read your thoughts aright,
For behold, I fly your presence,
  And you follow in my flight,
Till you find me by the lightnings,
  In the thunders of the night!

——o——

THE SHADOW.

There is but one great sorrow,
  All over the wide, wide world;
But that in turn must come to all—
The Shadow that moves behind the pall,
  A flag that never is furled.

Till he in his marching crosses
  The threshold of the door,
Usurps a place in the inner room,
Where he broods in the awful hush and gloom,
  Till he goes, and comes no more—

Save this there is no sorrow,
  Whatever we think we feel;
But when Death comes all's over:
'Tis a blow that we never recover,
  A wound that never will heal.

——o——

NOVEMBER.

THE wild November comes at last
  Beneath a veil of rain;
The night wind blows its folds aside,
  Her face is full of pain.

The latest of her race, she takes
  The Autumn's vacant throne:
She has but one short moon to live,
  And she must live alone.

A barren realm of withered fields,
  Bleak woods of fallen leaves,
The palest morns that ever dawned,
  The dreariest of eves:

It is no wonder that she comes,
  Poor month, with tears of pain:
For what can one so hopeless do
  But weep, and weep again?

CARMEN NATURÆ TRIUMPHALE.

MUSING in solitude the summer long,
Musing beside this sea, beneath these skies,
Whose gracious light upon my spirit lies,
My spirit has grown strong,
Grown strong, and calm, and wise,
With sharper, surer eyes,
And more capacious energies of Song.
Where I was blind I see,
And where I guessed I know;
For what was common then to me
Is now no longer so.
The outward world of sound and sight,
The shows of day, the pomps of night,
Are other than they seem;
The clouds around a hidden star,
The sleep around a dream.
The airs that fan the globe
Wrap it with Being like a robe.
It lives in dust, and grass, and flowers,
And in the trees,
And in the springs, and streams, and seas,
And in the mountains, Earth's Titanic Powers.
Throughout the Universe there is no spot
Where Life is not:
Nowhere is any death, Death does but seem,
A dream within the Dream:
Nothing but Life and Change, its heart and cause,
The adamantine base of crumbling laws.
The flowers may fade away, the woods may fall,
The sea may waste the land, the land the sea,
And men may feed the worms beneath the pall,
And Time may vanish in Eternity;

Still ocean-like the tides of Being lie,
Filled from exhaustless urns;
The flame of Life still burns,
And God still sits on high,
And watches Earth below with His Unsleeping Eye!

Why should I read what man has penned,
His speculations without end,
When here the Book of Nature lies,
Open to all her children's eyes,
No wire-drawn, narrow comments there,
Nor any warrant for despair?
I tell you, Nay! It cannot be,
Creation is enough for me:
I will not look
On creed or book,
Or aught beside the earth and skies;
There is no need
Of book, or creed,
To teach a man, and make him good and wise.
There is no need of temples built with hands,
To cast their shadows over subject lands;
No need of stolèd priests, and chanting friars,
Censers, and incense smoke, and altar fires;
No need of crucifix and beads,
No need of sacred bread and wine,
Of hymns, and psalms, and prayers supine,
And penances and fasts whereby our nature bleeds.
We should obey ourselves alone,
Nor ask what paths have others trod;
God wants no sign to know His own,
Nor they to know their God.
Better, far better now
The dew upon my brow,
Than all the ancient use and wont

Of water from the holy font,
Though shed by holiest hands on earth,
The symbol of a heavenly birth.
The bread and wine of quiet thought
Is sacrament enough for me;
Enough the temple of the world,
The sky, the land, the sea:
Whether the Spring perform her dewy rite;
Whether the Summer binds her brow with leaves;
Whether the Autumn stands amid his sheaves;
Or whether Winter plucks his locks of white.
God speaks to me in shouting winds,
And in the waves that shoreward come,
And in the little insect's hum,
And in the still small voice of human minds.
The year with all its train of nights and days
Is a perpetual service in His praise.
Morn comes from Him, as came the olden seers,
With fiery messages of awe and love;
From Him the golden Noon that climbs above,
Transfigured day by day from immemorial years.
And Night, incarnate Night,
Forever veiled and calm,
Eldest of all things that created be,
Night reads in silence her eternal psalm,
The gospel of the darkness, penned in light,
The starred evangel of Infinity!
The road to Heaven is broader than the world,
And deeper than the kingdoms of the dead,
And up its ample paths the nations tread,
With all their banners furled:
No saint nor angel sits beside its gate,
Holding the key within his griping hands:
The loving gate of Heaven wide open stands,
And never shall be closed by earthly hate:

For purified from all their grief and sin
The souls keep pouring in,
Singing melodious psalms,
While angels pitch their tents beneath the heavenly palms!

There be who love not Nature, souls forlorn
Who see no beauty in the smiling morn,
No joy in noon, no tenderness in night,
No pillared Cloud of Light!
Not such the little child, nor such the youth
Who has not done his childly nature wrong:
These Nature loves, and leads through realms of truth,
Forever flushed with atmospheres of Song.
Can I forget the wonder and the joy
That Nature roused within me, when a boy,
The gush of feelings, pure and undefiled,
The deep and rapturous gladness,
The nameless sadness,
The Vision that overpowered the visionary child?
Forget, forget, the very hour I do
May Heaven forget me too!
May Nature shut me in her wastes apart,
And press me never more on her maternal heart!

O Nature, Nature, I have worshipped thee
From being's dimmest dawn, perchance before,
Or ere my spirit touched this earthly shore,
Or time began with me.
When but a babe, (so say the ancient crones
Who nursed me then,) I watched the sky for hours,
Smiled at the clouds, and laughed in glee at showers,
And wept when winds were at their wintry moans.
A little truant child with trembling tread,
I sought the garden walks with wondering mind,
Perplexed to hear the fluting of the wind
In branches overhead:

I loved the wind, I loved the whispering trees,
I loved their shadowy shifting images,
And loved the spots of light that lay like smiles
Around the green arcades, and leafy forest aisles.
With bolder steps I tracked the meadows, deep
In fragrant grasses decked with daisies white,
And marked the mist on many a mountain height,
Melting away like Sleep.
The larks went up before me, and behind,
But not so fast as songs within my tuneful mind.
Through sweeps of landscape, over lawns and plains,
And where the birches walled their silver lanes
I passed, and down the gradual slope of vales,
Where tangled waters told their drowsy tales.
The river lay below in azure rest,
Sparkled the lake with lilies on its breast;
And where the jutting rocks o'errimmed the wall
Of abrupt gulfs I saw the waterfall,
With clouds of vapor blent,
A column of white light, a snow-like monument!
It mattered little where I went,
Everywhere I was content;
Everywhere I saw and heard
Sights and sounds divine;
Everywhere was Nature stirred,
And Nature's love was mine,
And I, what loved I not, O Nature, that was thine?
I held my peace, I sang aloud,
I walked the world as in a cloud.
I loved the Clouds.
Fire-fringed at dawn, or red with twilight bloom,
Or stretched above, like isles of leaden gloom
In heaven's vast deep, or drawn in belts of gray,
Or dark blue walls along the base of day,
Or snow-drifts luminous at highest noon,

Ragged and black in tempests, veined with lightning,
And when the moon was brightening
Impearled and purpled by the changeful moon.
I loved the Moon.
Whether she lingered by the porch of Even,
When Day retiring struck his yellow tents;
Whether she scaled the ancient peaks of heaven,
Whose angels watched her from its battlements;
Whether, like early Spring, she walked the night,
O'er tracts of cloudy snow;
Whether she dwindled in the morning light,
Like some departing spirit, loath to go;
Or sifted showers of silver through the trees,
Or trod with her white feet across the heaving seas!
I loved the Sea.
Whether in calm it glassed the gracious day
With all its light, the night with all its fires;
Whether in storm it lashed its sullen spray,
Wild as the heart when passionate youth expires;
Or lay, as now, a torture to my mind,
In yonder land-locked bay, unwrinkled by the wind.
I loved the Wind.
Whether it kissed my hair, and pallid brow;
Whether with sweets my sense it fed, as now;
Whether it blew across the scudding main;
Whether it shrieked above a stretch of plain;
Whether, on autumn days, in solemn woods,
And barren solitudes,
Along the waste it whirled the withered leaves;
Whether it hummed around my cottage eaves,
And shook the rattling doors,
And died with long-drawn sighs, on bleak and dreary moors;
Whether in winter, when its trump did blow
Through desolate gorges dirges of despair,
It drove the snowflakes slantly down the air,

And piled the drifts of snow;
Or whether it breathed soft in vernal hours,
And filled the trees with sap, and filled the grass with flowers.
Wind, sea, and moon, and clouds, and day and night,
The weeks, and months, and seasons of the year:
What was there was not dear?
What was not radiant with heavenly light?
What did not Nature cherish that was not mine?
What did not I adore, O Nature, that was thine?

My life with Nature now is blent,
She is a portion of my blood;
I am her passive instrument,
The creature of her every mood;
A part and parcel of her forms,
Of her calms, and of her storms.
To her my soul unfolds as violets do,
When April winds are low, and April skies are blue.
I am a harp whereon she plays,
When she accompanies her lays,
A sea of moon-like presence sways,
Shifting its tides a thousand ways.
Deep in her heart I live, and feel
All that she pleases to reveal;
And in my heart, with joy intense,
I paint her forms that fade not thence,
And in my thoughts see more magnificence;
My waking thoughts, and in my sleep
I carry on the marvel deep,
And dream all night of tropic seas and skies,
And Time immortal Youth, and Earth a Paradise!
A Presence fronts and haunts me everywhere,
Stands in the sun, and dips below the sea,
Fills all the voidest spaces of the air,

And lives in all things like Eternity.
The motes of dust on which I tread,
The floating stars above my head,
All without me, and within,
To Nature and to Man are kin.
Whence comes this strange affinity
That Man, O Nature, has for thee?
Forever unto thee we run,
And give ourselves away,
Like melting mists that seek the sun,
Like night that seeks the day.
To Nature do we turn, and minister,
Because we were of old a part of her.
It is a recognition,
A memory, an appealing,
An interchange of vision,
An interchange of feeling.
The soul of man detects and sympathizes
With its old shapes of matter, long outworn,
And matter, too, to new sensations born,
Detects the soul of man, with spiritual surprises.
Few understand their mutual dreams,
And few translate their speeches,
Save poets versed in Nature's themes,
And those whom Nature teaches.
They stare at us, and we at them,
We dare not slight, nor dare contemn:
We are the ripe fruit on the stem.
Not a leaf upon the tree,
Not a bird upon the bough,
But waves its little flag to me,
And sings within my spirit now;
Sings to itself in bowers apart,
Within the regions of my heart.
I am what winds and waters make me,

What the clouds and thunders please,
And what the changeful seas :
As Nature is so men must take me.
For I to Nature's self belong,
As much as any bud or bee ;
And when you do to her a wrong,
You do a wrong to me.
Be it sad, or merry, or sweet or strong,
She breathes her influence in my song,
And in my daily life she gleams,
And is the substance of my dreams.
I love her not as bard or painter might,
To spy and seize on sound and sight,
But for mine own delight.
The sun may burn, the stars may shine,
The pallid moon in heaven may pine,
The sea may wash a rocky shore,
The wind may howl, the tempest roar,
Nor I be other than before.
It may be day, it may be night,
Or foul or fair,
I do not care,
I go not there to learn, but for my own delight!
And yet I learn what books can never teach,
Nor any words express ;
A mystic love, a wordless speech,
For Nature teaches so in sacred silentness.
And when we seem asleep in dreams,
Our deepest lore is caught,
For Truth within man's nature dwells,
Her fabled fount, her well of wells,
Her crystal deep of thought.

In silent thought, that yearns to find a tongue,
Burthened with cares, and racked with cureless pains,

I rove to-day through Nature's wide domains,
No longer gay and young;
No longer moved with feelings undefiled,
No more, no more a child!
But wherefore grieve? The Past is past,
Nor can the Present always last;
It sows the Future in its seeds.
And flowers will grow where grow the weeds,
And suns will shine, and dews will fall,
And Love, the sum of human needs,
Love, comes to all:
Yea, even comes, so universal he,
To me, to even me!
Then let me dry again these gathering tears,
These bitter tears, and turn, Beloved, to thee,
For thee to live and die, in future years,
As thou for only me!
Meanwhile my soul to meditation given,
A many-sided mirror, broad and bright,
Reflects whatever meets my thoughtful sight,
The myriad shapes and hues of earth and heaven;
Diffused through all, like odors in the wind,
My mind the Universe, the Universe my Mind!

——o——

INVOCATION TO SLEEP.

DRAW the curtains round your bed,
And I'll shade the wakeful light;
'Twill be hard for you to sleep,
If you keep me still in sight;
But you must though, and without me,
For I have a song to write.
Then sleep, love, sleep:

The flowers have gone to rest,
And the birds are in the nest:
It is time for you to join them beneath the wings of
Sleep.

Wave thy poppies round her, Sleep,
Touch her eyelids, flood her brain,
Banish Memory, Thought, and Strife,
Bar the portals of her life,
Till the morning comes again;
Let no enemy intrude
On her helpless solitude;
Fear, and Pain, and all their train—
Keep the evil hounds at bay,
And all evil dreams away.
Thou, thyself, keep thou the key,
Or entrust it unto me,
Sleep, Sleep, Sleep!
A lover's eyes are bright,
In the darkest night,
And jealous even of dreams, almost of thee—Sleep!

I must sit and think, and think,
Till the stars begin to wink,
(For the web of Song is wrought
Only in the loom of Thought:)
She must lie and sleep, and sleep,
(Be her slumbers calm and deep!)
Till the dews of morning weep.
Therefore bind your sweetest sprite
To her service and delight,
All the night,
Sleep, Sleep, Sleep!
And I'll whisper in her ear,
Like a bee among the flowers,

What she loveth so to hear,
  In the night's impassioned hours,
News from my warm heart to hers,
Burthening Love's ambassadors—
  A happy sigh and smile;
Crooning to myself the while
Ditties delicate and free,
Dedicate to her, and thee,
    Sleep, Sleep, Sleep!
For I owe ye both a boon,
And I meant to grant it soon,
In my golden numbers that breathe of Love and Sleep!

——o——

THE STORK AND THE RUBY.

A CERTAIN prince, I have forgot his name,
Playing one morning at the archer's game,
Within a garden where his palace stood,
Shot at a stork, and spilled the creature's blood
For very wantonness and cruelty.
Thrice had he pierced his target in the eye
At fifty paces; twice defloured a rose,
Striking each time the very leaf he chose;
Then he set up his dagger in a hedge,
And split an arrow on its glittering edge.
What next to hit he knew not. Looking round
He saw a stork just lighted on the ground,
To rest itself after its leagues of flight:
The dewy walk in which it stood was bright,
So white its plumage, and so clear its eyes,
Twinkling with innocence and sweet surprise.
"I'll shoot the silly bird," the prince exclaimed:
And bending his strong bow he straightway aimed

His keenest arrow at its panting heart
The lucky arrow missed a vital part,
(Or was it some kind wind that pushed it by?)
And only struck and broke the creature's thigh.
The poor thing tumbled in a lily bed,
And its blood ran and made the lilies red.
It marked the changing color of the flowers,
The winding garden walks, the bloomy bowers,
And, last, the cruel prince, who laughed with glee—
Fixing the picture in its memory:
This done it struggled up, and flew away,
Leaving the prince amazed, and in dismay.

Beyond the city walls, a league or more,
A little maid was spinning at her door,
Singing old songs to cheer the long day's work.
Her name was Heraclis. The fainting stork
Dropped at her feet, and with its ebon bill
Showed her its thigh, broken and bleeding still.
She fetched it water from a neighbor spring,
And while it drank and washed each dabbled wing
She set the fractured bones with pious care,
And bound them with the fillet of her hair.
Eased of its pain again it flew away,
Leaving the maiden happier all the day.

That night the prince as usual went to bed,
His royal wine a little in his head.
Beside him stood a casket full of gems,
The spoil of conquered monarchs' diadems:
Great pearls, milk-white, and shining like the moon,
Emeralds, grass-green, sapphires, like skies of June,
Brilliants that threw their light upon the wall,
And one great ruby that outshone them all,
Large as a pigeon's egg, and red as wine.

At last he slumbered in the pale moonshine.
Meantime the watchful stork was in his bowers;
Again it saw its blood upon the flowers,
And saw the walks, the fountain's shaft in air,
But not the cruel prince, no prince was there:
So up and down the spacious courts it flew,
And ever nearer to the palace drew.
Passing the lighted windows row by row,
It saw the prince, and saw the ruby's glow.
Hopping into his chamber, grave and still,
It seized the precious ruby with its bill,
And spreading then its rapid wings in flight,
Flew out and vanished in the yawning night.
Night slowly passed, and morning broke again.
There came a light tap on the window-pane
Of Heraclis: it woke her, she arose,
And slipping on in haste her peasant clothes,
Opened the door to see who knocked, and lo,
In walked the stork again, as white as snow,
Triumphant with the ruby, whose red ray
Flamed in her face, anticipating day!
Again the creature pointed to its thigh,
And something human brightened in its eye,
A look that said "*I thank you!*" plain as words.
The virgin's look was brighter than the bird's,
So glad was she to see it was not dead:
She stretched her hand to sleek its bowing head,
But ere she could it made a sudden stand,
And thrust the priceless ruby in her hand,
And sailing swiftly through the cottage door
Mounted the morning sky, and came no more!

[ANTIQUE.]

WE are bent with age and cares,
In the last of our gray hairs,
And we lean upon our staffs,
Looking for the epitaphs;
For we are the last, the last,
In the ruins of the Past.

When our youth was in its prime,
Then it was a merry time;
Suns were golden, stars were bright,
And the moon was a delight,
And we wandered in its beams
In the sweetest, sweetest dreams.
Now our dreams are fled,
For the happy Past is dead,
And we feel it lived in vain,
And will never come again.
No, 'tis gone, and gone each trace
Of its once-familiar face:
Even the dust for which we yearn
Lost, and lost its very urn.
Nothing remains except the tomb,
  (Earth, and heaven so draped with clouds!)
And we who wander in its gloom,
  And soon will need our shrouds,
So pale are we, and so aghast
At the absence of the Past.

We had friends when we were young,
  And we shared their smiles and tears;

But they are forever flown,
We can only weep alone,
  For the unreturning years.
Roses come again with Spring,
And the summer birds do sing:
But the dead who loved them so,
They are in the winter's snow,
Far from birds, and far from flowers,
And this weary life of ours.
All is over! Naught remains,
Save the memory of our pains,
And the years that bear us fast
To the silence of the Past!

———o———

PAIN IN AUTUMN.

A DROWSY pain, a dull, dead pain
Preys on my heart, and clouds my brain;
And shadows brood above my dreams,
Like spectral mists o'er haunted streams.

There is no fire within the grate,
The room is cold and desolate,
And dampness on the window-panes
Foretells the equinoctial rains.
The stony road runs past the door,
Dry and dusty evermore;
Up and down the people go,
Shadowy figures, sad and slow,
And the strange houses lie below.

Across the road the dark elms wait,
Ranged in a row before the gate,

Giving their voices to the wind,
And their sorrows to my mind.
Behind the house the river flows,
Half unrest and half repose;
Ships lie below with mildewed sails,
Tattered in forgotten gales;
Along each hulk a whitish line,
The dashing of the ancient brine.
Beyond, the spaces of the sea,
Which old Ocean's portals be:
The land runs out its horns of sand,
And the sea comes in to meet the land.

Sky sinks to sea, sea swells to sky,
Till they meet, and mock the eye,
And where they meet the sand hills lie;
No cattle in their pastures seen,
For the yellow grass was never green.
With a calm and solemn stare
They look to heaven in blank despair,
And heaven, with pity dumb the while,
Looks down again with a sickly smile.

The sky is gray, half dark, half bright,
Swimming in dim, uncertain light,
Something between the day and night.
And the winds blow, but soft and low,
Unheard, unheeded in their wo,
Like some sick heart, too near o'erthrown
To vent its grief, by sigh or moan,
Some heart that breaks, like mine—alone.

And here I dwell, condemned to see,
And be, what all these phantoms be,
Within this realm of penal pain,
Beside the melancholy main:

The waste which lies, as legend saith,
Between the worlds of Life and Death;
A Soul from Life to Death betrayed,
A Shadow in the World of Shade.

THE FIRST SNOW.

TO-DAY has been a pleasant day,
  Despite the cold and snow;
A sabbath stillness filled the air,
And pictures slumbered everywhere,
  Around, above, below.

We woke at dawn, and saw the trees
  Before our windows white;
Their limbs were clad with snow, like bark,
Save that the under sides were dark,
  Like bars against the light.

The fence was white around the house,
  The lamp before the door;
The porch was glazed with pearlèd sleet,
Great drifts lay in the silent street,
  The street was seen no more.

Long trenches had been roughly dug,
  And giant footprints made;
But few were out, the streets were bare,
I saw but one pale wanderer there,
  And he was like a shade.

I seemed to walk another world,
  Where all was still and blest:

The cloudless sky, the stainless snows—
It was a vision of repose,
A dream of heavenly rest:

A dream the holy night completes,
For now the moon hath come,
I stand in heaven with folded wings,
A free and happy soul that sings
When all things else are dumb!

——o——

THE ABDICATION OF NOMAN.

NOMAN, the King of Hira, sat one day
In his pavilion, pitched at Karwanak,
With Bahram Gour, the son of Yezdejird,
And Adi Ibn Zeid, the Persian bard.
Cross-legged on scarlet cushions stuffed with down
They sat and smoked; the bubbling of their pipes
Was like a river in the land of sleep.
The curtain of the tent was drawn aside,
Looped up with golden cords; a twinkling gleam
Glanced from the tassels, smote the water-bowls,
And perished in the great sea-emerald
On Noman's turban: other light was none;
They lolled away the hours in purple dusk.

Before the doorway of the tent they saw
The palace park and garden bright with spring.
A pillared avenue of stately palms
Slept in the sun; a fountain rose and fell,
Breaking the silver surface at its base;
Gold-fish like sunken ingots lay in heaps
Beneath the fountain's rain; beside its rim,

Dipping his long bill in a lotus cup,
A black crane stooped; between the silent palms
A length of silken carpet was unrolled:
A white gazelle dangled a silver chain,
Picking its way through tufts of broidered flowers.
Flowers of all hues and odors streaked the ground,
Roses, fire-red, large tulips, cups of flame,
Banks of snow lilies turning dew to pearls,
And rolling rivers of anemonies,
The flowers that Noman loved; their crimson leaves
Were rubies set on stalks of emerald.
Broad meadows stretched afar, wherein, dim-seen
Through winking haze, the still Euphrates lay—
The great Euphrates fresh from Babylon.

Between their whiffs of smoke with happy eyes
They drank the landscape in; to Bahram Gour
It grew his father's garden at Madain—
Save that the Emir's daughter was not there,
Whereat he sighed: his long beard Adi stroked,
And thrummed his idle fingers in the air,
Turning a couplet in his tuneful brain.
Noman alone was sad, for he nor had
The poet's idleness, nor prince's youth;
Grown gray in troubled rule he longed for rest,
But found it never: fair things made him grieve,
Because their lives are short. He saw the end.

"Why grasp at wealth and power? Why hoard up gold?
Or make our whims a law for other men?
Earth hides her gold in veinèd rocks and hills,
Packs it in river sands: we dig it out,
And stamp our Kingly faces in its light,
And call it ours. Does Earth give up her claim?
Not she, she calmly waits, and takes it back.

We sift the sands, dive down into the waves,
Ransack the caves for gems ; Earth gives them up.
I have an hundred caskets full of pearls,
Ten chests of chrysolites, a turquoise plate
That holds a maund of corn, a chandelier,
The chains whereof are beryls linked with gold,
Its flame a ruby, found in Balashan.
Not mine, but Earth's ; for I shall pass away,
I, and my race, but Earth will still remain,
And keep my gems ; in palaces like mine,
To swell the treasury of future Kings,
Or, haply, in the caverns where they grew.

We build rich palaces, and wall them in,
Make parks and gardens near, plant trees, sow flowers,
And say, 'All this is ours!' But what says Earth?
She only smiles her still cold smile of scorn.
Forests a thousand parasangs in length
Are hers, and hers the tropic's zone of bloom,
And when we die our marble palaces:
She lets the jackal prowl about their courts.

My days have numbered five and sixty years.
Twenty and eight were passed upon the throne:
I count them lost. I may have gained some power,
Added a few wild tribes to those I rule,
And treasures to my treasure, but my life—
(I had so little time to think of that,)
Is not a whit the richer, save in cares.
Ah, who that knows himself would be a King?"

So spake the King the secret of his heart,
Like one who babbles to himself alone.
His head dropped on his bosom, and his beard
Hung in his lap: the shadow of his words

Drifted across the stream of Adi's thought,
And when the King had ended he began:

"Name me the King whose power was vast enough
To cope with Death, or cheat the Sepulchre.
Whither is Chosroes gone, the mightiest, he,
Of Persian Kings? Whither did Sapor go?
And they, the fair-haired race, the Roman lords—
Tell me why no memorial lives of them.
And he, the nameless King, who Hadhr built,
Where Khabur and the lordly Tigris flow.
He faced his palace walks with marble slabs,
Polished and white, and raised his roof so high,
His ridgy roofs, the birds made nests thereon.
The thought of dying never crossed his mind,
But not the less he died, and died alone;
For when Death came to that unhappy King
The very sentinels had fled his gates."

"The end of all things must be near at hand,"
Said Bahram Gour, half earnest, half in jest,
"For lo, the world hath now two Solomons,
Whose wisdom is compressed in three small words,
The knell of Folly, 'All is Vanity!'
It may be so, my dear philosophers,
But are you free from blame? What says the song?
'It is my sight that fails me, not the rose
That waxes pale; my scent that is too coarse,
No lack of odor in the heavenly musk.'
Cry down the world who will, but Bahram Gour
Will love it still." "And I," the poet said,
His fancied sadness dying with the words
That gave it birth, "and never more than now,
When to the quiet tent and drowsy pipe
Succeeds the eager life on flying steeds."

From out their marble stalls the dusky grooms
Led forth the royal stud of milk-white mares.
The falconers came next with hooded birds,
Each with a silver label on its leg;
And then the keepers with the beasts of chase
In chains, lithe panthers, and keen-scented dogs,
Tigers, whose tawny hides are mapped with black,
And lions trained to hunt,—the white gazelle
Fled from their cruel eyes to Noman's tent.
Slowly like one who wills away a dream,
Lifting his head the King called home his thoughts.
He saw the trembling creature at his feet,
And fondled it; the voice of Adi's lute,
Wooing a song, brought Adi to his mind,
The jingling of a scabbard Bahram Gour;
Adi still sat and smoked, but Bahram Gour
Had risen, and was girding on his sword.
"My sombre fancies led me from the chase;
But now that I have found myself once more
Let us depart at once. They wait for us."
He beckoned, and the grooms led up their steeds.
Between the palms whose shadows struck their brows,
Launching across the carpet's bed of flowers,
Around the fountain's glittering mist they rode.
The fretful panthers snuffed, and tugged their chains,
The calmer lions, quiet in their strength,
Strode on, and dragged their keepers after them.

Not far from Hira by the river's side,
Where stood a ruined city was a tomb.
Between the river and the tomb were trees
Whose twinkling leaves were shaken by the wind.
Dropping the hunt before the game was roused
Thither the King and poet rode alone;
They saw the shaken boughs, but felt no wind.

"The leaves are tongues," said Noman, "and they speak,
With some grave message charged, or prophecy.
You read the hidden meaning of the flowers,
Can you expound the language of the trees?"

"Many have here dismounted from their steeds
And kneeling camels in the days of old;
Have slaked their thirst with wine beneath our shade,
And led their camels to the limpid tide.
They strained their shining wine from precious flasks,
They tossed the splendid trappings of their steeds;
Gayly they lived, the pensioners of Time:
But ere life's noon they died, cut off by Fate.
Their ashes drift and waste like withered leaves,
Blown by the east wind now, now by the west."
So spake the trees to Adi. So he spake.

"All things are in a league with my grave thoughts
To make me think of death," replied the King.
"If leaves whose little lives of sun and dew
Last not the year out say that man is dust,
What must the dust, where men by millions sleep,
The dead of ages, say?" The poet stooped,
And scooped his two hands full of dry white dust,
And held it to his ear. "Interpret it."
"Know that the dust was once a man like thee,
Know, too, that thou wilt one day be but dust."
So spake the dust to Adi. So he spake.

"The words are changed," said Noman, "not the tune,
For that still urges man's mortality.
When man forgets his end, nor earth nor heaven
Can hold their peace. The tomb remains to speak.
I go to question that. Wait for me here.
Fear not to see me enter its dark walls;
The time will come when they will shut me in

Forever: now I shall return again."
He waved the poet back, and throwing wide
Its mouldering doors went down into the tomb.

Before the place a watchful sentinel
The poet paced his beat with noiseless steps,
Hearkening the while to catch the King's least call.
He heard the talking leaves above his head,
The river rippling on the sandy shore,
But not the King; the grass was growing thick
Around the tomb, but where the mares were hitched
It grew not; cutting with his sword a swath,
He bore an armful to the hungry mares:
But still the King nor called to him, nor came.
At last the fiery arrows of the noon
Drove back the lessening shadows of the trees,
And hemmed them in a circle round their trunks;
To this the bard retreated from the heat.
The happy light came down upon his heart,
And stretched at ease he sang a summer song.

"The morning moon is set, the stars are gone;
Beside the palace gate the peacocks strut,
And in the tank the early lotus wakes.

The dew fell all night long, and drenched my robe,
The nightingale complained to me, in vain:
I waited for the dawn to meet my love.

She stands before me in the garden walk,
Her blue robe bordered with a fringe of pearls;
She offers me a rose; I kneel to her.

'Nay, speak not yet, though all your words are pearls;
Your smiles outrun your speech, and greet me first:
But when you smile not, speak, or I shall die!

'I kiss the rose,—I would it were your lips!
But wherefore? Such a kiss would end my days.
Pity me, Sweet, my heart is at your feet!'

My long black hair is streaked with silver threads,
Years dim my eyes; yet still in thought I see
The Rose of Beauty in the garden walk.

She sleeps the long, long sleep; disturb her not
O nightingales, be silent, or depart:
And thou, my heart, be still, or moan and break."

The river rippled louder, but the leaves
Crowding together whispered, and the clash
Shook one at Adi's feet; the dust was stirred.
He raised his eyes, and lo, a cloud of dust
Blown from the clattering hoofs of flying steeds.
He knew the milk white mares, and knew the troop
That rode them—Noman's huntsmen; Bahram Gour
Trailing his spear rode wildly at their head.
"The King is lost," he shouted as he came:
"Not so," said Adi, pointing to the tomb,
"The King is there. He muses in the tomb,
Perchance he sleeps. I would have shared his dreams,
But he forbade, and made me wait him here."
Then Bahram Gour went down into the tomb,
To wake the King, and many of the lords
Went with him; those who stayed behind were hushed.
They heard the talking leaves above their heads,
The river rippling on the sandy shore,
But not the King. At length a voice was heard—
"*The King is dead!*" and Bahram Gour came out
Bearing a lifeless body in his arms.

THE CHILDREN'S PRAYER.

If there is any thing that will endure
The eye of God, because it still is pure,
It is the spirit of a little child,
Fresh from his hand, and therefore undefiled.
Nearer the gate of Paradise than we,
Our children breathe its airs, its angels see;
And when they pray God hears their simple prayer,
Yea, even sheathes his sword, in judgment bare.
Witness this story of a by-gone time,
Itself a song, though yet untold in rhyme.
  Where stretches Egypt, and its gardens smile,
Won from the desert by the lordly Nile,
Famine and Pestilence went hand in hand
Of old, and ravaged that unhappy land;
For lo, the Nile, wherein its plenty lies,
The fertilizing Nile forgot to rise.
Day after day it lay, a sluggish flood,
And slimy monsters wallowed in its mud.
When spread the news, and ill news fly apace,
A fearful panic seized the Moslem race,
For not alone its native tribes it fed,
But all the East to Egypt looked for bread.
In Cairo first, there most improvident,
Then in the towns, and in the wandering tent,
Under the palms, by many a shrunken well,
Fainting they fell, and perished where they fell.
  At first they only starved; but by and by
A dread infection brooded in the sky:
There was no time to starve, with every breath
They drew in death, a tainted, loathsome death.

All business ceased ; bazaars and mosques were closed ;
Somewhere about his tower the muezzin dozed.
No more the faithful bowed towards the East,
Was kept no more the Bairam's sacred feast :
(The fasts, alas, they could not help but keep !)
The land was shrouded in a deathly sleep.
You might have walked through Cairo, street by street
Nor met a soul,—'twere better not to meet :
The flying thief, the murderer abhorred,
Or plague-struck beggars—such were those abroad.
At length a sheik remembered what was writ,
(Through faith not doubt had he forgotten it),
That "Children are the keys of Paradise."
Also that "They alone are good and wise,
Because their thoughts, their very lives are prayer."
He sought the mosque, summoned the people there,
Told them his thought, and made its meaning plain,
That they by childish lips should pray again.
'Twas said, and done : the Emir gave command,
And straight the muezzins sang it through the land.
The hour was fixed at dawn. At last dawn came.
Slowly the sun arose, a globe of flame
Struggling with blood-red clouds : in every street
Was seen a crowd, was heard the tramp of feet :
Around the mosques they gathered with a sigh,
Waiting to know if they should live—or die.
The Imauns crowned the babes with early flowers,
And bore them up the minarets and towers,
Even to their topmost summits, where they stood,
And saw the Pyramids and Nile's black flood,
And Cairo at their feet, a breathless mass,
Dying to hear them pray, and see what came to pass.
It was a beautiful but solemn sight
To mark the trembling children robed in white,
Painted against the red and angry sky,

Stretching their arms to Him who dwells on high.
But there they stood, and there they knelt and prayed,
And from that hour the pestilence was stayed.
For while they prayed there came a rush of wind
That rent the clouds, and showed the sun behind;
They saw its broad, bright light, and seemed to hear
The wave of palms, the flow of waters near.
Yes, it was true: the Nile began to rise,
As if its springs were fed from the benignant skies!
It rose, and rolled, and ran before the breeze,
Its long waves furrowed like the stormy seas,
Its mud was swept away, its monsters sank,
It swayed and snapped the reeds along the bank,
Raging and roaring, rising higher and higher,
Far-flaming in the sun—a sheet of windy fire!
All wept with joy. And now there came a man
Wild with good news; he shouted as he ran,
"There is no God but God. Lo, God is Great.
There stands a row of camels at the gate,
Laden for all with sacks of wheat and grain."
They fell upon their knees and wept again.
But they, the children, meek and undefiled,
Went through the streets, and smote their hands and smiled.
Nor was there longer plague or famine there,
Thanks be to God, who heard the Children's Prayer!

———o———

By the margent of the sea
  I would build myself a home,
Where the mighty waters be,
  On the edges of their foam.
Ribs of sands should be the mounds
    In my grounds;

My grasses should be ocean weeds,
  Strung with pulpy beads;
And my blossoms should be shells,
    Bleaching white,
Washed from ocean's deepest cells
  By the billows morn and night.
Morn and night—in both their light,
  Up and down the paven sand,
I would tramp, while Day's great lamp
  Rose or set, on sea and land,
Through a sea of vapors dark
Glimmering like a burning bark,
Drifting o'er its yawning tomb
With a red and lurid gloom.
Seldom should the morning's gold
On the waters be unrolled,
Or the troubled queen of night
Lift her misty veil of light.
Neither wholly dark, nor bright,
Gray by day, and gray by night—
That's the light, the sky for me,
By the margent of the sea.

From my window, when I rose
  In the morning, I would mark
The gray sea in its endless throes,
    And many a bark.
As I watched the pallid sails,
  Bearing naught to me or mine,
I would conjure up the gales
  Soon to draggle them in brine:
Then, my cloak about my face,
Up and down the sands would pace,
Making footprints for the spray
    To wash away.

Waves might break along the shore,
  And thunders roar;
I should only hear aghast
The solemn moaning of the Past.
And if storms should come, and rain
  Pour in torrents down the sky,
    What care I?
What cares any one in pain?
  Are not tears still wrung from me,
Woe is me, and all in vain,
Falling faster than the rain
    In the sea?
But it would be over then,
  And I would no longer weep:
Grief is for the sea of men,
  By God's ocean it must sleep.
Happy, happy would I be
By the margent of the sea.

Up and down the barren beaches,
  Round the ragged belts of land,
In along the curving reaches,
  Out along the horns of sand,
Over the ledges of the rocks,
Where the surges comb their locks,
And their wreathèd buds remain,
  Not to bloom again;
Many a league and hour I stray,
And watch the madness of the spray,
  The caverns in its wall;
Its flame-like currents mounting slow,
Its rounding crest of frothy snow,
    Its crumbling fall;
The climbing sun in light betrayed
By a spot of thinnest shade;

The tossing foam, the wandering plain
Of the melancholy main;
The sea-mew darting everywhere,
Now on the water, and now in the air,
Vexing me with frantic scream,
Like a phantom in a dream—
In dreams I do behold them all,
  Mixed with wave and wind;
But hardly know, so strange they seem,
Whether I behold them there,
Or the sorrow and despair
    In my mind,
Wandering where its tortures be,
By the margent of the sea.

——o——

CHORIC HYMN.

THE little birds awake at peep of day,
When soft winds shake their nests, and leaves are stirred;
The buds unseal their lids beneath the spray,
Called by the dews, by mortal ears unheard.
But thou, though we have called thee, over-loud,
Thrice with our shrillest voices, thou art mute:
  But we will touch the lute,
And melt the dream that wraps thee like a cloud.
We passed along the borders of the vale,
And peeped into it from the misty hill;
Far in its depths we heard the nightingale
Muffled in song; we hear him singing still.
And when pale Hesperos with silver crook
Led forth his starry flock from out their fold,
We wept together in the bosky nook,
And linked our hearts with kisses, each thrice told.

Hast thou forgot our kisses, and thine own?
(We dreamed of those sweet kisses all the night!)
Forgot thy loving maidens, chaste and white?
Forgot the vale, whose depths are yet unknown?
It cannot be! Awake, and answer "No!"
O answer "No!" or we must wake, and weep:
Give us a little sign, before we go,
That we are not forgotten in thy sleep.
Think of us one and all as we of thee,
Both now, and evermore, Persephone.

Harken, our lutes are strung with silver wires,
  That nicely suit the strain;
Our voices melt therein like soft desires,
Or South winds dying in a vernal rain.
The sky-lark listens in the woods apart,
Since twilight sleeping in the falling dew,
And hoards our music in his brimming heart,
Meaning a sweet repayment from the blue.
But thou art bound in slumber, deaf to all,
Mute as a little maid beneath her pall,
Heedless of dear ones coming there to weep,
Locked in the cold and everlasting sleep.
If such should be thy sleep, O what should we
Say to Demeter, in her woe divine?
And to our hearts, and all that ask and pine,
For all would then demand Persephone.

Hark, hear ye not a stirring in her bower,
A rustling in the dimness of the leaves?
Ah yes, and see, the morning in its eaves,
Braids through the twinkling green a golden shower.
Strike all your lutes again, and break the bands
That Sleep has woven round her in the night;
Let melting Music with her loving hands
Slowly unwind his tangled skeins of light.

Up-gathering all thy poppies, drowsy-sweet,
And all thy syrop-urns of mandragore,
Fly, Morpheos, fly, ere Morning's wingèd feet,
Fire-sandalled, bear him to thy palace door,
Where waiting thee thy Dreams
Still linger, blinded by his dazzling beams;
Fly, Morpheos, fly, with heavy-lidded eyes,
The night is done, the maiden would arise.
Awake, Persephone! The finches round
Chirp to the swallows twittering overhead;
And little crickets answer from the ground,
Hidden in tufted mosses, crisp and red.
Awake, awake! Let sluggards weak and gray
Before their time drowse out the morning hours;
Health-loving maids are up before the day,
To trample in the dew, and gather flowers.
Flowers grow around in myriads, even here,
In this dark forest, beaded thick with dew,
They call for thee within thy spirit's ear,
And all the happy birds are calling, too;
And we thy loving maids, so dear to thee:
Then wake and rise, O rise, divine Persephone!

——o——

THE FISHER AND CHARON.

WHERE wild Laconia juts into the sea
The fisher Diotimus had his home.
Between the waters and the woods it stood,
A wattled hut, whose floor was strewn with leaves
And crisp, dry sea-weeds: when the tide came in
The surf ran up the beach even to the door.
Here lived the fisher and his aged wife,
Doro, his second self; she on the land,

And he upon the sea, their long lives passed.
He rose at early dawn and dragged his boat
Down to the water's edge, threw in his oars,
His lines, and bait, and then with lusty strokes
Pulled out into the gulf through clouds of mist.
From shore to shore he knew the gulf, the rocks,
The curling eddies and the isles of weed.
He knew the haunts and habits of the fish,
How best to catch them, and the bait they loved;
The sea-birds, too, his fellow fishers, they,
He knew them all. From Tenarus to Crete,
And where the beaches of Egilia break
The shining surge which dies among their shells,
He tracked the scaly tenants of the deep.
The summer smote him with its fiercest fires,
Burned his old face, and browned his sinewy arms;
The winter nipt him with its still, cold wind,
And drenched his cloak of mats with colder rain.
For days he saw no sun, so thick the clouds:
But, cloud or sun, he put to sea at dawn
Fearless, and with the dusk of eve returned.
The sunset was a torch to light him home.
His boat was guided by its golden flare
Straight to the shore; he saw his hut afar,
And Doro on the sands; she beckoned him:
His sharp keel cut the waves, and ere its wake
Sank in the blackness grated on the sand.
They lived the common life of little things
Summed up in poverty: like waves the days
The years went by, each day and year alike—
The last alone remembered. They were young;
Then crooked wrinkles crept about their eyes:
Then they were old. They lived, and loved, and died.
One autumn day, when tropic birds flew home,
The fisher sat beside his dying wife.

She lay upon a couch of withered leaves
That rustled as she moved; above her hung
A coil of line with sea-weed on its hooks;
A wicker basket was the fisher's seat.
Their dim eyes met, and both with tears were wet.
"Hereafter, Doro, I shall weep alone,"
Said Diotimus. "Not alone," she moaned,
"For I shall walk the solemn shore of death
In tears till you shall come." She clutched his knee,
Twisted her trembling fingers in his hand,
Looked in his face, and waited for the end.
The waters lapped the door stone, and went back,
The tide was slowly setting out to sea,
Leaving a narrow strip of barren sand.
When all was over Diotimus rose
And called the fishers' wives to wash the dead.
But first he placed the needful obolus,
The ferriage of the dead, beneath her tongue,
Her spirit else had wandered by the Styx
An hundred years among the wretched ghosts.
They buried her behind the fisher's hut,
Hard by the wood, among its fallen leaves.
The dead leaves rustled in the restless wind,
And mingled in the fisher's broken dream.
It seemed to him the leaves whereon he lay
Were stirred that night. The dead was by his side.
He rose at dawn, and rowed to sea again,
Scarce knowing what he did; a league from shore
He saw his net was lost, or left behind:
He dropped his oar, and let the crazy boat
Drift as it would, his idle thoughts the while
Drifting about the ocean of the Past.
The sea-birds knew him, and no longer shy
Swooped down, and snatched the fish around his boat;
Yea, lighted on his boat, his very oars,

And screamed, and chattered of their briny loves:
He harmed them not, his thoughts were in the Past.
"Could Time restore those days, or give her back,"
The fisher thought, "then I could die in peace;
But Time will not restore them, nor will she
Return to me: the dead return no more.
But there's a way to her," the old man thought,
And stared in the dark water. "Day and night
The gate stands wide; a sudden flaw of wind
Might send me through it, nay, a fish's fin
Rubbing against the bottom of the boat.
There are a thousand doors that lead to death.
I trail my fingers in the rippling brine
And dip my death; a cup of this salt wine
Drained in the sunless sea would end my days.
But would it help me to my wife again,
My dear, dear Doro? Does she wait for me,
There where my soul would land? I know not that."
He stared in the black water more and more,
He saw the tangled weeds, the glancing fish,
But Doro never; only in his dreams
Did he behold her, and she seemed to weep,
Walking alone the solemn shores of Death!
But now the tropic birds were all flown home,
The autumn leaves were shed, and wintry rains
Were sown in swelling seas; cold blew the winds.
It was too cold to live upon the sea;
The sea was full of ice, and every spray
That lifted his frail boat froze on the prow.
Besides his boat grew frailer day by day;
Old like himself, it scarcely rode the waves:
A storm would swamp it. "I should find my death
In the cold waters," Diotimus said,
"But not my dear, dead wife; for though I died
I could not join the souls across the Styx,

So poor am I. I have no obolus
To fee old Charon." So he sought the shore.
He hung his nets and lines within the hut
Stiffened with frost, made up his bed of leaves,
And gathered fagots in the windy wood
To feed his fire; he walked the bleak, bare wood,
Lone as the wind that snapped the withered limbs;
Also the barren beach, the stretch of sand
Close to the tumbling wall of roaring surf.
The surf, and sand, and melancholy wood
Troubled him less, so waste and grim were they,
Than did the hut; the memory of the dead
Peopled the lonely hut, and filled his thoughts.
He seemed to see, or saw, his vanished wife
About her household duties all the day.
She mended nets, she spun, she built his fires;
At night he dreamed of her; when the wind blew
'Twas she who shook his door: when fell the rain,
Trickling upon him through the crumbling roof,
'Twas she who wept—the tears he felt were hers:
She was the ghost of moonlight on the wall.
"I can no longer bear this loss of mine,
Here where it came upon me: I must go,
Whither I know not, but to sea, to sea;
There is no rest, no peace for me on land.
The winter winds may freeze me, or the isles
Of ice may crush my boat; I can but die.
But die I shall not yet, for I must seek
Charon, and ask him to forego his fee;
Not else can rest be mine when I am dead."
So spake the fisher one gray winter's day,
And straightway put to sea: the isles of ice
Parted before his prow and closed astern;
Behind the noisy shocks of spray his hut
Grew less and less: it disappeared: the beach

Sank in the sea: the woods alone were left—
The long, dark belt of woods and ragged hills.
At noon he doubled Tenarus, and beat
Northward along Laconia's western shore.
Somewhere along the shore, Tradition said,
Within a gorge the gates of Hades rose;
Where, no man knew—such knowledge suits not life.
Death brooded round that awful shore and sea.
The dreary woods were dead; nor leaf, nor limb
Stirred in the strong north wind that filled the sky:
Beaches were none, but rocks, a wall of rock,
With gaping caverns where the sea was lost.
No surf, no crested wave, no rippled swell
Wrinkled the sea's broad plain, and yet it moved,
Swept shoreward like a wind. There was a gulf
Between two barren mountains whose black jaws
Devoured the light; to this the current set,
Bearing the fisher's boat: for though his oars
Lay on the thwarts, and all his sails were furled,
He drove before the wind to the inner land.
Soon as he passed that portal of the sea
There came a change; the thought that led him on
Slackened, his mind grew weak, a drowsy weight
Hung on his lids: it was as he had crossed
The leaden portals of the Land of Sleep.
All memory of his former life was lost,
Sunk in his dream: only a sense of loss
Lived in his soul, a vague and muffled grief.
He bathed his eyes in that mysterious stream
To break his slumber; down his wrinkled cheek
The water trickled, and he tasted it:
'Twas sweet and bitter like forgetfulness,
A bitter sweet: he knew the river then—
Lethe, whose dreadful waters lead to Death!
At last the current emptied in the Styx—

A sluggish lake, whose nearer bank alone
Was seen; in mist the farther bank was hid.
He took his oars, and rowed to Charon's wharf.
A line of sickly willows fringed the shore,
Their ragged tresses draggling in the scum
That mantled the grim pool; a ghostly rank
Of poplars, like a halted train of shades,
Trembled; on one a raven sat, and slept.
And here and there were single ghostly shapes,
That wandered up and down like morning mists;
Others from somewhere inland through a gorge
Drifted and drifted down to Charon's wharf.
Charon himself was in his dusky barge,
Just touching land—returned from Hades: still
The furrow of his wake was on the scum.
His beard was long and ragged, and his hair
Hung o'er his brows; the wrinkles of his face
Seemed carved in bronze or stone: a stony light
Glinted in his hard eyes whose steady frown
Looked pity dead: no pity Charon knew.
"What man art thou? and wherefore art thou come?"
"My name is Diotimus, and my home
Is in Laconia; Doro was my wife.
She died: you ferried her across the Styx."
"Perchance, old man: but now so many cross
I cannot long remember single souls,
Or queens, or fisher's wives: but get thee back,
The dead and not the living come to me."
So Charon said, and waved the fisher back.
"Not back to earth again, O say not that!
He who has lived for threescore years and ten,
So old am I, and lived the poor man's life,
Once freed therefrom, not willingly returns.
From youth to age upon the dangerous sea
My days were passed; by suns of summer scorched,

By winds of winter numbed; and tempests rose,
Great whirlwinds in the sky, and in the sea
Chasms and gulfs of night; but all I bore,
For Doro lived; but now that she is dead
I long to die—there is no joy in life:
Pity me, then, and let me cross the Styx."
"*He will not pity thee*," a shadowy Voice
Breathed from the shore, "*but rather mock thy grief:*
There is no mercy shown to men in life,
Why should they look for any after death?"
Beneath the poplar where the raven sat
This hopeless Voice to Diotimus croaked:
The raven heard, and answered in his dream.
Meantime the wandering shapes had gathered round
To watch the issue; thin at first as smoke,
Against the swaying willow branches drawn,
Their dim uncertain outlines surer grew,
Grew firm and certain: wrapt in long white robes,
That swept the ground and o'er their faces fell
Hood-like, they stood: the wretched dead were they,
That wander by the Styx an hundred years.
"I bear the dead alone across the Styx,"
Charon replied, and smiled a grim, dark smile;
"Only the dead, nor all the dead, you see.
Prayers have been said to me, tears have been shed
For ages, as ye reckon time on earth;
In vain: I heed not human tears or prayers.
Great kings have laid their sceptre at my feet,
Pale queens have knelt to me and wrung their hands,
To die before their time: I sent them back.
What man art thou that I should let thee cross?
Go back, and live the remnant of thy life:
Live till the lords of life shall let thee die,
It cannot now be long, then come to me;
Not as thou comest now, but with the dead.

Come with an obolus, and thou shalt cross."
"I have no obolus, but I shall cross,"
The fisher said, "for Doro waits for me."
Above the dead the silent willows leaned;
The air was hushed; except the poplar rods,
High over all, naught stirred: the poplars shook,
Reached by the couriers of a coming wind,
Or some impending doom! A wind of doom
Swept through the gorge behind them, driving on
A sea of spirits and the noise of war:
In war two mighty kingdoms then were met;
These were the flower of both, slain in the shock.
Rushing from life to death they threw themselves
Straight into Charon's barge—or would have thrown—
But that his oar uplifted kept them off.
And now while clamor and confusion reigned,
Unseen, the wary fisher seized his oars
And pulled for the farther shore: before his prow
The scum was thick, and thick the matted weeds
Below the sliding keel: a faint dead scent
Burthened the waste; nor wave nor ripple there,
He tore his way through slime at every stroke.
Of all the slaughtered dead that stormed his barge
Not one would Charon ferry o'er the Styx,
For all were yet unburied in the field.
He stretched his hand in vain; no burial fee
Dropped in his greedy palm; he drove them back.
A single ghost, a slave that died in peace,
Wealthier with one poor obolus than they,
Heroes, and valiant captains, kings of war,
Stepped in the barge, and sat at Charon's feet.
The barge was turned, and now began the chase;
For Charon now the fisher missed, and saw
His laboring boat half-way across the stream:
He bent him to his oars that rose and fell,

Faster and faster raining strokes that shook
The sea of scum, and dashed its turbid waves,
Shouting great shouts to fright the daring man:
The shouts o'ertook the fisher in his flight,
And fright a little moment chilled his heart,
But soon was strangled by the iron will
That nerved his arm, half hope and half despair:
The crazy boat was strained in every seam,
And slow, great drops oozed through her trembling sides;
But not the less she flew, pursed by shouts,
And frowning Charon in his gloomy barge.
  But now the mist that veiled the further bank
Grew thin and thinner, and the fisher caught
The shore beyond, a green, low-lying shore,
Deep meadows, uplands, slopes, and happy woods
Steeped through and through with light; and stately Shapes
That came and went like gods: but one was still,
Hushed as a statute frozen in the moon.
It looked a woman, and her marble eye
Drank in that breathless chase across the Styx.
"Doro!" the fisher shouted, as he neared
The happy shore; the figure seemed to hear:
"Doro, dear Doro!"—but the rest was lost,
For Charon now had reached the fisher's boat—
His black barge struck it: down it sank like lead,
The fisher with it: but he rose again,
Breasting the surges to the blessed shore
Where Doro stood, and stretched her hands to him.
He lands—she falls upon his neck, and weeps:
Then hand in hand, their happy tears forgot,
The smiling spirits go to meet their judge.
But Charon goes back angry to the dead!

GREAT AND SMALL.

A LITTLE plot of garden ground
  Grew envious of bordering bowers,
  That cast their shade upon its flowers,
And thus its thoughts an utterance found :

"I envy you, ye stately bowers,
  Your royal growths of trunk and bough,
  With all the blooms that cluster now
Thereon, and those that fall in showers.

Far in the heavens ye lift your heads,
  Whatever wind blows, O, ye trees !
  But these my flowers, the lightest breeze
Dashes them on their dusty beds.

Within your branches lodge the birds,
  Rebuilding nests, and chanting lays ;
  And in your shade when summer days
Are sultry lie the drowsy herds.

Around my stalks the insects creep,
  Over my buds the beetles run,
  With moths that die when day is done,
And bees that hum themselves asleep.

Not all unloved by me the bees,
  Draining my cups of honey dry :
  But what are they, and what am I,
To herds, and birds, and giant trees ?"

But Nature, listening, "Thou art wrong,"
  Did say reproving: "Wrong," the herds;
  And "Wrong," the many-voicèd birds
Interpolated in their song.

"There is no difference with me,"
  Was whispered in the garden's ear.
  "The smallest blossom is as dear
To Nature as the greatest tree.

The pine and oak are only flowers
  Grown large: they drink the beads of dew
  Like little violets, meek and blue,
And battle with the stormy powers.

The insect with its gauzy wings
  Sings, and the moth and beetle grim;
  And for the bee, I doat on him,
And know by heart the tune he sings.

Then learn this truth, the base of all,
  That all are equal, so they fill
  Their proper spheres, and do God's will:
There is no other Great, or Small."

——o——

THE POPLAR.

THE poplar-tree that guards my house
  Looks in on me to-night,
As if it would divide my shade,
  Though based itself in light.
    Alas, poor tree,
    It knows not me—
A mystery few explain aright.

It stands out in the lamp-light there,
  And shakes its twinkling leaves,
And whatsoever the heavens send
  It patiently receives.
    Rain, hail, or snow,
    All winds that blow—
Whatever comes it never grieves.

For me, I cannot say the like,
  For I do grieve and pine;
There's not an hour but stirs a pang
  In this weak heart of mine:
    Even Pleasure pains,
    And Love contains—
How much of sorrow, though divine.

Even now they fill my aching heart
  With mingled gloom and flame;
And yet the poplar envies me
  My woe without a name.
    It sees my tears,
    Conceives my fears,
And yearns to bear the same.

No, poplar, no, rest where you are
  In wiser Nature's plan;
Man suffers so 'tis happier
  To be a tree than man.
    Your time will come,
    Your martyrdom:
Till then contented, happy be,
Nor seek to share my life with me.

MISERRIMUS.

He has passed away
From a world of strife,
Fighting the wars of Time and Life.
The leaves will fall when the winds are loud,
And the snows of winter will weave his shroud ;
But he will never, ah, never know
Any thing more
Of leaves or snow.

The summer-tide
Of his life was past,
And his hopes were fading, falling fast.
His faults were many, his virtues few,
A tempest with flecks of heaven's blue.
He might have soared to the gates of light,
But he built his nest
With the birds of night.

He glimmered apart
In solemn gloom,
Like a dying lamp in a haunted tomb.
He touched his lute with a magic spell,
But all his melodies breathed of hell,
Raising the Afrits and the Ghouls,
And the pallid ghosts
Of the damnèd souls.

But he lies in dust,
And the stone is rolled
Over his sepulchre dark and cold.
He has cancelled all he has done, or said,

And gone to the dear and holy Dead.
Let us forget the path he trod,
He has done with us,
He has gone to God.

——o——

THE SQUIRE OF LOW DEGREE.

The royal sunlight flushed the room,
From stainèd windows streaming down,
To where, rayed round in golden gloom,
The old king sat, and tried to frown.
Before him stood his daughter dear,
Her white hands folded on her breast,
And in her drooping eyes a tear,
The sign of love, and love's unrest:
For she was grieved as only maids can be,
That love, and lose, like her, a Squire of Low Degree.

[THE KING SPEAKS.]

"To-morrow we ride with all our train
To meet our cousin of Aquitain;
Be ready, daughter, to go with us there,
At the head of the train in a royal chair.
The chair shall be covered with velvet red,
With a fringèd canopy overhead,
And curtains of damask, white and blue,
Figured with lilies and silver dew.
Your robe must be purple, with ermine bands,
The finest fur of the northern lands:
Enamelled chains of rare device,
And your feather a bird of Paradise.

And what will you have for a dainty steed?
A Flanders mare of the royal breed?
An English blood? A jennet of Spain?
Or a Barbary foal with a coal-black mane?
We still have the Soldan's harness, Sweet:
The housings hang to the horse's feet,
The saddle-cloth is sown with moons,
And the bridle-bells jingle the blythest tunes.
Or will you on a palfrey go?
An ambling palfrey, sure and slow,
That shakes its head at every tread,
And tosses its heavy mane of snow?
Speak, my daughter! Or will you stay,
And make it a happy hunting day?
The huntsmen shall be gathered at dawn,
And the hounds led out upon the lawn;
When you and your bevy of dames appear,
We'll spur our steeds, and chase the deer:
Through meadows through woods away we'll go,
And shout while the merry bugles blow.
Or you shall lead us where you will,
Down in the valley, or up the hill:
Speak, and the hawks shall wait you there,
And a noble quarry in the air.
And O, but you are a lady bright,
On a green hill's side in the morning light,
Your rosy cheek by the soft wind kissed,
And a dappled falcon on your wrist.
After the chase we'll feast in the hall,
Under the antlers on the wall;
The trumpet shall wake its golden sound,
And the butler bear the dishes round,
Ribs of beef, so crisp and brown,
And a jug of Rhenish to wash it down,
Hares, and pheasants, and venison steaks,

And a boar with his skin peeling off in flakes,
And, to crown the whole, a peacock dressed,
With its starry plumes and a gilded crest.
For you and the maids, a store of spice,
Cloves, and the seed of Paradise,
Pots of ginger from over the seas,
Honeycombs from the English trees,
Plumbs, dim-seen through their misty streaks,
And dishes of peaches with bloomy cheeks,
Pears that smack of the sunny South,
And cherries, red as a maiden's mouth!
Grapes in salvers, with sprigs of vine,
And wine, wine, a river of wine,
Ripe and old, and brave and bold,
In cups of silver, and flagons of gold,
Red from Bordeaux, white from the Rhine,
Rumney, and Malmsey, and Malespine—
Every vintage of famous wine!"

[THE PRINCESS ANSWERS.]

"But I would rather have," said she,
"My loving Squire of Low Degree;
Nor gaudy trains, nor days of chase,
Reward me for his absent face.
They do but bring him back again,
And all the Past, a double pain.
I see him now, he is my page,
A dreamy boy of tender age:
His hair is long, and bright as gold,
And in his eyes are depths untold.
'Tis dangerous, believe me, Sire,
  The growth of two young hearts like ours:
We grow like flowers, and bear desire,
  The odor of the human flowers.

Eyes tell the tale, though lips say naught,
And it colors the very springs of thought;
I thought of him, and he of me,
The daring Squire of Low Degree."

The monarch's eye with anger burns,
Like one who hates yet hears a truth;
Besides his own sweet youth returns,
And pleads—but he despises youth.
The princess kneels before his chair,
And takes his heavy-hanging hand:
He does but smooth her ruffled hair,
And idle with its jewelled band:
And yet he loves her, angry though he be,
And bribes her to forget the Squire of Low Degree.

[THE KING SPEAKS.]

"You shall have a mantle, silver-green,
With clasps of gold, and gems between,
A cloak of scarlet, deep as flame,
And a wimpled hood to match the same,
A golden comb to crown your hair,
Or even a crown, like this I wear.
Or will you that every separate curl
Shall be inlaid with a priceless pearl,
Till you shine like night in the starry hours?
Or will you garland your brow with flowers?
But your stately throat, like a swan's afloat—
That must be circled with coral beads,
Or the ruby whose heart with passion bleeds.
Kerchiefs of Holland, Mechlin lace,
And a veil like mist to hide your face,
Embroidered gloves, and velvet hose,
And tippets to wrap you from the snows,

Eider shoes, lined from the cold,
And slippers of satin with buckles of gold.
Nor shall you tread on rushes more,
But cloth of gold shall cover your floor;
And when you please to take the air,
But name your path, and we'll spread it there.
Your garden walks shall be trimmed anew,
And we'll try if we can to keep the dew:
Plant new trees, of stronger shade,
And have the summer arbors made.
You shall have a fawn with a silver bell,
A delicate fawn, that knows you well;
A peacock, too, of the richest hue,
To strut before you, and spread its train,
Gay as the rainbow after rain.
The fountain shall play, the swans shall swim,
And feed from your hand at the basin's brim:
You shall have a shallop with silken sail,
And oars beside, if the wind should fail:
Shall float on the lake, with a rippling wake,
Shoot with the current down the stream,
And under the archèd bridges dream.
Or you shall land, if it please you more,
And have a pavilion pitched on shore,
Blue and white, like the sky in sight,
A couch of down, and a dreamy light:
An odorous silence, rapt and deep,
And sleep, the beautiful balm of Sleep!"

[THE PRINCESS ANSWERS.]

"But I would sooner have," said she,
"My loving Squire of Low Degree;
For in his faith my soul reposes,
Sweeter than in a bed of roses.

Nor balmy sleep, nor happy dream,
Nor shallop on a summer stream,
Nor garden walks, nor shaded bowers,
No, nor a perfect nest of flowers—
Nothing, my father, that is thine
Can make him any thing but mine.
You think us children, Sire, you men;
We want our playthings back again:
We must be pacified with show,
We are such simpletons, you know.
It may be so, it may be so,
But when the worst is known and told,
We cannot all be bought and sold;
Nor force nor art can make us part
From something holy in the heart—
The bright and beautiful love of old,
The deathless love I bear to thee,
My own dear Squire of Low Degree."

She leaned against her father's breast,
And in her virgin sorrow smiled;
Perplexed, distressed, and ill at rest,
He stooped, and kissed his weeping child.
Her arms around his neck she drew;
He felt her wild heart beat, and beat:
His own was touched, with pity, too:
He threw his kingdom at her feet:
And yet he held her suppliant soul in fee,
For still he plead against the Squire of Low Degree.

[THE KING SPEAKS.]

"The western wing, by the palace gate,
I give it to you, with all its state.
Deep are the halls, broad are the stairs,
And tables of oak, and walnut chairs,

With mirrors of Venice adorn the rooms,
That are hushed in the heart of purple glooms.
When the sun at his golden setting paints
The palace-panes, and we pray to the saints,
The Court shall in your chapel throng,
And hear the solemn even-song:
The priest before the altar stands,
And lifts the Host with reverent hands,
The little faery children sing,
And the incense burns, and the censers swing,
And the deep-toned organ thunders round,
Filling the aisles with a sea of sound.
You shall sup with me whenever you will,
And I'll pick you an arbor, green and still,
Drape it with arras down to the floor,
And spread your service by the door,
That when you eat you may behold
The knights at play where the bowls are rolled.
Then you shall to the drawbridge go,
And watch the sportive fish below,
Their glancing fins, their motions free,
Arrows of gold in a silver sea.
A beautiful barge shall meet you there,
With gilded pennons drooped in air,
And sturdy rowers, with lifted oars,
To pull you by the sedgy shores.
Step on deck, and mount your throne
Under the purple däis alone:
Your favored ladies, two by two,
And the knights you name shall follow you:
Wave your hand, the band shall play,
And the rowers speed you on your way;
Down the river, and past the lawn,
And up the lake where hides the swan;
Through glassy shadows, and drifts of light,

The bloom of eve, and the gloom of night,
Till rises the moon, when home you turn,
And land where the torches redly burn,
And the garden's roof and its leafy bars
Glitter with cressets, like colored stars:
Then to your chamber, chaste and white,
In the silent privacy of night.
Your room shall be hung with curtains of snow,
And a canopy over the couch shall flow:
The broidered sheets with pearls we'll strew,
Till it gleams like a lily edged with dew.
You shall have the finch that you desire,
In an ivory cage with golden wire;
It shall hang at the head of your bed, and cheep,
And meet your eyes when they close in sleep:
And to hasten sleep we'll make the room
Drowsy with shadow and perfume.
And you shall have the ripe delight
Of mellowest music all the night,
And when the songs of the minstrels fail
The sweeter songs of the nightingale:
And the heavenly strain will flood your brain,
Till heaven opens before your eyes,
And your spirit walks in Paradise!"

[THE PRINCESS ANSWERS.]

"But I would only have," said she,
"My loving Squire of Low Degree;
For I love him, and he loves me,
And what is life when love is flown?
We breathe, indeed, we grieve, we sigh,
And seem to live, and yet we die:
  There is no life alone.
Glory is but a gilded chain,

And joy another name for pain:
There is no joy alone!
But joy, or pain, it matters not,
Without my Squire of Low Degree;
All things are nothing now to me,
For I shall die, and be forgot.
You have another daughter still
To love you, Sire, and work your will;
For me awaits the convent cell,
And soon the mournful passing-bell.
No more a princess, when you hear
The woman's dirge, and see her bier,
Forget your pride, and all beside,
And but remember she was dear.
And when the ghostly mass is said,
And prayers are chanted for the dead,
O pray that she may happy be,
And all good souls shall pray for thee!"

——o——

IMOGEN.

UNKNOWN to her the maids supplied
Her wants, and gliding noiseless round
Passed out again, while Leon's hound
Stole in and slumbered at her side:
Then Cloten came, a silly ape,
And wooed her in his boorish way,
Barring the door against escape;
But the hound woke, and stood at bay,
Defiant at the lady's feet,
And made the ruffian retreat.
Then for a little moment's space
A smile did flit across the face
Of Lady Imogen.

Without the morning dried the dews
  From shaven lawns and pastures green:
  Meantime the court dames and the queen
Did pace the shaded avenues:
And Cymbeline amid his train
  Rode down the winding palace walks,
Behind the hounds that snuffed the plain,
  And in the track of wheeling hawks;
And soon in greenwood shaws anear
They blew their horns, and chased the deer.
    But she nor saw nor heard it there,
    But sat, a statue of despair,
        The mournful Imogen.

She shook her ringlets round her head,
  And clasped her hands, and thought, and thought,
  As every faithful lady ought,
Whose lord is far away—or dead.
She pressed in books his faded flowers,
  That never seemed so sweet before;
Upon his picture gazed for hours,
  And read his letters o'er and o'er,
Dreaming about the loving Past,
Until her tears were flowing fast.
    With aches of heart, and aches of brain,
    Bewildered in the realms of pain,
        The wretched Imogen!

She tried to rouse herself again,
  Began a broidery quaint and rich,
  But pricked her fingers every stitch,
And left in every bud a stain.
She took her distaff, tried to spin,
  But tangled up the golden thread:

She touched her lute, but could not win
A happy sound, her skill had fled.
The letters in her books were blurred,
She could not understand a word.
Bewildered still, and still in tears,
The dupe of hopes, the prey of fears,
The weeping Imogen!

Her curtains opened in the breeze
And showed the slowly-setting sun,
Through vines that up the sash did run,
And hovering butterflies and bees.
A silver fountain gushed below,
Where swans superbly swam the spray:
And pages hurried to and fro,
And trim gallants with ladies gay,
And many a hooded monk and friar
Went barefoot by in coarse attire.
But like a picture, or a dream,
The outward world did only seem,
To thoughtful Imogen.

When curfews rang, and day was dim,
She glided to her chapel desk,
Unclasped her missal arabesque,
And sang the solemn vesper hymn:
Before the crucifix knelt down,
And told her beads, and strove to pray;
But Heaven was deaf, and seemed to frown,
And push her idle words away:
And when she touched the holy urn
The icy water seemed to burn!
No faith had she in saints above,
She only wanted human love,
The pining Imogen.

The pale moon walked the waste o'erhead,
  And filled the room with sickly light;
  Then she arose in piteous plight,
Disrobed herself, and crept to bed.
The wind without was loud and deep,
  The rattling casements made her start:
At last she slept, but in her sleep
  She pressed her fingers o'er her heart,
And moaned, and once she gave a scream,
To break the clutches of a dream.
    Even in her sleep she could not sleep,
    For ugly visions made her weep,
      The troubled Imogen.

———o———

THE FLAMINGO.

[IN THE DESERT.]

THIN and pale the moon is shining
  Where the Arab tents are spread;
But the cloudy sky before me,
And around the burning desert,
    Both are red:
And where their hues are most like blood,
Mirrored in the sluggish flood,
Down the long, black neck of land,
I see the red Flamingo stand.

That bird accurst, I saw it first
  On a wild and angry dawn;
I was wakened from my slumbers
By Zuleika's stifled screaming—
    She was gone!

Stolen by a turbaned horseman,
  Mounted on a barb so black:
I saw her garments waving white,
And I followed day and night,
  In the red Flamingo's track.
Three whole moons have I pursued it,
  With a swift and noiseless tread;
Like a dreamer whom the demons
With a baleful lamp are leading
    To the dead.
Happy are the dead! But I—
I can never, never die,
    Until my hands are red.
But red they will be soon,
For I turn my back upon the moon,
And follow the bird that doubles its speed,
Eager to see the horseman bleed,
And dabble its beak, as I my hands,
In the blood that shall crimson the desert sands!

——o——

THE SERENADE OF MA-HAN-SHAN.

[CHINA.]

COME to the window now, beautiful Yu Ying!
The new moon is rising, white as the shell of a pearl.
    Your honored father and brother
      And the guests are still at table,
    Tipping the golden bottles,
      But I have stolen to you!
    The rose looks over the wall
      To see who passes near:

Look out of the window, you,
  And see who waits below.
I am a Mandarin: my plume is a pheasant's feather:
The lady who marries me may live at court, if she likes.

I stood by the pond to-day; hundreds of lilies bloomed,
And the wonderful keung-flower grew in the midst of all.
Whenever that marvel happens
  A wedding is sure to follow;
It rests with you, Yu Ying,
  Speak—is the wedding ours?
We will dwell in Keang-Nan,
  For I have a palace there;
My garden is leagues in length,
  Deer run wild in the parks:
Cages of loories, macaws; lakes of Mandarin ducks:
A lane bordered with peach-trees—all for sweet Yu Ying.

What means this wonderful light? Is it a second moon?
Yu Ying at her window! A million of thanks, Yu Ying!
Drop me your fan for a gift,
  Or better a tress of your hair:
It is but little to give,
  For I have given my heart!
The fire-flies twinkle, twinkle,
  Under the cypress boughs:
They are wedding each other to-night,
  The lights are their wedding lanterns.
When shall I order ours, and come in the flowery chair?
Name me the pearl of a day, my bride, my wife—Yu Ying!

THE SLEDGE AT THE GATE.

[LAPLAND.]

I WOULD run this arrow straight into my heart
  Sooner than see what I saw to-night.
I harnessed my rein-deer, mounted the sledge,
  And skimmed the snow by the northern light.
The thin ice crackled, the water roared,
    But I crossed the fiord :
I reach the house when the night is late,
What's this ? A deer and a sledge at the gate !

O the eyes of Zela are winter springs !
  But the wealth of summer is in her hair ;
But she loves me not, she is false again,
  Or why are the sledge and the rein-deer there ?
I throw myself down, face-first in the snow :
    "*Let the false one go !*"
She never shall know my love, or my scorn,
For I shall be frozen stiff in the morn.

The sharp winds blew, and my limbs grew chill.
  I knew no more till I felt the fire.
They rubbed my breast, and they rubbed my hands,
  And my life came back like a dark desire.
She spake kind words, and smoothed my hair,
    But the sledge was there !
"*Ah false, but fair !*" It was all I said,
I struck her down, and away I fled.

I mounted my sledge, and the rein-deer flew,
  In the wind, in the snow, in the blinding sleet :

The snow was heavy, the wind like a knife,
  And the ice like water under my feet.
The wolves were hungry—they scented my track—
    But I fought them back!
I fear neither wolves, nor the winter's cold,
For the faithless woman has made me bold.

——o——

THE GRAPE GATHERER.

[ITALY.]

WELL, I have met you, cousin,
  Where not a soul can see:
What do you want? "You love me?"
  You trifle, Sir, with me.
You love that grape-girl yonder,
  The one against the wall:
She climbs, and climbs; but have a care,
  A step, and she may fall.
You walked with her this morning,
  Her basket on your head:
"'Twas better than my coronet,"
  Or something so you said:
"And the grapes and yellow tendrils
  Tangled in her hair,
Were brighter than my ringlets,
  And all the pearls I wear."
You should have seen her lover,
  Hid in the vines hard by,
A swarthy, black-browed fellow,
  With a devil in his eye:
He clutched his grape-hook fiercely,
  And but that I were near,

He would have slain you, cousin,
  And will some night, I fear.
You think she loves you only?
  And so thought all the rest:
Why, you had hardly left her
  Before the Count was blest.
You doubt? Pray ask her sister,
  Or ask the jilted swains,
Or watch, when she's not watching,
  'Twill well be worth your pains.
I should be very angry,
  'Tis so unworthy you:
But since you say you jested,
  I must forgive, and do.
I own I love you somewhat;
  But ere you marry me,
You must do one thing, cousin—
  Let my grape gatherers be!

——o——

SICILIAN PASTORAL.

THE nests in spring were full of bluish eggs,
In summer full of birds: now autumn comes
The nests are empty, and the birds are gone.

The soft white clouds are flecked, the sky is bound
With belts of swallows, stretching from the west
To where the east is girded in with haze.

Stay, swallows, stay! The land is near and bright,
The sea is far, and dark, and perilous,
And all beyond is alien, and unknown.

Why should ye fly so soon? Why fly at all,
When ye might stay with us the long year through,
And be in deathless summer all the time?

Here all the vales are full of dewy flowers,
The orchard plots are full of juicy fruits,
The endless, purple woods are full of balm.

Stay, swallows, stay! The flowers and fruit and balm
Will fade and die, when ye have left the isle,
And winds will moan the absence of your songs.

Stay, swallows, stay! and hear the last year's birds:
"We flew o'er many an isle where summer broods,
But found no summer-land like Sicily."

They will not hear—we waste our words in air:
We might as well go chatter to the crows:
The crows would hear us, though they meant to go.

Go, swallows, go! and be it all your doom
To bear the memory of what ye leave—
For memory will cancel half the sin:

And be it all your punishment to sing
In tropic islands of Sicilian sweets,
And shame the tropic birds with summer songs.

———o———

[PERSIA.]

WE parted in the streets of Ispahan.
I stopped my camel at the city gate;
Why did I stop? I left my heart behind.

I heard the sighing of thy garden palms,
I saw the roses burning up with love,
I saw thee not: thou wert no longer there.

We parted in the streets of Ispahan.
A moon has passed since that unhappy day;
It seems an age: the days are long as years.

I send thee gifts by every caravan,
I send thee flasks of attar, spices, pearls,
I write thee loving songs on golden scrolls.

I meet the caravans when they return.
"What news?" I ask. The drivers shake their heads.
We parted in the streets of Ispahan.

——o——

THE SEARCH FOR PERSEPHONE.

BOOK II.

"Proserpine gathering flowers,
Herself a fairer flower, by gloomy Dis
Was gathered, which cost Ceres all that pain
To seek her through the world."

No more of rural song and pastoral,
Profuse or studied, but a higher strain;
Thee now I woo, divine Melpomene.
Thou didst inspire tragedians grave of eld,
To sing of Godlike suffering, and embalm
In monumental verse the woe of Gods;
Much did they sing, but much remains unsung,
And chief Demeter's woe, which now is mine.

O help me, as thou didst thine elder bards,
Order the lofty numbers, build the style
In naked and severe simplicity,
And lift my spirit to the argument,
Which deepens soon to tragic. Breathe through me,
Voiceless myself, and thine be all the wreaths.

Where is Demeter now? What troubled look
Burthens her face—what solemn words the air?
Demeter stands beside the spring which rose
Where Aides vanished with Persephone:
Of port superior to the loftiest
Of mortal mould, in Queen, or Amazon
Renowned, the light and pillar of the sex;
Deep-bosomed, and white-limbed, a supreme Shape.
Her face is pale with sorrow, yet she wears
Her sorrow grandly like a diadem,
Nor other crown, though Goddess of the Earth,
Except the simple tiar of golden hair
Coiled round her brow, an orbèd peak of thought.
Her voice is sadder than an autumn wind
In a lone land, not shrill, nor full of gusts,
But equal, and deep-toned, blown from all points.

"I have been listening, wrapt in searching thought,
To what, in trembling words, the nymphs revealed,
But where my child has gone I cannot tell;
My foresight failed me here, my knowledge fails.
Wisdom will come, till when its place usurped
Is filled by grief. Perchance some River God
Hath stolen my child, whom he will soon return,
Unharmed, for fear of me, so potent I.
This fountain must be questioned. Answer me,
Soul of this coil of foamy turbulence,
Whether thou art beneath the wide, waste sea,

With great Poseidon, and his finny train,
Or in the deeps of Earth, in caves obscure,
Up-hastening to the light, at this my call—
Speak, answer me, where is Persephone?
Thou hast beheld, and stolen her away,
Thou, or some other spirit mischievous,
Whose portal of retreat was opened here.
Where is my daughter? If I speak again,
The Earth will draw thy fountain to its source,
And cast thee from her bosom. Answer me!
In vain, in vain! The fountain hath no God,
And cannot answer; Godless let it be,
Stormy and bitter to the end of time.
But you, ye lesser spirits of the vale,
Cannot escape—I here compel ye all.
From rivers, brooks, and springs, you Naiads come,
With Napeads from the vale; and from the grove
The Meliads, who here for lack of flocks
Must tend the fruit; and you, ye Oreads,
Both from the valley and the mountain mists;
Hither, and tell me of Persephone."

The Goddess thus, and even as she spake
From rivers, brooks, and springs the Naiads came,
With water lilies tangled in their hair;
The Napeads from the vale in skirts of grass,
The Meliads with their white hands full of fruit,
And all the Oreads from the shifting mists,
Wringing their dewy tresses on the lawn;
Obedient to the power that summoned them,
They thus made answer in their several turns.

"We are the Naiads of the neighboring streams.
Below their wrinkled waves we live in grots,
Paven with furrowed sands, the shelvy rocks

Our thrones, our couches beds of humid moss.
We strain the water through our golden hair,
With flowers we sow the bottom, and with weeds
Whose blooms are full of wind. We love the fish
Whose little coats are sleek with glittering scales:
The plated turtles, and defiant crabs,
That lie, or crawl beneath the grayish stones,
The long-legged beetles skimming o'er the waves,
With other watery insects, are our care:
We know and love the least: but as we hope
To keep our silver urns forever full
We all are ignorant of Persephone."

"But I," said one, the Naiad of a lake,
"I saw the nymph, and she was lovelier
Than all my lilies, whiter than my swans;
But where she hides I know not, or may fires
Shed from the Dog-Star dry my fountains up,
And leave me shelterless on burning sands."

"And we," the drooping Napeads began,
"Surrounded by her train we saw the nymph
Trip down the vale. We woke the early flowers,
And turned the dew from their enamelled cups;
Not one but wanted to resign its life
Beneath her feet—to die such death were sweet:
She walked as lightly as the winds of Spring."

"The winds of Spring," the Meliads broke and joined
The broken thread of speech, "the winds of Spring
Blow in old Winter's teeth, and rouse the buds;
The winds of Summer overtake the Spring,
And swell the buds to fruit: both are our care.
We screen the buds with leaves, remove the worms,
And drive away the bees and angry wasps;

We feed the fruit with sun, and wind, and dew;
The rinds of some we gild, and some we kiss,
And leave our breath thereon in bluish mist.
We saw at dawn the nymph Persephone
Lost in our orchards; figs, and plums, and pears
Lay round in heaps; we rained the olives down,
The red pomegranates split, and pierced the myrrh
And manna-tree whose veins are full of balm.
With many a sweet delay the virgin passed,
But where she hides we know not, or may blight
Shrivel our leaves, the north winds nip our buds,
And worms destroy our fruit—henceforth to be
More rich and luscious than in other years."

"We dwell in mists," began the Oreads next,
"In vale and mountain mists; a streak of gold
Betrays our presence there; in hollow glens
We couch when dews are dried: among the hills,
From peak to peak, we float across the gulfs,
And leap in cataracts down the untouched crags.
May all our dews and exhalations fail
But we are ignorant of Persephone."

"Infirm, and idle, wherefore do ye live,
If not to see, and succor Excellence,
When Excellence may need your timely aid?
Is it for this that Earth's maternal care
Protects and clasps ye to her loving heart?
For this Heaven holds ye in its sacred charge?
But thou, O Earth, great Mother of Mankind!
If these, thine own appointed ministrants,
Neglect their calling, thou shouldst rise thyself,
And save the heavenly ones whose lives are thine,
And unto thine add joy and length of days.
Back to your homes, and little tasks again,

Ye spirits of this dark, accursèd vale,
And leave me in my loneliness alone!
To be a Goddess now avails me not,
Nor yet to have a Goddess for my child.
With sleepless eyes the island must be searched.
Obscure and wild the dark retreat must be
For me to fear; a mother's eyes are keen,
A mother's heart is strong to save her child.
Farewell ye groves of Enna, where we dwelt!
Farewell, ye meadows! When I come again,
I bring Persephone, or come no more."

Thus spake Demeter as she crossed the vale
To search its northern bounds, which lovelier grew
At every step, the home and haunt of Spring.
Through groves and orchards full of piping birds,
That dropped from bough to bough like falling buds,
Through emerald meadows sown with silver dew,
And golden pastures resonant with bees,
The Goddess passed, with keen and anxious eyes
Perusing all; nor did she cease to call
"*Persephone!*" But trace of her was none,
Save in her shoutings, which the vale retained,
As hollow shores the voice of ebbing seas.
Then through a gorge along the east she went,
The mountains on her right fledged with dark pines,
And on her left the long Nebrodian range,
The craggy barriers of the northern sky;
The wind blew downward from their summit snows
Freighted with winter, and the melting mist,
Heavy and damp, rolled up and down the gorge;
And up and down the gorge the Goddess went,
Scanning the figures shrouded in the mist.
And one by one the Hours with solemn pace
Did come and go, and Morning was no more.

There was a wild and desolate ravine
That wound along the bottom of the pass;
Its misty sides were dark with shaggy woods,
And from its verge, headlong, a river plunged
Through clouds of spray, deep down a troubled lake,
Dammed up with rocks, down which it plunged again,
In ragged cataracts, sullen and hoarse.
A narrow pathway coiled on rocky shelves
With steep descents traversed the precipice:
Down this with wary feet Demeter trod,
And searched the old and melancholy woods
Burthened with endless shade and solitude,
And searched the clouded lake and waterfall,
And all the cavernous bases of the hills,
Deep-sunk in earth; no nook, nor secret cleft,
In which a spotted adder and her brood
Could coil away, escaped her sharpened eye,
That found no traces of Persephone.
So up the pass with slow and toilsome steps
She clomb again, and reached at last a plain
That stretched along the west, and slept in light.
Till now nor sight nor sound of man appeared,
But now at intervals shepherds were seen,
And notes of shepherd's flutes were heard afar.
Here dwelt a pastoral race that worshipped Pan,
Nor far the Goddess journeyed ere she found
A group around his altar,—reverent swains
With sacrificial goats, and pious maids
With urns of honey wreathed in sprigs of pine;
And in their midst the venerable Priest.
Deep awe pervaded all as thus she spake.

"Shepherds, since dawn the nymph Persephone
By hostile force from Enna has been ta'en;
If any man has seen her, let him speak,

Let him not fear, but speak, and name her path.
We both are kind to you, nor love you less
Than if you worshipped us instead of Pan;
Witness the bees I charmed from Hybla here,
When last the sun flamed in the vernal signs,
With all that shall hereafter come of good
To him, whose happy knowledge touching her—
If any such there be—lightens my heart;
Good, if he speak, evil, if he speak not,
To him, and all his kindred after him;
But such there cannot be. Speak, shepherds, speak!"

The Goddess thus, and paused, but none replied,
So deep the dread that fell upon all hearts.
At length the Priest ventured with faltering tongue.
"O great Demeter! Goddess of the Earth!
Impute not sin to silence, neither charge
Thy loss to us, participants therein—
For who but suffers when the good are wronged?
Forgive our ignorance of Persephone,
And elsewhere let thy just displeasure fall."

To whom Demeter, mild and sad, returned;
"Old man, 'twould ill become the race divine,
Divine no less through justice than through power,
Instead of Wrong, to punish Ignorance.
For if the Gods unjust and cruel prove,
How shall their worshippers be good and kind?
But fear not that; lifted above the world,
No mortal frailties their perfections mar.
Though sad at heart, right glad am I withal
To see ye love and reverence the Gods;
No grateful heart enjoys the least of gifts
Without returning to the giver thanks,
And offering in return the best it can.

Not that the Gods are ever paid thereby,
For what to them are honey, goats, or bulls?
They need them not, nor need they hymns of praise,
For they are all sufficient in themselves.
Yet dear to them the clouds of sacrifice,
That waft above the prayers of thankful hearts;
It is their due, the makers of mankind."

Thus through her grief accents of wisdom fell.
Assured thereby they bowed, and worshipped her:
But mindful of her search, too long delayed,
She journeyed o'er the plain with added speed,
Till many-wooded Etna came in sight,
And the hot sun rounded the arch of Noon,
Descending to its western base of sea.

Ten leagues from Enna blue Simetos rolled
Through osier banks his current to the main.
Bathing her burning forehead in the waves,
She saw the image of the River God,
Obliquely mirrored in a bed of reeds;
Him she addressed, and at her call he rose,
With dripping locks crowned with a wreath of sedge.
"Son of Oceanos, whom ocean owns
No longer for its God, but still doth hide
In some deep cavern, while Poseidon rules
His sovereignty of sea—beloved of both,
Divine Simetos, if thou hast beheld
Since early dawn the nymph Persephone,
Stolen from Enna by some Power unknown,
Haply from spring, or stream, or far-off main,
Unfold what thou dost know: or knowing naught,
Since I would cross thy current in my search,
Draw back thy waters to their mountain source,
And let me pass; so may the mountain snows

Fail not to brim thy fountain, and thy mates,
Camsorus, Chrysos, and bright Eryces,
Empty their urns of tribute at thy feet."

"O great Demeter! Mother of the Earth!
Sower of seed, and source of fruitfulness,
With grief I hear thy melancholy voice
Laden with loss, which I cannot repair,
For naught hath passed since dawn. I will draw back
My current to its source, and let thee cross."

Thus he, and northward buffeted the waves,
Till lost around the river's westward curve;
Reaching its source he sealed its secret urn,
And stayed the current, which rolled on below,
And left a gulf, through which the Goddess passed,
With unwet sandals over waves of grass,
Through rounded walls of crystal, rolling down
Tumultuous in her rear in crumbled foam,
That shut the pass, and followed in her path,
Until she gained the river's eastern bank,
And shouted to Simetos, who unsealed
The dripping urn, when all the waters closed,
And sought the sea again as she her child.
Her path now wound about the southern base
Of Etna, sloping to the river's edge.
Here Polyphemos fed his numerous flock,
That lay like drifts of snow in dreamy vales,
Until Demeter's shadow, dark and tall,
Searching the uplands chased them o'er the hills;
All fled in fear save one whose lamb was lost,
A fearless ewe that to the Goddess came,
And made its sorrow known with piteous tears.
She would have left it in the fields, but lo,
It followed her, and bleated for its lamb.

So towards the sea they went, and reached at last
Its rippled margent where the Cyclops lay,
Under a ledge of rocks that made a cave;
Beside his feet a nameless river ran,
Now named and known from Acis, buried there.
Here Polyphemos languished in the sun,
Like some rude idol dusk barbarians
Adore no longer, tumbled from its base.
Thrice did the Goddess shout a mighty shout
Above his couch before he stirred a limb,
Then slow, and sullen, he arose and frowned.
But she stood calm as Thought, nor feared his strength.

"O Polyphemos, great Poseidon's son!
Noblest of all the Cyclopean race!
Shepherd of Etna, and its thousand flocks,
From thee Demeter claims a patient ear,
Attentive to her sorrow and despair,
That seek the footprints of Persephone,
Stolen from Enna by some wanton Power,
Not thee she fain would hope, since thou art great,
And should'st be kind, for kindness is the star
That crowns all greatness, therefore crowneth thee,
If thou hast harmed not her defenceless child,
Sunk, as thou seem'st, in sorrow and despair,
From ills unknown to her, for which nathless
She grieves, and pities thee, as thou dost her,
Meaning to tell her of Persephone;
Till when she waits, a-hungered for thy voice."

Thus with wise words, like oil upon the sea
Swollen with storm, she laid his rising ire,
And smoothed his rugged features to a calm.

"Not I," he said, "not I have done this thing,
Whoever may; not I go stealing maids;

I live and die for Galatea alone.
Why, I have lain all night in falling dew,
And sang of Galatea to every star;
And I have shouted from the cloven peaks
Until the Thunder answered from his cave,
While startled Lightnings glared from parting clouds.

O Galatea, divinest Galatea!
Well I remember when I saw thee first!
'Twas when at noon I lay along the bank
Of blue Simetos, where my thirsty flock
Crowded and pushed until the lamb fell in,
To drown, but for thy help, so strong the tide
That bore it out beyond my reaching crook,
But not beyond those delicate hands of thine,
Reaching from out the lilies that concealed
Thy whiter breast, to which the lamb was drawn,
Bleating for joy, and safely borne ashore,
Beneath thy loosened hair, that like a veil
Fell to thy feet, and sowed a shower of pearl.
O Cyclops, Cyclops, it were well for thee
Had thy one eye been blinded like Orion's,
Or ever thou hadst seen that fatal sight!

But hearken yet, Demeter, let me speak,
And I will guide thee to the mountain path
That winds about the forges of Hephaestos.

Again at noon she came, and fed the lamb
With handfuls of long grass, and wove the flowers
To crown her dripping tresses while I went
Through Hybla, drumming on the hollow oaks
Swarming with bees, till I had filled my cup
With lucent honey, which I gave to her;
For then she did not fear to let me sit

Beside her feet, nor fear my gifts of love :
But when she left me, floating like a swan
To seek the sea again blew kisses back.
Had I been blest with fins, like happy fish,
I would have followed in her glittering wake,
And scared away the amorous River Gods.
But had I been a River God myself,
I would have dived to her in the cold deeps.
Be sure I had not failed to find her there,
For ruffled waves are clear as air to me ;
And oft at noon I watched her rising slow
Through shimmering leagues of water like a star.

I gave her ten young fawns as black as night,
Soft-eyed and delicate with silver feet,
With each a collar, and a chain of pearl.
She clapped her hands for joy, and smoothed my cheek
Until I laughed and wept : her hands were soft,
But mine are rougher than the mountain briars.

But hearken still, and let me speak again,
For now I touch upon my grief and loss,
Which had not been but for another's love
Thrust in between mine own and Galatea,
Whom all the shepherds worshipped, but afar,
Till Acis came, and spake. How did he dare
Step in between the Cyclops and his love ?
And how could she endure his boyish face
Half-hid in yellow ringlets after me,
Whose mighty heart pulsed fire at every beat!

But let me speak again, and I have done.
I sat last eve upon the slope of hills,
What time the sunset tipped, as now, the woods,
And saw a double shadow on the mead—

Two shadows clasped in one, with kissing lips;
'Twas Acis, and the faithless Galatea.
They were too busy then to think of me,
But I, I saw them there, and spake no word,
But crept in silence up from peak to peak,
Till, with sore labor, straining all my strength,
I lifted from its bed a crag of rock,
And cast it down upon the dreaming fools,
Thinking to crush them both, nor had I failed,
But that its falling shadow like a cloud
Startled the nymph, who suddenly leaped aside
To see him crushed and buried where he stood,
Jammed in the hard, cold earth, despite his moans;
Nor might her tears, which fell around like rain,
Nor all her prayers, restore him to her arms,
Unless she found him in the turbid stream
Which gushed from out the rock, and followed her,
Flying with shrieks of terror to the sea!

But come, Demeter, let us rise and go;
The lean, gray wolves will soon begin to prowl,
And I must pen my flocks; but let us go."

Thus Polyphemos told his tale of love:
And spying at his feet the bleating ewe,
He lifted it with care in his rough arms,
And led the Goddess from the foamy beach,
Full to the west again, where now the Sun
Had plunged his broad red disc in seas of cloud.

ON A CHILD'S PICTURE.

I LAY his picture on my knee,
  The knee he loves to sit upon.
  It is the image of my son,
And like the child a world to me.

He fronts me in a little chair,
  In careless ease, and quiet grace,
  A courtly deference in his face,
A glory in his shining hair.

An infant prince, a baby king,
  To whom his ministers relate
  Some intricate affair of state :
He hears, and weighs the smallest thing.

Happy the day when he was born,
  Two summers since, my summer child :
  Two Junes have on his cradle smiled,
A rose of June without a thorn.

I stood beside his mother's bed
  When he was born, at dead of night.
  My heart grew faint with its delight ;
I heard his cry : he was not dead !

And she, his mother, dearer far
  Than this poor life of mine can be,
  She lives, she weeps, she clings to me,
Her dim eye brightening like a star.

We heard his low uncertain moan,
  In both our souls it smote a chord
  Not reached by Love's divinest word;
It stirred, and stirs to him alone.

"*We have a child!*" We smiled and wept.
  He slept: God's Angel in the dark
  Pushed down the stream his little bark,
And with it ours: with him we slept.

At last the lingering summer passed,
  The summer passed, the autumn came,
  The dying woods were all a-flame,
The leaves were whirling in the blast.

He lived; our loving spirits wore
  A royal diadem of joy:
  Time laid his hands upon the boy,
And day by day he ripened more.

His dreamy eye grew like the sky,
  A liquid blue, half dark, half bright;
  Now like the moon, and now like night
With silver planets sown on high.

His thin, pale ringlets turn to gold,
  And gleam like suns on autumn eves;
  Or like the sober autumn sheaves,
Whose strawy fires are faint and cold.

I take his picture from my knee,
  And press it to my lips again:
  I see an hundred in my brain,
And all of him, and dear to me.

He nestles in his nurse's arms,
  His young eyes winking in the light:
  I hear his sudden shriek at night,
Startled in dreams by vague alarms.

We walk the floor, and hush his moan;
  Again he sleeps: we kiss his brow.
  I toss him on my shoulder now,
His Majesty is on the throne!

His kingly clutch is in my hair,
  He sees a rival in the glass:
  It stares, and passes as we pass;
It fades. I breathe the country air.

I see a cottage leagues from here,
  A garden near, some orchard trees,
  A leafy glimpse of creeping seas,
And in the cottage something dear.

A square of sunlight on the floor,
  Blocked from the window; in the square
  A happy child with heavenly hair,
To whom the world is more and more.

He sees the blue fly beat the pane,
  Buzzing away the noon-tide hours,
  The terrace grass, the scattered flowers,
The beetles, and the beads of rain.

He sees the gravelled walk below,
  The narrow arbor draped with vines,
  The light that like an emerald shines,
The small bird hopping to and fro.

He drinks their linkèd beauty in,
  They fill his thought with silent joy:
  But now he spies a late-dropped toy,
And all his noisy pranks begin.

They bear him to an upper room
  When comes the eve; he hums for me,
  Like some voluptuous drowsy bee,
That shuts his wings in honeyed gloom.

I see a shadow in a chair,
  I see a shadowy cradle go,
  I hear a ditty, soft and low:
The mother and the child are there.

At length the balm of sleep is shed.
  One bed contains my bud and flower.
  They sleep, and dream, and hour by hour
Goes by, while angels watch the bed.

Sleep on, and dream, ye blessèd pair!
  My prayers shall guard ye night and day;
  Ye guard me so, ye make me pray,
Ye make my happy life a prayer.

Dream on, dream on! and in your dreams
  Remember me,—I love ye well:
  I love ye more than tongue can tell,
Dear Souls, and ere the morning beams

My soul shall strike your trail of sleep,
  In some enchanted, holy place,
  And fold ye in a fond embrace,
And kiss ye till with bliss I weep!

THE KING'S BELL.

THE KING'S BELL.

> "*For Heaven's sake, let us sit upon the ground,*
> *And tell sad stories of the death of kings.*"
> SHAKESPEARE.

PRINCE FELIX at his father's death was King.
So he commanded all the bells to ring
A jubilant peal, and bade his heralds say
From that time forward every happy day
Should so be honored. "Not an hour will pass,
Nay, scarce the turning of the smallest glass,
Without the merry clamor of my bells.
In sooth I think they'll banish funeral knells,
And set the mourners dancing. I shall be
So happy the whole world will envy me."

Thus spake the new-made monarch, and indeed
He had some grounds to justify his creed.
Imprimis, he was young, and youth, we know,
Cannot be wretched, if it would be so,
For grant it sometimes weeps, and seems to pine,
It feels through all its royal self like wine.
Then he was rich as Crœsus: bags of gold
Heaped up his treasury, and wealth untold
Smouldered in guarded chests of precious stones,
And blazed like stars in sceptres, crowns, and thrones.

Powerful, and rich, and young—in short a King,
O happy man, why should his bells not ring?

He built himself a palace, like his state,
Magnificent, with many a marble gate;
A great dome in the centre, and thereon
A gilded belfry, shining like the sun,
And in it hung a bell of wondrous tone,
From which a silken cord ran to his throne:
Nor only there, but o'er his royal bed.
(O how unlike the sword above the head
Of that unhappy King of olden time!)
"My people will be deafened by its chime,"
Quoth he, when all was done. And now began
That perfect life not yet vouchsafed to man.
He chose his ministers as monarchs should,
Among the oldest men, the great and good,
And, placing in their hands the reins of State,
Charged them to make his people good and great.
"For me," he thought, "an idle life is best:
They love to bustle—let them, I shall rest."
He lolled upon his couch with dreamy eyes,
Watching he cared not what—the summer skies,
The nest of swans, the fountain's rise and fall,
The light and shadow shifting on the wall.
Perchance he ordered music; at the word
His fancy flattered from its trance was stirred
And quickened with sweet sounds, from harp and lute,
Or some rich voice that chid the music mute.
Ten times a day he stretched his hand to ring
The bell, he felt so glad, but some slight thing,
A buzzing gnat, the wind too cold, or hot,
Deterred him till the impulse was forgot.
"Have you been happy?" something seemed to say
At night: "I see you have not rung to-day."

"I must have been too idle," he replied.
And then, at dawn: "I will arise, and ride
A league or two in the dew and morning wind,
'Twill freshen and revive my drowsy mind."
He called a sleeping groom who cursed his fate,
And bade him take his courser to the gate,
That he might mount unseen, and ride away,
Before the court was stirring for the day.
The courser soon was saddled, and the groom
Returned, still yawning, to the monarch's room,
But found him fast asleep, so back he crept,
And late that day both groom and monarch slept.

The listless hours in idle reveries spent
Stung Felix to a noble discontent,
For shamed to think he loved his ease so well,
And longing for the music of the bell,
He charged the groom to bring his steed once more,
And if he slumbered thunder on his door
Until he woke. "And harkee, sirrah, see
That I rise, too, or 'twill be worse with thee."
'Twas done. Adown the palace walk he spurred
Into the misty dark, unseen, unheard;
Through meadows where the trampling of his steed
Fell muffled, noiseless as a wingèd seed,
Sown by soft airs where endless summer smiles;
Through forest shades, like dim Cathedral aisles
Arching beneath a sky of brightening blue.
Sometimes he touched a spray and showers of dew
Baptized him, or some small bird, half awake,
Twittered an early ditty for his sake.
How sweet the morning was, how cool the wind!
A weight seemed lifted from his waking mind,
And faster flowed the current of his blood.
His proud steed bore him onward like a flood,

Shaking from his champed bit the snow-white foam.
The larks up-springing from their grassy home,
Winging the deeps of air, a jubilant choir;
The leaden clouds consumed with morning's fire,
Melting in seas of gold: the silver rills,
The broad champaign, the woods, the purple hills—
He saw, and felt them all, and filled with joy
Forgot the King, and shouted like a boy,
And rising in his stirrups clutched the air
As if to ring his bell—ah, why was it not there?

Was Felix happy? Had you asked him then
He would have said, "The happiest of men."
But when a league was past, and he rode back,
His brow was knitted, and his bridle slack,
His little burst of happiness was o'er,
And he was sadder, idler than before;
For what but pain could this remembrance bring—
Thou art a boy no longer but a King?

Returning gloomy to the court he sought
The crowded Council-chamber, grave with thought,
But meeting at the door a merry lord,
Who made a lowly bow and begged a word,
He stopped and heard, alas, with greedy ear,
A trifling tale, not meet for him to hear,
A bit of scandalous gossip, then a jest.
The laughing pair linked arms: you guess the rest,
That day the Council met without the King.
At night there was a sound of revelling
Within the banquet-chamber, loud and late.
There Felix sat, oblivious of his state,
Carousing with the roysterers of his court,
And what a drunken King should be—their sport.
They clinked their glasses with him, or they sang

Light songs, and shouted till the palace rang,
Or stamped in chorus when he rose to speak.
At last the boldest, in a tipsy freak,
Would play the King himself; he touched the crown,
But Felix, roused a moment, smote him down
Bleeding among the wine cups. "Fool, lie there!
Crowns were not made for such as you to wear."
He spurned him with his foot. A draught of wine
Washed out the insult to his right divine,
And set his swimming thoughts adrift again;
The purple sea kept mounting to his brain.
"I hear," he said, "a buzzing in my ears,
The echoed music of the happy spheres:
What waves of sound, and how they sink and swell!
It must be time to ring my golden bell."
He rose, and staggering to his chamber-door
To ring the bell he fell upon the floor,
And while his soberer guests their revels kept
He lay and moaned for help. At last he slept.

What cup shall he drain next? What chase pursue,
Whose end is happiness, and pleasure, too?
The bell is silent still, ah, who can tell
What he must do to ring the happy bell?
He rose betimes and rode, no more alone,
For when his taste for horsemanship was known,
The court was seized o'th' sudden with the whim
Of early rising, and would hunt with him;
So when day broke you might have seen a train
Of lords and ladies spurring o'er the plain,
With hawks upon their wrists, or hounds behind,
The ready puppets of the royal mind.
The court of Felix, histories say, was then
Famed for its lovely dames and gallant men.
His first temptation was a merry face,

Crimsoned with healthful roses in the chase:
His next a little tress of dangling hair,
Blown o'er plump shoulders with a jaunty air:
His third a white hand on a palfrey's mane,
Or small foot peeping from a flowing train.
Or it may be on some sweet night in June,
When o'er the park there hung a yellow moon,
While on the banks reclined maids told their tales,
Or singing hushed the amorous nightingales,
He came on beauty, grace, perfection there,
In ripe, round forms, white robes, and night-dark hair;
Or met a mask, in some dim nook apart,
Whose lustrous eyes shot passion to his heart.

Not his a lesser lover's doubt and pain,
He was assured of being loved again,
For was he not a King? What woman would
Withhold her heart from him? No woman could.
His first love was a fair, but fragile maid,
With drooping, violet eyes, half light, half shade,
A sweet, pale face, a little touched with care,
And nothing bright about her save her hair.
Poor, fading flower, she had not time to die
Before the fickle Felix cast her by,
And plucked another, eager for her fate,
A full-blown beauty, made of love and hate,
With bold, black eyes, that smouldered with desire,
Or through its ashes flashed a dangerous fire;
About her brow great coils of midnight hair,
With one fierce ruby like a comet there;
Cheeks brown as olives, with a bloomy streak
Like twilight burning in each dusky cheek:
A passionate, scornful mouth, a hand superb,
Moulded to grasp a sceptre, or to curb

The tameless spirit of a desert steed :
A heart that loved to make the hearts of others bleed !
"The King should wed," the people thought at last;
"'Tis time the follies of his youth were past,
And something better grafted in their stead.
We need a Prince to rule when he is dead."
"O mighty Felix!" Thus his Poet sung,
(His glowing fancy showed that he was young,)
"Until they see a bud upon the tree
They fear that beauty's rose will die with thee;
Put forth a bloom to comfort them, and save
Thy rich remembrance from the sullen grave.
An hundred fair princesses whose bright eyes
Are dowered with kingdoms waste their days in sighs,
Thinking of thee, great King! O, let thy heart,
Maugre its royal rigor, take their part
Against itself, and thy too-cruel mind;
If not to all, to one, at least, be kind.
Select a Queen, the fairest of the fair,
To grace thy marriage-bed, and bear an heir.
Thereby thou liv'st again, but dying now,
Thou art but ashes—dust, no Phœnix, thou,
That after crumbling on the funeral pyre,
Rises triumphant by its own bright fire.
Then leave a son when thou art laid to rest,
Whose golden plumes shall light thy royal nest."

The Council, too. Not in such dainty words,
But in the pithy phrases of grave lords,
Who thinking much say little. "He must wed."
The reasons followed. One grave seignor said,
"The State demands it," (words of awful weight!)
Another, "Yes, the welfare of the State."
Carried at last he weds. With whom? They scanned
Each marriageable princess in the land.

One brings five duchies, and a million down,
And one a kingdom, but disputed crown,
The third a silver mine, (but she is old,)
The fourth, (still older,) several mines of gold.
They chose a maid whom Felix had not seen,
More fitted for an Abbess than a Queen,
For in a cloister's shade her youth had passed,
In virgin dreams of Heaven—too bright to last.
When Felix heard their choice, (the Council found
The royal idler playing with his hound,)
He sighed, and said, "I wish the lady joy!
We look for folly in a beardless boy,
And wisdom in gray hairs; but yours, I see,
Thatch something worse than folly—cruelty.
Cruel, I say, for can she hope to be
Happy (she can not) with a man like me?
Enough; I take the sacrifice ye bring,
And though no lover I am still a King."

He sent a lord who grew up by his side,
With a long train of knights, to wed the bride.
Were I to paint them on their merry way,
The time should be the lover's season—May,
The sky an arch of sapphire, set in light,
Birds singing in the trees, the hedges white.
Then I'd describe the pile wherein they wed,
The fretted arches stretching overhead,
The saints and martyrs in the blazoned panes,
Through which in a rich dusk the sunlight rains,
The organ's burst, the choir, the hymn, the prayer,
The mitred Abbot, and the noble Pair!
Then over many a river and wide plain
Back to the court again should sweep the train,
With purple banners dancing in the air,
And proud steeds tramping to the trumpet's blare,

And in the midst the lady, riding slow,
Checking her ambling palfrey white as snow.
"Long live the Queen!" She knows the city near,
Before she sees its gleaming towers appear
Above the belt of woods that shut it in,
For the wind bears her snatches of the din
That welcomes her approach: a noise of bells
Blended with shouts and music sinks and swells,
Until the city bursts upon her sight,
Towers, temples, palaces, a-blaze with light.
The wall is hung with broidered cloths of gold,
And she can see her name on every fold;
"AGNES AND FELIX" glitters everywhere.
White hands strew flowers upon her till the air
That stirs her veil grows languid with their sweets;
Triumphal arches span the spacious streets,
Alive with merry faces, and bright eyes,
And clapping hands, and shouts that rend the skies.
When she draws near the palace from the crowd
A herald steps, and blows his trumpet loud,
Thrice at the gates, which on their hinges swing,
Opening within where she beholds the King,
Who, waiting her approach, in royal state,
Comes like the Sun through Morning's golden gate.
Dismounting from her steed the trembling bride
Gives him her hand, and slowly, side by side,
They cross the palace-threshold, and the gate,
Still to the trumpet's clang, closes behind like Fate.
He led her straightway to the balcony,
A robed and crownèd Queen for all to see.
"Long live the Queen!" "Long live the happy King!"
The bells, a moment mute, began to ring
Louder than ever, whirling round and round,
Drunken, delirious in the storm of sound
That rocked the lofty belfries to and fro.

And up and down the living sea below
Ran a great wind of shouts, and, wrapt in smoke,
From throats of grim black cannon thunders broke.
The streets were full of shows, and all were free,
Rope-dancing, juggling, mumming, minstrelsy,
Soldiers, and music's merriment divine,
And, better still, the fountains flowed with wine.
So passed the day; at night the palace park
Was hung with lamps that lit the leafy dark,
And showers of stars, from hissing rockets shed,
Mocked with their rainbow fires the stars o'erhead.
Meanwhile the bells kept ringing in their towers,
Hailing with jubilant throats the joyous hours.
But one was still—(it would have struck a knell,
Had Felix touched the cord,)—the happy bell!

And is he then so wretched? Nay, not so.
Between the neighbor lands of Joy and Wo
There is a middle state where many dwell,
Benumbed as in a dream by some strange spell.
And thus it is with Felix, whose desires,
Raging intensely like volcanic fires,
Have burned away, and left a waste behind,
A heart of ashes, and a barren mind.
He does not love the woman he has wed,
For love with him like happiness is dead.
If she loves him—she may—she loves not well.
How could a maid bred in a convent-cell,
And schooled by priests, know what a man demands
In her he loves—what work of heart, or hands?
She knew to count her beads, and say her prayers,
But not to share his joys, and soothe his cares.
Wavering between her faith and what she felt,
When he was near her tender heart would melt,
But thoughts of Heaven would check her sinful bliss,

For she loved him and Heaven, and both amiss.
Unhappy pair, I pity your sad fate,
Not wise enough to love, too wise to hate.
God made ye both unlike, in brain and heart,
But Man hath joined what God would keep apart.
The wrong is common, common, too, the cure;
There is but one—forgive, forget, endure,
So shall the heart its fruitless struggles cease,
And, if not happy, be at least at peace.

But peace was not for Agnes. She was one
Who could be only what she was—a nun.
She made the court a convent. Tolerant, wise,
Poor Felix stood aloof, with watchful eyes,
Guarding his wife as if she were a child,
A kind but thoughtful man, who seldom smiled,
But as his hopes of happiness grew less,
Labored to give his people happiness.
And they were happy. Well they might be so;
No wars, large harvests, and their taxes low.
Their King was just, their Queen was good and fair,
Besides, there was a promise of an heir.
"God send a boy!" they said. The days went by
Like withered leaves when autumn winds are high,
Or whirling snow flakes: autumn, winter passed,
Snows melted, budded leaves, spring came at last.

The long-expected child was born with spring.
They bore the joyous tidings to the King,
Who paced his chamber with an anxious brow,
And gravely wondered: "Am I happy now?
A father, tell me"—But his challenged heart,
Disdaining parley, took the infant's part,
Whose cry he heard, and forced him to confess
A natural, manly thrill of happiness.

He stretched his hand to ring the silent bell,
But the grasped cord from out his fingers fell,
For entering now the grave physician said,
"Forbear your joy, my liege, the Queen is dead!
A deathly pallor seized him when he heard
These doleful words: he neither spake, nor stirred,
But stood transfixed to marble—all surprise,
Two great tears welling from his blinded eyes.
Why did he weep? He did not love the Queen.
What could she be to him? What had she been?
Why should her death so move him? It may be
He sees therein his own mortality,
Or, sadder still, the solemn doom of all,
If so, his not unmanly tears may fall.
But be more just, and say his heart is wrung
With natural pity that she died so young.
He weeps to think his joyless marriage-bed
Has borne at once the living and the dead,
That she has died to give his infant life,
In short he weeps because he loved his wife!
Yes, Felix loved her, strange as it may seem,
His long indifference was a troubled dream;
It left him darkly in his sorest strait,
He woke at last, but woke, alas, too late.
He loved her now, the bitter Past forgot,
Nor owned there was a time he loved her not.
"But grant it true," (here Conscience seemed to wake,)
"I would have loved her for the Prince's sake."
All this and more, a world of hopeless pain
Brooded like death upon his heart and brain,
Until he heard his new-born infant's cry,
Which called him back to life with many a sigh.
"Be calm, the child is living, Sire." He smiled:
"But she is dead!" then went to see his child.

She lay in state, beneath a canopy,
Three mortal days for all the court to see,
In royal robes, her crown upon her head,
With holy tapers burning round her bed;
And prayers were said, and heavenly hymns arose,
And mass was chanted for her soul's repose.
Ah, Requiescat! Then the funeral show,
The gorgeous pageant of a nation's wo,
The slow, sad march, the tap of mournful drums,
The death-like hush that tells the body comes,
The great car, seen afar, the turbaned grooms,
The led steeds, haughty with their ostrich plumes,
The King in his black coach—Why do they bring
In Death's triumphal march the happy King?
Deep in an old Cathedral's holy gloom
They buried her with tears, and on her tomb
Carved in white marble like a drift of snow
An *Agnus Dei*, with her name below—
"AGNES, THE WIFE OF FELIX," (wretched wife!)
The rest was written in the Book of Life.

A dreadful shadow in the palace lay
Long after the poor Queen had passed away,
And the court doffed its customary black:
Yea, till her virgin dust had mouldered back
To the cold dust it sprung from! It was not
That Felix missed her in some hallowed spot,
And peopled it with memories, (say, her room,)
But that her image filled the haunted gloom.
He saw her as she used to be in life,
A loving woman, but a troubled wife,
Bent o'er her broidery frame, while roses grew
Beneath her fingers, wet with silver dew:
Or where like nuns her spotless lilies stood,
The beauteous abbess of the sisterhood;

Or in her chapel with ecstatic air,
Telling her rosary, each bead a prayer;
Or standing saintly in the moon's faint light,
Beside the cradle at the dead of night;
The ghostly mother kissed her sleeping child,
That in its dream stretched out its arms and smiled.

What Felix felt, his wo or happiness,
Only a father's loving heart can guess.
Be sure he loved the babe, whose helpless life
Cost it, poor thing, its mother, him his wife,
And when his State-craft could be brushed away,
Stole in to see it twenty times a day,
Hung o'er its slumbers, if perchance it slept,
And gazed till called, then out on tip-toe crept;
Returning soon to gaze his fill again,
Perchance to still its little cry of pain,
With infant lullabies and drowsy charms;
Or, sweeter far, to take it in his arms,
And pace the floor until it sank to rest,
A smiling burden on his aching breast.
The love he would have lavished on the Queen,
But for that dreadful cloud that came between,
Clung to the child as if his heart would break:
He loved it madly for its mother's sake.
To paint his passion in its fond extremes,
The hopes, the fears, the endless golden dreams
He built on that frail life an hour might blight;
Haunting the Prince's cradle day and night,
Outwatching all the nurses; as he grew
Fetching him costly playthings, quaint and new,
Teaching him pastimes full of merry noise,
Devised by fathers to divert their boys;
Making grim shadows that awoke his fears,
The heads of rams or, sheep with monstrous ears,

Browsing along the wall with piteous bleat;
Trotting him now a cock-horse on his feet,
With breathless shouts, and eager, clapping hands,
Through wondrous ways in undiscovered lands,
The fairy world of Nowhere : dropping now
A crown of kisses on his baby brow,
Then lifting him sedately to his throne,
The strong, broad shoulder where he sat alone,
Fearless and proud—he knew his royal part,
The king, the tyrant of his father's heart :
To tell how Felix as the years went by
Watched the soul brightening in his soft blue eye ;
How while he smoothed his darkening hair, and smiled,
He breathed the sigh, "Thou hast no mother, child!"
How wandering in the Past with vain regret,
He asked the heavens, "Has she forgiven me yet?"
The volume of his life where this was writ,
Could I but open, and decipher it,
(Be sure the pages of the wasted years
Where that dead flower was pressed were wet with tears !)
Would make a story, sadder, sweeter far
Than any I may try to tell, and mar ;
A sad, sweet story, worth a famous pen,
The tears of women, and the thoughts of men.
Write it who can, let me go on to tell
How and when Felix rung the happy bell.

Ten years or more, (the time concerns us not,
Our epochs are the feelings, Life the plot,)
He schooled himself in all the craft of State,
The little business of the would-be great.
Not from a royal fondness for intrigue,
To break a useless make a useful league,
Or strike the sceptre from a brother's hand,
But for the good and glory of his Land,

Holding his people's happiness his own,
Their love the best foundation for his throne.
No King of all his race so shrewd as he,
So great a master of diplomacy.
It mattered little whom his rivals sent
To sound his secrets, as they came they went,
Ambassadors, who cunning trains had laid
How to betray, and not to be betrayed,
Old, crafty ministers with stealthy eyes,
Skilled in the courtly art of hinting lies;
He baffled all, not by a deeper art,
But by a clearer brain, and larger heart.
Nor better fared the servants of his throne,
If they mistook their wishes for his own,
Plotting to serve themselves, and not the State;
Poor fools, they did but trifle with their fate.
'Tis said his Council was corrupt at first,
And the Bench, too, with venal judges cursed,
Hucksters who Law, and sometime Justice sold,
Also, that in the Church, God's earthly fold,
Thieves in the guise of shepherds oft did creep,
Not to keep out the wolves, but fleece the sheep.
If this, alack, were true, (who will may doubt,)
He found a way to weed the culprits out,
And make his people happy. All went well,
Yet somehow Felix did not ring his bell.

At last there came a war. What led thereto
I have forgotten, if I ever knew.
Doubtless the cause was just, or said to be,
Alike by Felix and his enemy,
The gray-haired father of his sainted Queen,
Whose death had broken the last bond between
Their rival kingdoms. Having striven in vain
To keep the early promise of his reign,

And live and die beneath a peaceful star,
Felix, prepared, resolved on sudden war,
And marched his armies on the unready foe,
Who fled before the shadow of his blow.
He overran his royal kinsman's land,
Until his coward forces made a stand
For very shame, within an old, walled town
Famous for strength. Here Felix sat him down
For a long siege, as was the custom then.
The country round about swarmed with his men,
Felling old forests, filling swampy grounds,
Digging great trenches, throwing up huge mounds,
Drawing their circles closer day by day
Around the foe who kept them still at bay,
Safe in his stronghold. Nor less busy he,
Thinning their ranks with his dread enginery
That thundered all day long: and oft at night
He sallied from his gates in desperate fight,
That smote the darkness with a burst of flame,
That died in rolling drums as sudden as it came.
Their girding cannon batter at the walls,
That slowly crumble; now a bastion falls,
Anon a turret; still the foe defies,
Though low in dust his bravest captain lies.
Hour after hour the bloody work goes on.
Another day—the fated town is won.
But see, the gates are opened! Who are these?
The oldest burghers bringing out the keys.
"We would not yield," they say, "till we were dead,
Did not our wives and children starve for bread:
We yield to Famine, Felix, not to thee."
"Your children and your wives are safe with me,
I only war with men. Take back your keys,
Bread, also." Amazed, they fell upon their knees.
His soldiers shouted as the tidings flew,

They heard it on the walls, and shouted, too :
Trumpets were blown, and bells began to ring.
" Long live the King! Long live the happy King!"

His clemency and the prowess of his arms
Distracted the old King with fresh alarms;
Repulse he might have schooled himself to meet,
But not defeat, such merciful defeat.
" What shall be done with one who can subdue
Not only us, my lords, but himself, too?
Advise me." And they did. "We must pretend
His mercy is a cloak to some dark end,
(Say your dethronement, Sire,) as time will show."
So they conspired against their generous foe.
The silly people (were they ever wise?)
Of course believed them, for a monarch's lies
Pass current, like his coin, from hand to hand,
However base the metal. The whole land
Bankrupt awhile through fear, but affluent now
With spurious courage, raised they knew not how,
Rose to defend,—each man declared, his hearth,
And sweep the tyrant Felix from the earth.
The good King Felix heard the wicked cry
With noble anger, dying in a sigh.
" Since they belie us so there is no way
To bring them to their senses, but to slay.
They must be taught to fear, as well as hate;
Who speaks of pity now, he speaks too late.
What says the stern commandment of the Lord?
' Who take the sword shall perish by the sword.' "

At last it came, the dark, the fatal day,
When, face to face, in battle's dread array,
For the first time the hostile armies stood.
The low and sullen East was red as blood

Behind the ghostly tents of the old King,
O'er which a raven flapped its funeral wing,
Affrightened by strange thunders from below,
And puffs of driven cloud, up-mounting slow.
For now the glimmering field was rolled in smoke,
And heavily the boom of cannon broke,
Shattering the startled air, shaking the ground,
Pouring, whole parks at once, destruction round.
Then came the sharp fire of the musketeers,
And flights of arrows, and the thrust of spears;
Steel rang on steel, drums beat, the trumpet's blare,
Ominous, threatening, smote the trembling air.
At first they fought by rule, the wings, the van,
As had been planned and ordered, every man
A tutored puppet in his captain's hand,
And all obedient to their King's command.
Did Felix say, or sign, "Go there," 'twas done,
A thousand men marched to the spot as one.
Where they should stand they stand, firm as a wall,
Closing their shattered ranks fast as they fall;
Where they should move they move: the cannon roar,
Ploughing them down, the spears grow more and more,
Bristling before them, clouds of arrows fly,
Darkening what little day is in the sky:
In vain, they still encroach upon their foes.
So for awhile the tide of battle flows.
But by and by it takes a wider sweep,
Rolling its waves towards the eastern steep,
A raging sea, that swayed, and surged, and reeled,
Bursting tumultuous over the whole field.
Ere long the struggling hosts, on carnage bent,
So broken were, in such disorder blent,
That neither King could say, "These are my own,"
Or whether he were victorious, or o'erthrown.
Against the cannon archers twanged their bows,

Where blows were thickest standards sank and rose,
White crests were lost like foam-flecks in the sea,
And here and there were bands of cavalry,
Whose dreadful, flashing swords were dripping red,
Galloping o'er the dying and the dead!
'Twas chaos all. At noon there came in sight,
Swift-marching from the west, fresh, full of fight,
A second host which Felix had concealed,
To turn the doubtful fortunes of the field,
Rushing with glittering weapons, and a shout,
Which heard a league off put the foe to rout,
For as the red leaves, in an autumn gust,
Whirl round the self-same spot, in clouds of dust,
Till sweeping all before it like the sea,
Comes the north wind, when suddenly they flee;
So, panic-struck, the old King's forces fled,
A coward mob, to honor, manhood—dead!
In vain their captains strove to check their flight,
They turned on them the fury of the fight,
And cut them down—each man in that wild strife
Braving a thousand deaths to save his worthless life!
When Felix saw the field was won, his heart,
Glorying a moment, took the old King's part
For sheerest pity. "Death to him," he said,
"Who dares to hurt a hair of his gray head!"
Then spurring his white steed away he went,
The first to find and save him. In his tent,
Girt by the few that scorned to fly, he lay,
Bathed in his blood that swiftly ebbed away,
His son, Prince Irac, stooping at his side.
"Felix!" as he drew near, the old man cried.
Prince Irac started up, and snatched a spear—
Rage in his eyes and soul. "Rash boy, come here,"
His father groaned. "You dare to disobey?
Sir, I command you." Felix turned away,

His sweet thoughts changed to gall. "Like sire, like son,
They hate me—the whole race. There was but one
Who knew me as I am, and she is dead."
"Felix! Go, call him back," (he raised his head,
The King still regnant in his fading eye,)
"For I must speak with him before I die.
Felix, I know thee now, and long have known,
True man and good, too good to fill a throne,
Above the petty lust of Power, which brings
Such wo to nations, and such death to Kings.
For this bad war, O, let it end to-day!
Not thine, but mine, the sin is mine, I say.
Irac, I made this war for selfish ends,
They fail, death comes—be you and Felix friends."
He clasped their hands in his, as they drew nigh
To catch his faltering words, and see him die,
And while they knelt he bade them swear to be
"Brothers in heart, and live in amity,
They and their people"—Here his spirit fled,
For when they looked again the poor old King was dead!

When, treaties signed with Irac, Felix came
Back to his kingdom, with a conqueror's fame,
Each man rejoiced, his cup filled to the brim,
As if some special good had fallen to him;
The women laughed, the children clapped their hands,
It was a holiday throughout the lands,
Triumphal arches, banners, music's swell,
And all the bells were rung—except the happy bell!

The happy bell—what tales it could have told
Of what it saw below its house of gold,
Since first, in youth, Prince Felix hung it there
Above his palace towers in the wide air.
Beneath it and around, a league each way,

Mapped out in small the mighty city lay,
A stretch of roofs, with slips of street between,
Glimpses of trees, and summer squares of green,
Cool, bosky places, sacred to repose,
Wherein, like shafts of silver, fountains rose.
And here and there a golden gleam of fire
Betrayed the cross on some Cathedral spire;
And bells were round, in tower and turret hung,
Great, brazen bells, whose ponderous iron tongue
Proclaimed the flying hours, by day and night,
The honeyed joys that wait the marriage rite,
(Ah, dreams of youth and love too early fled!)
And man's unspeakable sorrow for his Dead!
Year in and out the changeful sea of sound,
Fed from below, kept flowing, circling round;
Freighted with human life it rose and fell,
But drew no answer from the royal bell.

When first 'twas hung there in its airy hall
The park below, new-planted, was so small
Its trees, from that far height, were shadowy stalks
Drawn on the emerald grass and gravelled walks.
But by and by they grow more tall and dark,
The glossy rind becomes a wrinkled bark,
Tangled the boughs, and thicker the green leaves,
Through which the sun glints, and the soft wind grieves,
And birds are glancing. Soon the shady places
Are lighted by bright eyes and laughing faces,
And knots of beauteous dames, in merry talk,
Go sauntering, arm in arm, from walk to walk,
With fluttering scarfs, rich robes, and jewelled sheen,
Brilliant as tropic flowers! Then comes the Queen,
Chaste as her bridal lily, and as pale,
A nun who wears a crown instead of veil.

It hears her marriage peal, her funeral knell,
But never rings itself—that silent bell!

Years pass without a sound from that high tower.
The bell hangs dumb, like some great drooping flower,
That never knows the bloom and blight below,
Now bright with sunshine, and now white with snow.
At last the snow and sun and the wild rains
Clouded its burnished sides with darkening stains,
And muffled thick with dust its iron tongue,
And birds built there, and reared their clamorous young.

What good King Felix and his life had been
Through all these silent changes, we have seen.
Not much, perhaps, but still enough to see
He always missed his wished felicity.
We might have found, or made, a happier lot,
Born to the throne he filled, but *he* could not.
Ah, more's the pity, since his youth was past,
And manhood--age came stealing on at last.
First in a few gray hairs, a gleam of white,
That made his brown locks richer in the light;
Against the corners of his eyes a line
That could not be a wrinkle 'twas so fine;
A step that lost a little of its spring,
Measured, deliberate, as became a King.
These shadows, say, of change, before his prime,
Ere one could think it was the work of Time.
For still his eyes were keen, his cheeks were red,
No leaf yet of their princely roses shed.
As year by year went by with all its care,
Thinner and whiter grew his wintry hair,
And Time, or Sorrow holding his old plough,
Did turn great furrows in his faded brow.
His stooping shoulders and his tottering gait,

His head that seemed to droop with its own weight,
Dim eyes, and trembling hands, so icy cold,
All these declared that he was growing old.

Such was the hapless King in his decay,
Suffering and silent, till one summer's day,
When weary of his cares he stole apart,
And paced his chamber with an aching heart.
Backward and forward with a listless tread,
With many a sudden stop, and shake o'th' head,
He paced the lonely chamber, so forlorn
He wished that he were dead, or never had been born.
The darkest corner seemed to suit his gloom,
No fitter nook for sorrow, save the tomb ;
Then he affected brightness, just to see
His shadow creep beside him wearily :
Anon he halted in his shifting mood,
Where some fresh landscape hung, or statue stood,
Taking their beauty in with vacant eyes,
Lost to the fairest shapes, the brightest skies.
His windows opened on a balcony,
Whence, under silken awnings, he could see
His slope of lawns, his gardens, and between
The winding, wooded walks, cool avenues of green.
He threw a casement up in his despair,
To watch the clouds, perchance, or feel the air,
Which blowing freshly o'er his royal grounds
Came freighted with fine odors, and sweet sounds,
The breath of flowers and dew, the song of birds,
The low (or did he dream ?) of distant herds,
Shouts near at hand, (it was a holiday,
And the whole city was alive and gay,)
"Long live the happy King!" He bowed his head.
"The happy King, O mockery!" he said.
"What is this thing called Happiness ? And where

Does it abide, and who shall guide me there?
My feet have never struck the path thereto,
My groping hands have never found the clue,
Or, finding, straight have lost it. Who can tell
Why I have never rung my golden bell?
Perhaps I asked, in youth, what could not be,
A bliss too great for man, at least for me,
Raptures, for which all language would be weak,
Striking a sudden color to the cheek,
A swelling of the heart not felt before,
Like the sea's setting to a summer shore,
A dance o'th' pulse, a brightening o'th' eye,
A light like endless morning in the sky,
Something which should compel me to confess
What I am dying to—This, *this* is Happiness!
It may be so: youth is not over wise,
Nor Kings content with common destinies.
There lies, methinks, the secret, everything
Summed up at last in that one word—a King!

O wretched state of Kings! O doleful fate!
Greatness misnamed, in misery only great!
Could men but know the endless wo it brings,
The wise would die before they would be Kings.
Think what a King must do! It tasks the best
To rule the little world within his breast,
Yet must he rule it, and the world beside,
Or King is none, undone by power and pride.
Think what a King must be! What burdens bear
From birth to death! His life is one long care.
It wears away in tasks that never end:
He has ten thousand foes, but not one friend.
Not for himself he lives, but for the State,
To make his thankless people good and great,
The head that guides their hands—to plough to-day,

To-morrow to grasp the dreadful sword and slay:
What's good in them must foster, check what's ill,
And save them from themselves against their will,
Do many things they cannot understand,
And rule, when need is, with an iron hand,
Look for revolt at home, and war abroad,
Prepared to strike at both, and strike like God.
O doleful state of Kings! O dreadful fate!
O hell in which we wake, like damnèd souls—too late!

Would I could doff my royal robes, and be
One of the people who are ruled by me,
Long leagues away from this great city's roar,
No matter who, so I were King no more.
I'd rise when dawn was glimmering in the blue,
And drive my flocks a-field through mist and dew,
Stopping to bind my crook with nameless flowers,
Or harken to the birds in neighboring bowers.
Watching the snowy lambs that round me feed,
On some low knoll I touch my rustic reed,
Or sing old ditties with a quaint refrain,
How Corydon did Phyllis love in vain,
Till Cupid, smit with ruth, becomes his friend,
Bringing his troubles to a blissful end.
My Phyllis sits with me, a blushing lass,
Plucking with down-cast eyes the blades of grass,
Listening the tale I whisper in her ear,
How dear she is to me—and am I dear?
Nor does she fear my arm around her waist,
Nor start when kissed, nor shrink to be embraced.
Ye know not, O my people, cannot guess
How much I envy you your happiness,
Your calm, contented days, your dreamless nights,
Your power to make life's little things delights,

Your wakes, your festivals, your antique play,
The dance upon the green around the Queen of May!

I saw to-day a father at his door,
A simple clown, the poorest of the poor:
He stared upon me as I hurried by,
And I stared back at him with wistful eye.
Ah, why should I not sit like him, and see
My chubby children clamber up my knee?
No more a child, my boy a man has grown,
And soon will follow me upon the throne.
What I could do to make him good and wise,
Fit to shape out his people's destinies,
I've done; he's generous, has a loving heart,
A scorn of low intrigue, the courtier's art;
Commands his passions better than his Sire;
Not quick to take offence, though full of fire;
Expert in arms and fearless in the fray,
(I know he'll win the jousting prize to-day:)
Indeed, a noble Prince, who'll not disgrace
The kingly glories of his name and race.
This he is now, but who, alas, can say
What he may be when I have passed away,
As soon I must, his tutor, and his friend?
Woe's me, my son, I cannot see the end.
Knowing my own life, I am full of fears,
Nor can I help, to-day, at least, my tears,
Breathing in prayer my last, my sole desire—
May you be happier than your hapless Sire!

Happy, alas, who's happy here on earth?
Why, man is wretched from his very birth.
Frail as a flower's his hold of life, none know
Whether the human bud will fade or blow;
For hours on hours his lids are sealed in sleep,

And when at last he wakes—it is to weep.
And now begins his endless quest of joy.
At first he finds it in the simplest toy,
His rattle, bells, a string of tangled beads,
The beetle in the grass, a knot of weeds,
The letters in old books begirt with gold,
In everything that he can snatch and hold:
Yet brief as bold his sallies of delight,
For even when he laughs he weeps outright.
Youth comes, and then as childhood went before,
Why, so youth goes in turn, to come no more;
Its little blisses never known, and prized,
Or only known amiss—to be despised.
But wiser manhood soon will make amends,
Has riper purposes and richer ends;
We shall be fortunate and happy then,
Be all we would as soon as we are men.
One, seeking pleasure, to the wine-cup flies,
Another drinks his bane from woman's eyes,
A third hoards gold, a fourth is mad for fame,
All aiming at one thing, whate'er their aim,
All mocked and baffled by it, (me, no less,
Me, most of all!) the phantom—Happiness!

At last old age; gray hairs, a wrinkled brow,
The wreck of what he was—what I am now.
Then the last sickness, and the hour of death,
The slowly-glazing eye, the fluttering breath,
The swoon in which the senses slip away,
No pulse, heart stopped—a lifeless lump of clay
That stirs no more, the feet that ran to ill
Still, and the busy, guilty hands,—*all* still,
Dead-cold from head to foot, a frozen form,
Twin of corruption, brother of the worm,
Dust, ashes,—nothing! Happy with all this?

Let me behold the wretched man who is.
There's no such man, he must be more, or less;
There's no such thing as Death and Happiness!"

So said, or thought, that day the poor old King,
Sick of himself, and life, and everything,
Crushed by the secret that he seemed to know,
The solemn mystery of human wo.
Tortured in heart and brain he totters back,
Like one just lifted broken from the rack,
And falling on a couch which near him stands,
Buries his face forlornly in his hands;
Then closing his dim eyes that would not weep,
Drops in a moment into happy sleep,
So deep it looks like death. They find him there,
The night-wind blowing in his snowy hair.

'Twas known next morning that the King was ill.
The people caught the whisper as they will,
But caring little for the affairs of Kings,
Soon went their ways, and thought of other things.
In his still chamber, darkened from the day,
Low in his bed of state the sick man lay;
A grave physician stood beside his bed,
(He who first told him that the Queen was dead,
The Prince was born,) the Prince, too, pale, distressed,
But hoping, as youth always does, the best.
"You took the prize, I hear." His father spoke.
"Yes, Sire, but rather by a lucky stroke
Than any skill or prowess of my own."
"You'll have another soon—I mean the throne."
"May Heaven preserve you long!" He quickly chid
The foolish, loving prayer: "May Heaven forbid!"

Next day "The King is worse," the rumor ran.
And now it touched the people, who began

To ask his ailment. Would he soon be well?
What did the doctor think? But none could tell.
He knew not what to think, with all his skill
He only knew with them—the King was ill.
The third day's rumor was "The King will die."
It passed from mouth to mouth with many a sigh;
Each had some tale to tell, some proof to bring,
How happy all had been since he was King.
"Do you remember now seven years ago,
The famine-winter when we suffered so,
He melted up his plate to buy us bread,
And sold the golden crown from off his head
To keep life in us, who must else have died?"
"God bless him, yes!" his earnest listener cried.
"And, later, when the Pestilence was here,
(I never shall forget that fatal year,
My wife died then, God rest her soul above!)
There never was such courage, so much love
As his for us, his people, when we lay
Crowding with deaths each minute of the day.
Fear made all selfish, flying for their lives.
Wives from their husbands, husbands from their wives,
The mother from her child, despite its moan;
The dying and the dead were left alone.
But he—was ever such a King before?
He went from street to street, from door to door,
Physician, nurse, and friend; no wretched den
Passed by, nor shrunk from the most desperate men,
Moistened their lips with water, brought them wine,
And talked—the Bishop never talked so fine
In his long robe at Easter, when he stands
Blessing the world with much-bejeweled hands.
Don't tell me, sirs,—he is the best of Kings."
From this the gossip passed to other things.
One of the youth of Felix strove to tell,

Another babbled of his famous bell,
(All knew, alas, that folly of their King,)
How strange it was they never heard it ring,
Not even when the victory was won,
Nor on his marriage, no, nor birthday of his son.
And now their thoughts the Prince and Queen divide,
How fair and good she was, how young she died,
How valiant he, no knight could ride him down,
So handsome, too, his golden hair his crown.
"What better King than he can we desire?
May he be happy, happy as his Sire!"

Felix meanwhile was dying. Day by day
His strength, his life had slowly ebbed away,
No wave returning from the shoreless sea
To which his soul was drifting wearily.
Pale, pale his sunken cheek, and sharp his chin,
His long, thin hands so white, more long and thin,
(Like knotted cords their large, blue arteries rise,)
And what great orbs are in his pits of eyes,
Draped in the wrinkled lids whose fringes meet,
As dreadful as the dead beneath the winding sheet.
Ah yes, and when at last the lids are stirred,
Lifting at some soft step, or loving word,
(Say, when the Prince is by,) more dreadful yet,
Filled with such solemn light, such strange regret,
Unearthly, wild—as if the dead arose,
And stared about them in their burial clothes.
For hours he spoke not, moved not, shunning all,
He turned his face in sorrow to the wall,
And, lost in shadow, slept, or seemed to sleep:
He murmured "Agnes" once, and woke to weep.
Then, rest denied, he tried to dream of rest,
Stretched on his back, his hands across his breast
Clasped as in prayer, his upward-pointing feet

Drawing in long, white folds the marble sheet;
Pale, cold, dumb, dead—as awful in the gloom
As if he had become the statue on his tomb.
Vainly his books the sage physician read,
Not written for the living, but the dead,
The dreams of ancient fools reputed wise,
That nor diseases knew, nor remedies.
"Give over, sir," the sick man said at last.
"The hour when drugs would do me good is past.
You know not my disease, and yet 'tis rife."
To which the leech: "What is it, Sire?" "'Tis Life."
"There is no cure for that." "There is but *one*."
"Dear Father, say not so," exclaimed his son,
His sorrow fainting in a storm of sighs,
The wild tears raining from his clouded eyes.
"There's nothing, boy, to weep for, if there be,
'Tis Life, not Death; weep for yourself, not me.
That I must die is but a little thing,
Not so that you must live—and be a King!"
Here some one entered with a smirking face,
To say the Bishop waited. "Tell his Grace,
With all the reverence that befits his state,
The great, good man,—he comes too soon, or late,
Too soon to bury me, too late to save:
But bid him come to-morrow—to my grave.
Enough of him. Who'll lift me up in bed?
I'm troublesome, I know." He raised his head—
The weeping Prince—with more than woman's care,
Kissing with loving lips his silver hair.
And there he sat, a piteous sight to see,
Propped up beneath his gilded canopy
Whose purple shadow o'er his features fell,
And near him hung the cord to ring the happy bell!
"Look up, my son," the dying King began:
"Weep not, but take what's coming like a man.

I do, and have; you do not hear *me* sigh,
I know too much of life to fear to die,
Enough to say some bitter things—all true:
But wherefore should I say them, and to *you?*
You could not look at life through my old eyes,
Nor would my early follies make you wise.
Youth will be youth, however age may prate;
'Twill learn like age, perchance, but learn too late.
Besides, I love you so I can not bear
To darken your young days with future care.
No, keep the dew, the freshness of your heart,
As something precious, which must soon depart.
Be happy, if you are so, while you may:
For me, I have not seen one happy day.
Start not, nor ask the solemn reasons why—
Time flies too fast—you'll know them by and by.
You'll wear my crown to-morrow—Take it now,
O, may it sit less heavy on your brow
Than mine! (See, feel how thin my hair is worn,)
Why every jewel in it is a thorn!
Remember what I've taught in my poor way—
(Would I had strength, I have so much to say!)
The office of a King—what he must be—
How good and wise a man, how—unlike me!"
"Dear Father!" cried the Prince, up-looking then
With reverent eyes, "you are the best of men.
May I be half so good!" "Be better, sir.
Follow—but hark, what's that? I hear a stir,
A sound like summer rain of many feet,
And the low hum of voices in the street."
"It is your people, Sire, who gather there,
(Throw up the casement, you, and give him air,)
Knowing how ill you—were, (the news *would* fly,)
To show their love, they say, before you die."
"My people love me, then?" "Ah Father, yes."

"Well, that is something,—if not Happiness."
He closed his eyes a moment, bowed his head,
And moved his silent lips; at last he said:
"Sit by my side—just there, and now your hand.
When one is going to a distant land,
As I am now, he loves to have a friend,
A son, say, as he starts, to cheer him to the end.
Speak kindly of me after I am gone,
And see my name be graven on the stone,
'INFELIX,' mind, not 'FELIX'—that would be
A cruel, lying epitaph for me,
And yet I know not, for methinks I seem
Slowly awaking from the strangest dream;
The mystery of my life is growing clear.
Something—it may be Happiness—is near.
I hear such heavenly music! Did you speak?
Who's shining yonder? Look!" His voice grew weak,
Died to a whisper, while his swimming sight
Strained through the darkness to a shape of light,
Floating across the chamber to his bed.
"*Agnes!*" He clutched the cord, and fell back—dead,
Striking in death the first stroke of his knell.
Thus Felix rang at last the Happy Bell.

THE BOOK OF THE EAST.

PERSIAN SONGS.

SWEET are the garden spaces,
Lighted with happy faces:
Long may their faces shine,
The merry drinkers of wine.

The wind of the morning blows
Out of the heart of the rose:
My heart, or the rose at my feet,
Which is the sweetest, Sweet?

But the rose will soon depart,
And leave its thorns in my heart;
Then I shall sigh, and wail,
And bleed, like the nightingale.

O nightingale, come with the dews,
Thy coming will be good news;
For lovers that cannot sleep
Listen to thee, and weep!

——o——

THE heart where love and patience dwell,
(But such there cannot be,)
I hold it not a heart, but stone,
It will not do for me.

Ah, no, a thousand pharsangs part
The loving and the patient heart.

What discipline shall I adopt
  To ease this woe of mine?
I harken to the harp in vain,
  And drain the cups of wine;
I love, but cannot patient be,
Nor can the patient love like me.

———o———

NOT wholly, poet, from the eyes
    Doth love arise:
For words create, though ne'er express,
    This happiness.
Once at the portal of the ear,
    Let love appear,
There is no rest for heart, or brain,
    Till loved again.
No need of sight, enough for me
    To hear, not see.
The god I serve is painted blind,
To show his eyes are in his mind.

———o———

MY little soul, my lover,
  He does not hear me sigh:
Tell me the street he lives in,
  At once to him I'll fly.

If I can only find him,
  He's sure to hear my prayer:
Tell me the street you live in,
  O Mirza, tell me where.

Give me a cup of wine, dear,
  And listen to my plea;
Say, when you love another,
  You want no more of me!

——o——

TWO strings for my guitar
  I will spin from your hair;
What else can you expect
  From a lover in despair?

You grant a "Yes" to all,
  But the man that is your own;
When I ask for a kiss,
  It is "No" to me alone.

Were I marble I would be
  A floor where you might walk,
As stately as a cypress,
  With an eye like a hawk.

You said that you would come,
  Where is your promise, dear?
For lo, I am alone,
  And the midnight is here.

——o——

YOUR hands are red with henna,
  And you wear a Cashmere shawl;
Such gay and cruel colors
  Become you best of all.

You stand in blooming beauty,
  Like a mulberry-tree, my dear:
I've eaten mulberries often,
  But not enough this year.

We did not sit together,
  Nor touch our knees again:
I talked with you so little
  I could not tell my pain.

Come to me in the morning,
  Again when day doth end:
Nobody, love, will mind it,
  They'll say you are my friend!

——o——

SHE does not hear my sighing,
  My rose, my willow leaf;
And if she heard, what matter?
  She would not heal my grief.

Come to me, dear, when day breaks,
  And come when day doth close;
I'm drunken with your beauty,
  O European Rose!

And if she's from Arabia,
  This little love of mine,
Her mouth shall be my wine-glass,
  Her kiss shall be my wine!

Her travelling-packs are ready,
  She fastens on her shawl;
Were I the shawl I'd hold her,
  She should not go at all.

When shall I see thee, darling,
  And lighten my poor heart?
I come once more to whisper
  Its secrets—and depart.

——o——

Do not yet put on your slippers,
      I shall die :
Do not take your veil, belovèd,
      Do not fly!
Ah, so sweet your conversation,
      Do not go;
Stop a minute, Rose, my darling,
      Leave not so!
'Tis the very hour for prattle,
      'Tis the hour,
O my darling! O my sweetest
      Poppy flower!
See, the ceiling of the chamber
      Painted fine;
Rose was never like your blushes,
      Rose of mine!
O my sunflower! My belovèd!
      Linger here :
Linger, I have lost all patience,
      All, my dear.
Sweetheart, 'tis a lonely chamber,
      No one near :
Rose of Khansar, sweet as amber,
      Blossom here!
Hurry, hurry on the wedding,
      Or I die;
I am dying, dead already,
      If you fly!

Sweetheart, with your eyebrow bending,
Like a bow;
And your arrowy glances flying,
So, and so;
Stop, my love, another minute,
Do not go!

——o——

I FELL in love with a Turkish maid,
(She sleeps, she does not wake,)
A scarlet turban covers her head,
(She sleeps, she does not wake.)
My eyes are red with tears,
And my sighs like smoke are driven,
The smoke of my burning heart
Reaching the seventh heaven.
The happiness of the world
Awakes for her sweet sake;
But she, she,
Who is more than happiness to me,
She sleeps, she does not wake.

I came and saw the maid asleep,
(For sometimes eyes forget to weep,
And hearts forget to ache;)
My arms embraced
Her slender waist,
And with my hands I pressed
The citrons of her breast;
(She slept, she did not wake).
Who weds, they say, a maiden,
Has a world of sweets in store,
Fresh as the buds in May;
But the riper charms of widows

Are like the fruits of autumn
  That drop from day to day.
I measure with my steps the shore,
I hearken to the ocean's roar,
  My heart is like to break—
She sleeps, she does not wake!

—o—

It is a morn in winter,
  The air is white with snow,
And on the chinar branches
  Jasmines seem to grow.

The furrowed fields and hill-tops
  With icy treasures shine,
Like scales of silver fishes,
  Or jewels in a mine.

The bitter wind has banished
  The silent nightingale,
And the rose, like some coy maiden,
  Is muffled in a veil.

Its silver song of summer
  No more the fountain sings,
And frozen are the rivers
  That fed the baths of kings.

No flower-girls in the market,
  For flowers are out of date;
And the keepers of the roses
  Have shut the garden gate.

No happy guests are drinking
  Their goblets crowned with wine;
For gone are all the merchants
  That sold the merry wine.

And gone the dancing maidens
  Before the winds and snows:
Their summer souls have followed
  The nightingale and rose!

——o——

JOY may be a miser,
  But Sorrow's purse is free.
I had two griefs already,
  He gave two more to me.
He filled my eyes with water,
  He filled my heart with pain;
And then, the liberal fellow,
  He promised to again.

——o——

THUS to waste the precious hours,
With the hues and scents of flowers,
Captured by the woman's eyes
That bestows them, is not wise.

Take the flowers that longest live,
And the sweetest odors give;
Scarce a summer's day they bloom,
Frailer still is woman's doom.

Therefore keep thy fancy free,
Woman knows not constancy:
This the soundest wits approve,
This is wise—but not to love!

———o———

DAY and night my thoughts incline
To the blandishments of wine:
Jars were made to drain, I think,
Wine, I know, was made to drink.

When I die, (the day be far!)
Should the potters make a jar
Out of this poor clay of mine,
Let the jar be filled with wine!

———o———

IN the market-place one day
I saw a potter stamping clay,
And the clay beneath his tread
Lifted up its voice, and said,
"Potter, gentle be with me,
I was once a man like thee."

———o———

(*Sadi.*)

APART from all the creatures of the earth
I sit and weep aloud, and in my grief
My eyes send up to heaven their hopeless tears.

Even as a little boy whose bird is flown
From out his hand still weeps for that same bird,
So I bewail my sweet but vanished life.

———o———

(*Hakim Sanayi.*)

WHAT sweetness is there in the honeycomb,
That is not tasted, Sweetest, in thy kiss?

What beauty is there in the pheasant's walk
That is not seen, belovèd, in thy step?

What heart in all the city is not thine?
The heart that is not thine no longer beats.

The bird that flies not to thy nest of love
Deserves to fly no more: why has he wings?

———o———

TARTAR SONGS.

YES, we are merry Cossacks,
  Though not the Russian breed;
But bring a steed from Ilmen,
  And fatten the lean steed.

When we come back with plunder,
  We are true Cossacks then:
We sleep in the arms of beauties,
  My merry, merry men.

———o———

THE merry spring is here,
  Then come before it fades,
Pluck handfuls of red roses,
  And kiss the lips of maids.

The lips of maids in spring
  Are cardamoms and cloves;
Let each fair maid come hither,
  And kiss the man she loves.

——o——

I AM drunk with thy fragrant breath,
  Come hither, my girl, to me;
Of all the girls that I know,
  I have given my heart to thee.

In the fruits of beauty around,
  Thou art my peach, and my pear;
O when wilt thou lie on my breast,
  From dusk till dawn, my fair?

——o——

I WANDERED by a river,
  And met a lady fair,
And she was busy bathing
  Behind her veil of hair.

"If I should buy, sweet idol,
  Your ringlets long and rare,
Tell me the price." She answered,
  "A pearl for every hair."

——o——

O FOLLOWER of the Prophet,
My heart is again on fire;
A certain man has a daughter
Who kindles my desire.

How shall you find the Houri?
Easy enough, d'ye see;
Before the door of her dwelling
There grows a mulberry-tree.

——o——

HE rode from the Khora Tukhan
On his nimble bay steed,
For the eyes of his mistress, Girgalla,
Forsaking his creed.

He gave his broad belt to his comrade.
Why scoff you? he said.
The sheep are all killed for the wedding,
The dishes are spread.

I have sat in the rains and the thunders,
Alone since she went.
I would I could sit down beside her,
Beneath the white tent!

When I lift to my lips the red tea-cup,
Slow sipping the tea,
I think of the lips of Girgalla,
And sigh, "Woe is me!"

I peeped through the snowy tent curtains,
  Girgalla was there :
She stood like a peacock before me,
  No peacock so fair.

Your head on the lap of Girgalla,
  Stretched out at your ease,
No cushion, you say, of swan's feathers
  So soft as her knees!

——o——

BLOW, Wind, blow,
And carry news of me
Away to Astrabad,
Away to my Sakina;
And soon as you have seen her
Say, " A Tartar lad
Sends this kiss to thee."
Then, your sweet lips pressed
To her snowy breast,
Kiss her so—and so!

——o——

MY war-horse was fond of my singing
  The free songs of yore :
But now he'll remain in the stable—
  I shall ride him no more.

My Tartar girls, fair as the billows,
  In the tents will remain;
They will find a new lord, and the horse
  A new rider again.

But my mother, dear heart, when she loses
  Her rider so brave,
Will be true to the love that she bears me—
  She will find a dark grave!

—o—

I AM a white falcon, hurrah!
  My home is the mountains so high;
But away o'er the lands and the waters,
  Wherever I please, I can fly.

I wander from city to city,
  I dart from the wave to the cloud,
And when I am dead I shall slumber
  With my own white wings for a shroud,

—o—

I AM dying of the brand
  Love has burned upon my heart;
Let me come to my death
    By the girdle that you wear.
I must see you twice, or thrice,
  Ere the day can depart,
Or I ask after you,
    Of the birds in the air!

—o—

WAIL on, thou bleeding nightingale,
  I join my wail with thine;
Deplore thy passion for the rose,
  And let me weep for mine.

Lament thy rose for seventy days,
  She lives, and may reply;
But mine is dead, and I must weep,
  Or break my heart, and die!

——o——

FORGIVE me, mother dear,
  For the days of unrest
And the sleepless nights you passed
  When I sucked from your breast.

Dig my grave on a hill,
  On the summit let it stand,
That the wind may blow my dust
  To my own Tartar land.

——o——

ARAB SONGS.

O LOVELY fawn! O my gazelle!
  O moon on summer seas!
Full moon whose beauty doth surpass
    The Pleiades!

I swear an oath to fast a month
  The day that I am blest,
The happy day I press thee, dear,
    Upon my breast!

——o——

BREAK thou my heart, ah, break it,
  If such thy pleasure be;
Thy will is mine, what say I?
  'T is more than mine to me.

And if my life offend thee,
  My passion and my pain,
Take thou my life, ah, take it,
  But spare me thy disdain!

——o——

BELOVED, since they watch us,
  For all we meet are spies,
And we can have no messengers,
  Except our loving eyes,

I check my fiery feelings,
  The words I must not speak,
Content to see, I dare not pluck,
  The roses of thy cheek.

Give me a glance, belovèd,
  Now none are near to see:
My downcast eyes will read my palms,
  I will not look at thee.

It is not resignation,
  It is the deepest art:
Be wary, then, and doubt no more,
  But trust my loving heart.

——o——

THOU art my only love,
  The world is nothing now:
In no walled garden grows
  So fair a branch as thou.

Thou hast forgotten all,
  Ah yes, it must be so.
She should have been my friend,
  She has become my foe.

I've drunk the bitter cup,
  Since we were parted, Sweet;
The tears I shed have made
  This river at my feet!

Ah, long, long hours of love!
  Ah, nights we stole from sleep!
When such sweet nights are gone,
  It is no shame to weep!

———o———

I HID my love when near you,
  My pain for your sweet sake;
But now that you are absent,
  My heart must speak, or break.
God save you from such passion,
  It never knows despair,
For whether kind or cruel,
  You are the only fair.

You will not see me, Sweetest,
  Nor answer, when I call;
But I will follow, follow
  Beyond the giant's wall.
Go, shut your door against me,
  I will not doubt, or fear;
God still leaves one door open,
  The door of hope, my dear!

Could I have loved another,
  That time is now no more ;
I cover with my kisses
  The threshold of your door.
Open the door of pity,
  And hear my burning sigh,
For absent from you longer
  Is sadder than to die !

——o——

"GIRL, I love thee!" Her reply
Was the saucy one, "You lie!
If you love me, as you say,
Why are you alive to-day?
I will tell you what to do:
There will be no love in you
Till your blood is weak and thin,
And your bones prick through your skin;
Till you wither, heart and mind,
And are nearly deaf and blind,
Scarcely hear them when they call,
And not answer them at all;
Till you never prate again
Of your love, and my disdain,
No, nor breathe it in your sighs;
Or at least until your eyes,
Blind with tears that rain for me,
Shall your only vouchers be."

Master of the Universe!
If there be a deeper curse
Than this terrible despair,
(Burden more than I can bear,)
O let Leila have her share!

Let my love divided be,
Half to her, and half to me;
Or, if this be not her fate,
Let her neither love nor hate,
Only be indifferent,
I will try to be content.

"Ah, but she is sick," you say.
Why was I not sent for, pray?
There is danger in delay.
I have taken my degree
(Leila knows, my master, she,)
Let me her physician be.
These diseases of the heart
Are beyond the reach of art:
He who gives can cure the smart.

——o——

If you meet my sweet gazelle,
By these signs you'll know her well:
Eyes like arrows, black and bright,
Cheeks the fiery rose of night,
And her voice a silver bell.

I am burning with desire,
Like a parchment in the fire;
I am dying, hear my cry,
'T is for love of thee I die,
Emir's Daughter, Peacock's Eye!

Hearts of rocks, be soft to me,
Or my tears will soften thee,
In my passion and my pain
Flowing down my cheeks like rain,
And they will not flow in vain!

I know where her palace stands,
It is in the far-off lands,
Over mountains, over sands:
Seldom letters reach her there,
Never wretched lover's prayer.

I am dying, for no art
Can relieve my broken heart.
What I suffer none can tell,
Blasted by the fires of hell,
By the love of that gazelle!

There's a stately palm that grows
Where the purest water flows:
She's its fruit: her lips are red
As the blush that rubies shed,
Or the west when day is dead.

Life and death are met in me,
But I only think of thee.
Let the happy fool complain,
What is dying? Where's the pain?
I have lived, and loved in vain!

CHINESE SONGS.

UP in an old pagoda's highest tower
I sat, and watched the falling shades of eve.

Long curls of smoke, and sounds of distant lutes
As faint as smoke, spread through the lonely wood.

The evening wind blew over the cool stream,
Troubling the pallid pin-flowers on its bank;

And where the autumnal hills were thickly strewn
With faded, fallen leaves the hoar-frost fell.

Naught could I see in all that cloudless sky
Except the wild goose flying to the South.

Harkening in bright moonshine I heard the sound
Of distant villagers beating out their rice.

Then, thinking of the friend, whose absent face
The long year through, not once has brightened mine,

I sought the window shaded o'er with pines,
And struck the strings of my melodious lute.

——o——

(*Soo Hwuy.*)

WHAT time my husband went to banishment,
I followed to the foot of yonder bridge;
I bore my grief, but could not say "Farewell!"

Ah, why have you not written me, my love?
Our couch, remember, even in spring is cold.
The staircase that you built has crumbled down,
And dust has soiled the windows and white curtains,

My mind is sore perplexed; I would I were
The shadow of the moon upon the sea,
The cloud that floats above the lofty hills.
The careless clouds behold my husband's face,

And she, the sea-moon, in her monthly round;
They know the man a thousand leagues away.

The tall green rushes by the river's side
Have faded, since we parted; but the plum—
Who would have thought before we met again
The plum-tree would have blossomed many times?

The flowers unfold themselves to meet the spring;
Our hearts unfold in vain, no spring is ours.
My thoughts are busied so with your return
The willow at the door droops to the ground,
And no one sweeps away its fallen leaves.

The grass before the house grows thick and rank;
My husband's flute hangs idle in the hall;
He sings no more the songs of Keang-nan.

Because no letter comes to me, my lord,
My silver dress that on my pillow lies
Is dyed with tears, and tears have spoiled the flowers
Broidered in gold upon my satin robe.

Thrice have I heard in spring the wild-fowl's cry,
Crossing the swollen stream. I sing old songs;
My heart-strings seem to break upon the lute.
I faint with love, and grief; grief ends my song.

Forget not, O my lord, your own true wife,
Your wife, whose love is firmer than the hills,
Whose thoughts are filled with you. She weaves this song
To win the gracious ear of Majesty.
O Son of Heaven! Let him return, and soon!

——o——

("*Kang Chi.*")

I.

MOULAN is weaving at her cottage door.
You cannot hear the weaving shuttles fly,
You only hear the young girl sigh and moan.

"What are you thinking of? Why do you moan?"
The young girl thinks of nothing, yet she moans.

"I saw the army record yesterday;
The Emperor is levying troops again;
The book has twelve long chapters, and in each
I saw enrolled my honored father's name.

What can be done to save the poor old man?
Thou hast no grandson, father, no, not one.
Thou hast no elder brother, O, Moulan!
What shall I do? I will arise, and go,
And buy a horse and saddle. I will go,
And serve and fight in my dear father's stead."

She buys a swift horse at the eastern market,
A saddle and a horse-cloth at the western,
And at the southern a long horseman's whip.
When morning comes she smiles and says, "Farewell,
Father and mother." She will pass the night
Beside the Yellow River. She hears no more
Father, or mother, calling for their child;
The hollow murmur of the Yellow River
Is all she hears. Another morning comes;
She starts again, and bids the stream farewell.
She journeys on, and when the evening comes

She reaches the Black River. She hears no more
Father, or mother, sighing for their child;
She hears the savage horsemen of Yen Shen.

II.

"Where have you been, Moulan, these twelve long years?"
"We marched and fought our way ten thousand miles.
Swift as a bird I cleared the gulfs and hills.
The north-wind brought the night bell to my ear,
The moonlight fell upon my iron mail.

Twelve years are past. We meet the Emperor
When we return; he sits upon his throne.
He gives this man a badge of honor, that
An hundred or a thousand silver ounces.
'And what shall he give me?' And I reply:
'Nor wealth, nor office; only lend Moulan—
She asks no more—a camel, fleet of foot,
To lead her to her honored father's roof.'"

Soon as the father and the mother learn
Moulan's return they haste to meet their child;
Soon as the younger sisters see them go
They leave the chamber in their best attire;
Soon as the brave young brother hears the news
He straightway whets a knife to kill a sheep.

"My mother takes my warrior's armor off,
And clothes me in my woman's garb again:
My younger sisters, standing by the door,
Are twining golden flowers in their hair."

Then Moulan left the room, and went to meet
Her fellow-soldiers, who were much amazed;
For twelve long years she marched and fought with them,
And yet they guessed not Moulan was a girl.

(*Yuen Yuen.*)

WE started when the clarion of the cock
Was ceasing, and the first thin curl of smoke
Rose from the village; not a withered leaf
Waved in the frozen forest, and no bird
Sang there, but flocks were lighting on the plain.
In vain they pecked for food, the barren plain
Bore naught but rotten grass; frost hid the roots;
So back they hastened to their empty nests.

The gray-haired village farmer, up at dawn
To fondle his grandchildren, hears the shout,
"A Mandarin is passing!" Staff in hand
He gazes, leaning on his matted door.
West of his house we see great stacks of straw,
And in the east the golden beams of day;
His thick warm garments and his ruddy face
Are signs of plenty, and, I shrewdly guess,
That somewhere in his house could still be found
One measure more of rice, stowed in the bin.

——o——

(*Keaa.*)

MILLIONS of flowers are blowing in the fields.
On the blue river's brink the peony
Burns red, and where doves coo the lute is heard,
And hoarse black crows caw to the eastern wind.

Under the plane-tree in the shaded grove,
Screened from the light and heat, the idler sits,
Brooding above his chess-board all day long,

Nor marks, so deep his dream, how fast the sun
Descends at evening to its western house.

When autumn comes men close their doors and read,
Or at the window loll to catch the breeze
Freighted with fragrance from the cinnamon.

The snow is falling on the balustrade
Like dying petals, and the icicle
Hangs like a gem; all crowd around the fire:
Rich men now drink their wine with merry hearts,
And sing old songs, nor heed the blast without.

———o———

(*Too-Mo.*)

THE shadows of the swallows
Have crossed the autumn rivers,
Then let us climb the mountains,
    And friend with friend carouse:
We'll take a bottle with us,
And drink like merry fellows,
And stagger back at sunset,
    With flowers about our brows.

But no, let's drain our bottles
At noon in this bright garden,
For dark and sad the sunsets
    On distant mountains shine.
The days of old have vanished,
Then drink, and laugh, to-day, boys,
Nor stain with tears your garments,
    They're better stained with wine!

———o———

(*He-Kwan.*)

THE farmer cuts the So leaves,
  And weaves his rainy cloak;
His cot is on the hillside,
  You see it by the smoke.

His rustic wife soon hails him,
  "The nice boiled pears are done."
The children from the pea-field
  To meet their daddy run.

In the shaded lake the fishes
  Are swimming to and fro;
The little birds brush each other,
  As back to the hills they go.

Crowds will be going and coming,
  In the happy season of flowers;
But could I find the philosopher's stone,
  I'd fish in the brook for hours.

— o

EAST, or west, to the pastures,
  We lead our herds at ease;
Having no master to goad us,
  We spend the time as we please.

In the green bamboos together
  We cut our reeds, and play;
Or sit in the long grass patching
  Our cloaks for a rainy day.

Or twist the ropes of the heifers,
And make them stout and long,
Tuning our merry voices
To sing the herdsman's song.

We point at the restless miser,
And laugh in his face with glee.
"Your legs are mighty travellers,
What can the matter be?

"Ride who will on horseback,
The cow is sure and strong."
Thus, by the springs in the coppice,
We sing the herdsman's song.

———o———

HE saw in sight of his house,
At dusk, as stories tell,
A woman picking mulberries,
And he liked her looks right well.

He struggled out of his chair,
And began to beckon and call;
But she went on picking mulberries,
Nor looked at him at all.

"If Famine should follow you,
He would find the harvest in;
You think yourself and your mulberries
Too good for a Mandarin.

I have yellow gold in my sleeve."
But she answered, sharp and bold,
"Be off! Let me pick my mulberries,
I am bought with no man's gold."

She scratched his face with her nails,
  Till he turned and fled for life,
For the lady picking mulberries
  Was his true and virtuous wife!

——o——

BEFORE the scream of the hawk
  The timid swallow flies;
And the lake unrolled in the distance
  Like a silver carpet lies.

The light that sleeps in the air
  Like the breath of flowers is sweet;
The very dust is balmy
  Under the horses' feet.

We sit in the tennis court,
  Where the beautiful sunlight falls;
The mountains crossed by bridges
  Come down to the city walls.

The houses are hid in flowers,
  Buried in bloomy trees;
But under the veils of the willows
  Are glimpses of cottages.

What makes the wind so sweet?
  Is it the breath of June?
'T is the jasper flute in the pear-tree,
  Playing a silent tune!

——o——

THE dark and rainy weather
  That now has taken flight
Has made the sunshine brighter,
  And filled our hearts with light.

The groves are full of song-birds,
  And troops of butterflies
Are hovering o'er the peach-trees,
  Like blossoms of the skies.

The flowers that have not faded,
  But to the boughs still cling,
Are hanging every garden
  With tapestries of spring.

And see, the happy students,
  Have met by scores to dine
Beneath the willow branches,
  And drain the cups of wine.

———o———

STRETCHED in flowers and moonlight,
  The poet took his lute;
His mind was full of sweetness,
  A salver heaped with fruit.

"The odor of the blossoms,
  It breathes upon my heart;
But the thoughts it quickens
  No language can impart.

The whiteness of the blossoms,
  The young moon's virgin light,
They make me think of marriage,
  The happy bridal night.

I see a troop of damsels,
  My own dear love I see :
They are willow branches,
  A peach blossom, she."

——o——

IT grieves the bee and butterfly
  Because they strive in vain
To hoard the scent of flowers,
  Whose honeyed cups they drain.

The swallow and the loriot
  Are not so swift of wing,
For the summer overtakes them,
  As they chase the sweets of spring.

It is the King of the East, dear,
  That makes the flowers to grow;
Nor can the rains prevent them,
  Nor all the winds that blow.

——o——

NOW the wind is softest,
  Lightest now the shower,
And in an hour the barren boughs
  Begin to bud and flower.

Happy thoughts are brooding
  On the song I sing,
As to the arch of yonder bridge
  The mists of morning cling.

Pitiful the miser,
  Who digs the earth for gold;
I would sooner hoard the snow,
  So barren and so cold.

No, I love thee, Sweetest,
  And the wandering dove—
I send her with a sigh to thee,
  A little verse of love.

"Go count the silken tresses
  That hang on yonder tree;
So many are my loving thoughts,
  And so they cling to thee!"

———o———

THE grove is crowned with hoar-frost,
  And clothed in robes of snow;
But buds of tender purple
  On all the branches blow.

They rain upon the river,
  As winds go sweeping by,
Redden the waves a moment,
  And then like torches die.

At the foot of yonder gallery
  I see a beauteous girl;
She has a thousand garments
  Of satin and of pearl.

The blossoms blush to meet her,
  It is the maiden Spring,
For hark, among the branches
  I hear the cuckoo sing!

——o——

(" *Shi King.*")

I HEAR the sacred swan,
  In its river island sing;
I see the modest maiden,
  A consort for a king.

The tendrils of the Hang
  Are green and white below,
Along the running waters
  Swaying to and fro.

The king has sought the maid,
  His passion is so strong:
And day and night he murmurs,
  "How long, alas, how long!"

He turns him on his bed,
  He tosses in his woe;
His thoughts are like the Hang plants,
  Swaying to and fro.

Again I hear the swan,
  In a palace garden sing;
Again I see the maiden,
  The consort of the king.

The king is happy now,
  For see, the maiden comes,
And hark, the bells are ringing,
  And hark, the noise of drums!

——o——

A WOMAN'S POEM.

You say you love me, and you lay
  Your hand and fortune at my feet:
I thank you, sir, with all my heart,
          For love is sweet.

It is but little to you men,
  To whom the doors of Life stand wide;
But much, how much to woman! She
          Has naught beside.

You make the worlds wherein you move,
  You rule your tastes, or coarse, or fine;
Dine, hunt, or fish, or waste your gold
          At dice and wine.

Our world (alas, you make that, too!)
  Is narrower, shut in four blank walls:
Know you, or care, what light is there?
          What shadow falls?

We read the last new novel out,
  And live in dream-land till it ends:
We write romantic school-girl notes,
          That bore our friends.

We learn to trill Italian songs,
  And thrum for hours the tortured keys:
We think it pleases you, and we
          But live to please.

We feed our birds, we tend our flowers,
  (Poor in-door things of sickly bloom,)
Or play the housewife in our gloves,
          And dust the room.

But some of us have hearts and minds,
  So much the worse for us and you;
For grant we seek a better life,
          What can we do?

We cannot build and sail your ships,
  Or drive your engines; we are weak,
And ignorant of the tricks of Trade.
          To think, and speak,

Or write some earnest, stammering words
  Alone is ours, and that you hate;
So forced within ourselves again
          We sigh and wait.

Ah, who can tell the bitter hours,
  The dreary days, that women spend?
Their thoughts unshared, their lives unknown,
          Without a friend!

Without a friend? And what is he,
  Who, like a shadow, day and night,
Follows the woman he prefers—
          Lives in her sight?

Her lover, he: a gallant man,
  Devoted to her every whim;
He vows to die for her, so she
    Must live for him!

We should be very grateful, sir,
  That, when you 've nothing else to do,
You waste your idle hours on us—
    So kind of you!

Profuse in studied compliments,
  Your manners like your clothes are fine,
Though both at times are somewhat strong
    Of smoke and wine.

What can we hope to know of you?
  Or you of us? We act our parts:
We love in jest: it is the play
    Of hands, not hearts!

You grant my bitter words are true
  Of others, not of you and me;
Your love is steady as a star:
    But we shall see.

You say you love me: have you thought
  How much those little words contain?
Alas, a world of happiness,
    And worlds of pain!

You know, or should, your nature now,
  Its needs and passions. Can I be
What you desire me? Do you find
    Your all in me?

You do. But have you thought that I
  May have my ways and fancies, too?
You love me ; well, but have you thought
          If I love you?

But think again. You know me not :
  I, too, may be a butterfly,
A costly parlor doll on show
          For you to buy.

You trust me wholly? One word more.
  You see me young : they call me fair :
I think I have a pleasant face,
          And pretty hair.

But by and by my face will fade,
  It must with time, it may with care :
What say you to a wrinkled wife,
          With thin, gray hair?

You care not, you : in youth, or age,
  Your heart is mine, while life endures.
Is it so? Then, Arthur, here's my hand,
          My heart is yours.

——o——

WITHOUT AND WITHIN.

I.

THE night is dark, and the winter winds
  Go stabbing about with their icy spears;
The sharp hail rattles against the panes,
    And melts on my cheek like tears.

'Tis a terrible night to be out of doors,
But some of us must be, early and late;
We needn't ask who, for don't we know
It has all been settled by Fate?

Not woman, but man. Give woman her flowers,
Her dresses, her jewels, or what she demands:
The work of the world must be done by man,
Or why has he brawny hands?

As I feel my way in the dark and cold,
I think of the chambers warm and bright,
The nests where these delicate birds of ours
Are folding their wings to-night.

Through the luminous windows, above and below,
I catch a glimpse of the life they lead:
Some sew, some sing, others dress for the ball,
While others, fair students, read.

There's the little lady who bears my name,
She sits at my table now, pouring her tea;
Does she think of me as I hurry home,
Hungry and wet? Not she.

She helps herself to the sugar and cream
In a thoughtless, dreamy, nonchalant way;
Her hands are white as the virgin rose
That she wore on her wedding day.

My clumsy fingers are stained with ink,
The badge of the Ledger, the mark of Trade;
But the money I give her is clean enough,
In spite of the way it is made.

I wear out my life in the counting-room
  Over day-book and cash-book, Bought and Sold;
My brain is dizzy with anxious thought,
    My skin is as sallow as gold.

How does she keep the roses of youth
  Still fresh in her cheek? My roses are flown.
It lies in a nutshell—why do I ask?
    A woman's life is her own.

She gives me a kiss when we part for the day,
  Then goes to her music, blithe as a bird;
She reads it at sight, and the language, too,
    Though I know never a word.

She sews a little, makes collars and sleeves,
  Or embroiders me slippers (always too small,)
Nets silken purses (for me to fill,)
    Often does nothing at all

But dream in her chamber, holding a flower,
  Or reading my letters—she'd better read me.
Even now, while I am freezing with cold,
    She is cosily sipping her tea.

If I ever reach home I shall laugh aloud
  At the sight of a roaring fire once more:
She must wait, I think, till I thaw myself,
    For the nightly kiss at the door.

I'll have with my dinner a bottle of port,
  To warm up my blood and soothe my mind;
Then a little music, for even I
    Like music—when I have dined.

I'll smoke a pipe in the easy-chair,
And feel her behind me patting my head;
Or drawing the little one on my knee,
Chat till the hour for bed.

II.

Will he never come? I have watched for him
Till the misty panes are roughened with sleet;
I can see no more: shall I never hear
The welcome sound of his feet?

I think of him in the lonesome night,
Tramping along with a weary tread,
And wish he were here by the cheery fire,
Or I were there in his stead.

I sit by the grate, and hark for his step,
And stare in the fire with a troubled mind;
The glow of the coals is bright in my face,
But my shadow is dark behind.

I think of woman, and think of man,
The tie that binds and the wrongs that part,
And long to utter in burning words
What I feel to-night in my heart.

No weak complaint of the man I love,
No praise of myself, or my sisterhood;
But—something that women understand—
By men never understood.

Their natures jar in a thousand things;
Little matter, alas, who is right or wrong,
She goes to the wall. "She is weak," they say—
It is that which makes them strong.

Wherein am I weaker than Arthur, pray?
He has, as he should, a sturdier frame,
And he labors early and late for me,
But I—I could do the same.

My hands are willing, my brain is clear,
The world is wide, and the workers few;
But the work of the world belongs to man,
There is nothing for woman to do!

Yes, she has the holy duties of home,
A husband to love, and children to bear,
The softer virtues, the social arts,—
In short, a life without care!

So our masters say. But what do they know
Of our lives and feelings when they are away?
Our household duties, our petty tasks,
The nothings that waste the day?

Nay, what do they care? 'Tis enough for them
That their homes are pleasant; they seek their ease:
One takes a wife to flatter his pride,
Another to keep his keys.

They say they love us; perhaps they do,
In a masculine way, as they love their wine:
But the soul of woman needs something more,
Or it suffers at times like mine.

Not that Arthur is ever unkind
In word or deed, for he loves me well;
But I fear he thinks me as weak as the rest—
(And I may be, who can tell?)

I should die if he changed, or loved me less,
  For I live at best but a restless life;
Yet he may, for they say the kindest men
    Grow tired of a sickly wife.

O, love me, Arthur, my lord, my life,
  If not for my love, and my womanly fears,
At least for your child. But I hear his step—
    He must not find me in tears.

——o——

ON THE TOWN.

THE lamps are lighted, the streets are full,
  For coming and going like waves of the sea,
Thousands are out this beautiful night;
  They jostle each other, but shrink from me.
Men hurry by with a stealthy glance,
  Women pass with their eyes cast down;
Even the children seem to know
  The shameless girl of the town.

Hated and shunned I walk the street,
  Hunting—for what? For my prey, 'tis said;
I look at it, though, in a different light,
  For this nightly shame is my daily bread:
My food, my shelter, the clothes I wear,
  Only for this I might starve or drown;
The world has disowned me—what can I do
  But live and die on the town?

The world is cruel. It may be right
  To crush the harlot, but, grant it so,
What made her the guilty thing she is?
  For she was innocent once, you know.

'Twas love! That terrible word tells all.
  She loved a man and blindly believed
His vows, his kisses, his crocodile tears;
  Of course the fool was deceived.

What had I to gain by a moment's sin
  To weigh in the scale with my innocent years,
My womanly shame, my ruined name,
  My father's curses, my mother's tears?
The love of a man! It was something to give,
  Was it worth it? The price was a soul paid down,
Did I get a soul, *his* soul in exchange?
  Behold me here on the town!

"Your guilt was heavy," the world will say,
  "And heavy, heavy your doom must be;
For to pity and pardon woman's fall
  Is to set no value on chastity.
You undervalue the virgin's crown,
  The spotless honor that makes her dear."
But I ought to know what the bauble is worth,
  When the loss of it brings me here!

But pity and pardon? Who are you
  To talk of pardon, pity, to me?
What I ask is justice, justice, sir,
  Let both be punished, or both go free.
If it be in woman a dreadful thing,
  What is it in man, now? Come, be just.
(Remember, she falls through her love for him,
  He through his selfish lust.)

Tell me what is done to the wretch
  Who tempts and riots in woman's fall?
His father curses, and casts him off?
  His friends forsake? He is scorned of all?

Not he. His judges are men like himself,
  Or thoughtless women who humor their whim.
"Young blood," "Wild oats," "Better hush it up."
  They soon forget it—in him!

Even his mother, who ought to know
  The woman-nature, and how it is won,
Frames a thousand excuses for him,
  Because, forsooth, the man is her son.
You have daughters, madam, (he told me so,)
  Fair, innocent daughters—"Woman, what then?"
Some mother may have a son like yours,
  Bid them beware of men!

I saw his coach in the street to-day,
  Dashing along on the sunny side,
With a liveried driver on the box:
  Lolling back in her listless pride
The wife of his bosom took the air.
  She was bought in the mart where hearts are sold:
I gave myself away for his love,
  She sold herself for his gold.

He lives, they say, in a princely way,
  Flattered and feasted. One dark night
Some devil led me to pass his house.
  I saw the windows a blaze of light;
The music whirled in a maddening round,
  I heard the fall of the dancers' feet:
Bitter, bitter the thoughts I had,
  Standing there in the street.

Back to my gaudy den I went,
  Marched to my room in grim despair,
Dried my eyes, painted my cheeks,
  And fixed a flower or two in my hair.

Corks were popping, wine was flowing,
  I seized a bumper, and tossed it down:
One must do something to kill the time,
  And fit one's self for the town.

I meet his boy in the park sometimes,
  And my heart runs over towards the child;
A frank little fellow with fearless eyes,
  He smiles at me as his father smiled.
I hate the man, but I love the boy,
  For I think what my own, had he lived, would be:
Perhaps it is *he*, come back from the dead—
  To his father, alas, not me!

But I stand too long in the shadow here,
  Let me out in the light again.
Now for insult, blows, perhaps,
  And bitterer still my own disdain.
I take my place in the crowded street,
  Not like the simple women I see:
You may cheat them, men, as much as you please,
  You wear no masks with me.

I know ye! Under your honeyed words
  There lurks a serpent; your oaths are lies.
There's a lustful fire in your hungry hearts,
  I see it flaming up in your eyes!
Cling to them, ladies, and shrink from me,
  Or rail at my boldness. Well, have you done?
Madam, your husband knows me well,
  Mother, I know your son.

But go your ways, and I'll go mine:
  Call me opprobrious names if you will;
The truth is bitter, think I have lied:
  "A harlot?" Yes, but a woman still.

God said of old to a woman like me,
  "Go, sin no more," or your Bibles lie.
But you, you mangle his merciful words
  To "Go, and sin till you die!"

Die! The word has a pleasant sound,
  The sweetest I've heard this many a year.
It seems to promise an end to pain,
  Anyway it will end it here.
Suppose I throw myself in the street?
  Before the horses could trample me down,
Some would-be friend might snatch me up,
  And thrust me back on the town.

But look—the river! From where I stand
  I see it, I almost hear it flow.
Down on the dark and lonely pier—
  It is but a step—I can end my woe.
A plunge, a splash, and all will be o'er,
  The death-black waters will drag me down;
God knows where! But no matter where,
  So I am off the town!

——o——

THE BALLAD OF VALLEY FORGE.

It was a night in winter,
  Some seventy years ago;
The bleak and barren landscape
  Was blurred with driving snow.

You caught a glimpse of uplands,
  And guessed where valleys lay;
The trees were broken shadows,
  A house was something gray.

Only the western forests
  Stood sharply, black and bare;
For there the blood-red sunset
  Still shot a sullen glare.

In an old New England farm-house,
  That snowy winter night,
In the spacious chimney corner,
  Where the logs were blazing bright,

An aged man was sitting
  In the cherry light and heat,
With his head upon his bosom,
  And the watch-dog at his feet.

Beside him sat his grandson,
  In a high-backed oaken chair,
And the glow of ten sweet summers
  Was golden in his hair.

The man was Nathan Baldwin,
  And many a tale is told
Of how he marched, and suffered
  With hunger and with cold.

Of brave old Gran'ther Baldwin
  Shall be the song I sing,
Who fought for Independence
  When George the Third was King.

Before him hung two muskets,
  With clumsy, dinted stocks,
The bayonets were mounted,
  The flints were in the locks;

Two rusty Queen Anne's muskets,
  Whose pans were smoky still,
The spoil of British soldiers
  Who charged at Bunker Hill.

They fell by Nathan's rifle,
  He snatched their dropping guns,
And sent them to the farm-house
  To arm his stalwart sons.

They hung against the chimney
  That windy winter night,
Unseen by Nathan Baldwin,
  Who saw another sight.

He sat there in his settle
  Before the dancing flame,
And on the wall behind him
  His shadow went and came.

He dozed behind his grandson,
  Whose thoughts were on the snow,
While his eyes were on the muskets,
  And the powder-horns below.

"Tell me a story, Gran'ther,"
  The little dreamer said;
But Nathan did not answer,
  Though he smoothed his curly head.

He heard the shrill winds whistle,
  He saw the embers glow,
And dropping down the chimney
  The ragged flakes of snow.

The sap in the back-log spluttered,
  And through the puffs of smoke,
Like a sharp discharge of rifles,
  A crackling volley broke.

"Tell me a story, Gran'ther.
  Not that of Riding-Hood,
Nor how the robins buried
  The Children in the Wood.

"But how you fought the Indians,
  So many years ago;
Or Valley Forge in winter,
  And all about the snow."

"In the fall of seventy-seven
  (My little Abner, hear,)
In the middle of November
  Of that unhappy year,

I marched with Morgan's Rifles,
  A corps of gallant men,
To join our wretched army
  In the Quaker State of Penn.

By forced and rapid marches,
  (We took the shortest way,
A crow-flight through the Jerseys,
  And added night to day,)

By long and weary marches
  We crossed the dreary plain:
The winds were wild with winter,
  And the sky was dark with rain.

There was no sun in the daytime,
At night there was no moon:
So Morgan told the fifer
To blow a merry tune.

Our poor old regimentals
Were more like rags than clo'es:
Just fit to flap in cornfields
And scare away the crows.

You knew our halting-places
By the tatters lying round.
When we came in sight of White Marsh
Our feet were on the ground.

We scarcely saw the army
That cheered as we drew nigh;
But we marched with flying colors,
And our powder, boy, was dry!

One morning in December
The British came in sight.
Said Morgan, 'Load your rifles,
For here's a chance to fight.'

Six hundred stout militia,
With Irvine at their head,
Sneaked out to take a volley—
Of course the cowards fled!

Howe changed his ground at midnight,
For at the break of day
We saw that he was nearer,
Though still a mile away.

All day he lay and watched us,
  But changed again at night.
When morning came ('twas Sunday)
  We saw he meant to fight.

'Be ready, boys,' said Morgan,
  'And let your aim be true.'
At noon the word was '*Forward!*'
  And then the bullets flew."

"I guess," said Abner, warming,
  "You showed 'em how to fight."
"At dusk they lighted watch-fires,
  And vanished in the night.

The General called a council
  To meet him in his tent,
And choose our winter quarters,
  And all the generals went.

They sat with maps before them,
  And knit their brows awhile;
Some thought of York and Reading,
  And others of Carlisle.

But Washington decided,
  When all had spoken round,
That Valley Forge, in Chester,
  Should be our winter ground.

We heard the news at supper,
  And said 'twas time to go,
For winter was upon us,
  And the sky was full of snow.

So when the dead were buried,
 Some ninety men in all,
We took the road to Chester,
 As the snows began to fall.

It was a sight to see us,
 That dreary winter day,
As we broke up our encampment,
 And stretched for miles away.

The files that came and vanished,
 The banners on the wind,
The gallant van of light-horse,
 The rifles close behind.

Then Poor's brigade, and Glover's,
 The heavy guns of Knox,
The train of baggage-wagons,
 And the teamsters in their frocks,

Climbing the whitened hill-tops,
 And swarming on the plain;
And Washington on horseback,
 With Harry Lee and Wayne.

We crossed a wasted country,
 With a farm-house here and there:
No smoke-wreaths from the chimneys
 Went curling up the air.

No face at door or window
 Looked out as we passed by;
But through the battered sashes
 We saw the blank of sky.

We pushed ahead till nightfall
  Closed round our straggling lines,
Then halted in the shelter
  Of a ragged belt of pines.

We lighted fires of brushwood,
  And stacked our muskets round;
The teamsters lent us fodder,
  And we spread it on the ground.

'Twas bitter, bitter, Abner,
  On the frozen ground to lie,
No pillow but a knapsack,
  No blanket but the sky!

We took the road at daybreak,
  In the blinding snow and wind;
The wounded went in wagons,
  We left the dead behind.

The fifers screamed their loudest,
  But the winds alone were heard;
The drums in snow were muffled,
  And no man spake a word.

We marched in gloomy silence,
  A sort of grim despair,
That nerved the weak to suffer,
  And fired the strong to dare.

You might have tracked us, Abner,
  By the trail of blood we shed;
We bled at every footstep,
  The snow for miles was red!"

"O Gran'ther!" Abner whispered,
  But Gran'ther did not speak,
For the tears of eighty winters
  Were trickling down his cheek.

The tender child was troubled,
  He knew not what to say;
So he clambered up and kissed him,
  And wiped his tears away.

"On the seventeenth of December
  (The day was still and bright)
We crossed the swollen Schuylkill,
  With Valley Forge in sight.

We saw the smoke of the forges,
  We heard the anvils ring;
You should have seen us, Abner,
  And hear us shout and sing.

We pitched our tents by the river,
  In a row along the street,
Built fires, and cooked our dinners,
  And dressed our bleeding feet.

Some sat apart with their muskets,
  Rubbing the rusty stains;
The teamsters stood by their horses,
  And combed the snow from their manes.

One chopped a stack of brushwood,
  Another blew a brand;
I fell asleep at dinner,
  With my ration in my hand.

The next day was Thanksgiving,
  And the valley bells were rung;
The farmers drove to meeting,
  And a goodly psalm was sung.

The drummers beat the roll-call,
  We gathered in the air;
The chaplain preached a sermon,
  And made a touching prayer.

Next morning we were stirring
  As the cocks began to crow,
With our shovels on our shoulders,
  To clear away the snow.

It was a dreary prospect,
  For the winds were sharp and cold,
And we were nearly naked,
  And some, alas, were old.

The General planned our village,
  The streets were east and west.
We dug the snow in trenches,
  A dozen men abreast.

By night the white embankments
  Were piled above our heads.
The roads were black with soldiers,
  And blocked with carts and sleds;

With ox-carts of provisions,
  With sleds of wood and hay,
And officers on horseback
  That slowly cleared the way.

And in the windy forest,
  Whose moan was like the sea's,
We heard the stroke of axes,
  And the crash of falling trees;

The lowing of the oxen,
  That hauled the timber down;
The noise of saws and hammers,
  And the forges in the town.

Our huts were built by Christmas,
  Rough logs, a slab the door;
The cracks with clay were plastered,
  The frozen ground the floor.

All through the happy valley
  The Christmas cheer was spread;
The farmers ate their turkeys,
  And we our mouldy bread.

Well, there we were all winter,
  Ten thousand men, or more.
Ah, how can I remember,
  Or speak of what we bore?

The stupor that benumbed us,
  The pains that drove us wild,
The hunger and the sickness,
  The—all but death, my child!

We made us shoes of raw hide,
  That stung our tender feet;
We limped about on crutches,
  We stumbled in the street.

I had a burning fever,
  I had a freezing chill,
I dreamed of killing Indians,
  I dreamed of Bunker Hill.

One night, when I was better
  The guard was ordered out
In front of Varnum's quarters,
  Before the Star Redoubt.

I thought I heard them call me,
  (It was my turn to go,)
So I snatched a hat and musket,
  And hobbled through the snow.

Along the grim abatis
  That faced the windy street,
To where the gloomy forest
  And swollen river meet.

Along the roaring river,
  Beyond the narrow ford,
Till near the outer picket—
  When all at once I heard

The General's voice. I harkened,
  And through the darkness broke
His tall, commanding figure,
  Wrapt in a martial cloak.

'Good evening, Nathan Baldwin.
  I'm glad to see you out.'
'It is my night on guard, sir,
  Before the Star Redoubt.'

And he: 'Did Morgan send you?
The snow is drifted there.'
I felt he saw my tatters,
And pitied my gray hair.

'I'll do my duty, General.'"
"What did the General say?"
"He threw his cloak about me,
And slowly walked away.

'God bless you, sir!' I shouted,
And as I strode along
I laughed and cried together,
And hummed a battle-song.

I felt my way before me,
It was too dark to see,
I floundered in a snow-drift,
I ran against a tree.

The March winds, sharp and cruel,
Their stormy trumpets blew;
Came charging down the hillsides,
And stabbed me through and through.

I heard the drums in the distance,
I heard the river roar,
I heard the wolves in the forests,
And then I heard no more.

I woke in your father's barrack,
I was lying in his bed;
He stood beside me crying,
Because he thought me dead.

But hark, I hear him coming,
  And mother's drawing the tea;
His step is on the scraper,
  Run to the door, and see."

The outside latch was lifted,
  A draught blew in the room;
They heard him calling "Mother!"
  And "Abner, fetch a broom."

He stamped his feet in the entry,
  And brushed his homespun clo'es.
"Well, boys." "Good evening, Reuben.
  What news to-night?" "It snows!"

The dog barked, Abner tittered,
  But Gran'ther shook his head.
Now mother brought the candles,
  And the table soon was spread:

With the dishes on the dresser,
  The loaf of wheat and rye,
The baked beans from the oven,
  And a royal pumpkin-pie.

"Draw up, we're ready, Reuben."
  "But where did Abner go?"
With Gran'ther's crutch for a musket,
  He was marching sad and slow,
Freezing in thought at midnight,
  At Valley Forge in the snow.

THE WINE-CUP.

LYCIUS, the Cretan Prince, of race divine,
Like many a royal youth was fond of wine;
So when his father died and left him King,
He spent his days and nights in revelling.
Show him a wine-cup, he would soon lay down
His sceptre, and for roses change his crown,
Neglectful of his people and his state,
The noble cares that make a monarch great.

One day in summer, so the story goes,
Among his seeming friends, but secret foes,
He sat, and drained the wine-cup, when there came
A gray-haired man, and called him by his name,
"Lycius!" It was his tutor, Philocles,
Who held him when a child upon his knees.
"Lycius," the old man said, "it suits not you
To waste your life among this drunken crew.
Bethink you of your sire, and how he died
For that bright sceptre lying by your side,
And of the blood your loving people shed
To keep that golden circlet on your head.
Ah, how have you repaid them?" "Philocles,"
The Prince replied, "what idle words are these?
I loved my father, and I mourned his fate;
But death must come to all men, soon or late.
Could we recall our dear ones from their urn,
Just as they lived and loved, 't were well to mourn;
But since we cannot, let us smile instead:
I hold the living better than the dead.
My father reigned and died: I live and reign.
As for my people, why should they complain?

Have I not ended all their deadly wars,
Bound up their wounds, and honored their old scars?
They bleed no more; enough for me, and mine,
The blood o' th' grape, the ripe, the royal wine.
Slaves, fill my cup again!" They filled and crowned
His brow with roses, but the old man frowned.
"Lycius," he said once more, "the State demands
Something besides the wine-cup in your hands;
Resume your crown and sceptre, be not blind.
Kings live not for themselves, but for mankind."

"Good Philocles," the Prince, ashamed, replied,
His soft eye lighting with a flash of pride,
"Your wisdom has forgotten one small thing,
I am no more your pupil but your King.
Kings are in place of Gods; remember, then,
They answer to the Gods, and not to men."
"Hear, then, the Gods, who speak to-day through me,
The sad but certain words of prophecy:
'Touch not the cup; small sins in Kings are great;
Be wise in time, nor further tempt your fate.'"

"Old man, there is no Fate, save that which lies
In our own hands that shape our destinies.
It is a dream. If I should will and do
A deed of ill, no good could thence ensue;
And, willing goodness, should not goodness be
Sovereign, like ill, to save herself, and me?
I laugh at Fate." The wise man shook his head.
"Remember what the oracles have said:
'What most he loves, who rules this Cretan land,
Shall perish by the wine-cup in his hand.'"
"Prophet of ill, no more, or you shall die!
See how my deeds shall give your words the lie,
And baffle Fate, and all who hate me—so!"

Sheer through the casement, in the court below,
He dashed the half-drained goblet in disdain,
That scattered, as it flew, a bloody rain.
His courtiers laughed. But now a woman's shriek
Rose terrible without, and blanched his cheek.
He hurried to the casement in a fright,
And lo, his eyes were blasted with a sight
Too pitiful to think of—death was there,
And wringing hands, and madness, and despair.
There stood a nurse, and on her bosom lay
A dying child, whose life-blood streamed away,
Reddening its robe like wine. It was his own,
His son—the Prince that should have filled the throne
When he was dead, and ruled the Cretan land,
Slain by the wine-cup from his father's hand!

THE KING'S SENTINEL.

UPON a time, unbidden, came a man
Before the mighty King of Teberistan.
When the King saw this daring man he cried,
"Who art thou, fellow?" Whereto he replied,
"A lion-hunter and swordsman, I,
Moreover, I am skilled in archery:
A famous bowman, who of men alone
Can drive his arrows through the hardest stone.
Besides my courage, tried in desperate wars,
I know to read the riddle of the stars.
First in the service of Emeer Khojend,
Who, friend to none, has none to be his friend,
Him have I left, I hope an honest man,
To serve, if so he wills, the Lord of Teberistan."
To whom in answer: "I have men enow,

Stalwart like thee, apt with the sword and bow;
These no King lacks, or need to: what we need
Are men who may be trusted—word and deed,
Who, to keep pain from us, would yield their breath,
Faithful in life, and faithfuller in death."
"Try me." As thrice the monarch claps his hands,
The Captain of the Guard before him stands,
Amazed that one, unknown of him, had come
In to the King, and fearful of his doom.
Sternly his lord: "You guard me, slave, so well
That I have made this man my sentinel."
Thus did the happy archer gain his end,
And thus his sovereign find at last a friend,
Who from that hour was to his service bound,
Keen as his hawk, and faithful as his hound.

Now when a moon of nights had ta'en its flight,
Amid the darkness of a summer night,
The King awoke, alarmed, with fluttering breath,
Like one who struggles in the toils of death,
And wandered to his lattice, which stood wide,
Whence, down below him in the court, he spied
A shadowy figure with a threatening spear.
"What man art thou? if man, and wherefore here?"
"Your sentinel, and servant, O my lord!"
"Harken." They did. And now a voice was heard,
But whether from the desert far away,
Or from the neighbor-garden, who could say?
So far it was, yet near, so loud, yet low.
"Who calls?" it said. It sighed, "*I go, I go!*"
Then spake the pallid King, in trouble sore,
"Have you this dreadful summons heard before?"
"That voice, or something like it, have I heard
(Perchance the wailing of some magic bird)
Three nights, and at this very hour, O King!

But could not quit my post to seek the thing.
But now, if you command me, I will try,
Where the sound was, to find the mystery."
"Go, follow where it leads, if anywhere,
And what it is, and means, to me declare.
It may be ill, but I will hope the best:
But haste, for I am weary, and must rest."
Softly, as one that would surprise a thief,
Who might detect the rustling of a leaf,
The sentinel stole out into the night,
Nor knew that the King kept him still in sight,
Behind him, with a blanket o'er his head,
Black-draped down to his feet, as he were dead;
But the spear trembled in his hands, his knees
Weakened; at length he sank beneath the trees.
Again the voice was heard, and now more near
Than when it faded last—it was so clear.
"*I go! What man will force me to return?*"
"Now," thought the wondering soldier, "I shall learn
Who speaks, and why." And, looking up, he saw
What filled his simple soul with love and awe,
A noble woman standing by his side,
Who might have been the widow or the bride
Of some great King, so much of joy and woe
Hung on the perfect lips that breathed "I go,"
Shone in the wondering eyes, dimmed the bright hair,
No woman, born of woman, half so fair.
"Most beautiful, who art thou?" "Know, O man,
I am his life, who rules in Teberistan,
The spirit of your lord, whose end is nigh,
Except some friend,—what friend? for him will die."
"Can I?" But she: "'Tis written you must live."
"What, then, my life rejected, can I give?"
"You have a son," she whispered in his ear,
Feeling her way, it seemed, in hope and fear,

Lest what she would demand should be denied.
He pressed a sudden hand against his side
Where his heart ached, but spake not. "Fetch your son,
And I remain; refuse, and I am gone
Even while we parley." Stifling the great sigh
That heaved his breast, he answered, "He shall die."
And now for the first time he was aware
Besides themselves there was a Presence there,
Which made his blood run cold, but did not shake
His resolution that, for the King's sake,
His boy must perish. So he said, "I go,"
And like the swiftest arrow from his bow
The phantom vanished, and he went to bring
His sleeping child as ransom for the King,
Leaving that strange, bright woman there alone;
Who, smiling sadly, soon as he was gone
Ran to her lord, fallen upon the ground;
And while she lifted his dead weight, and wound
Her arms around him, and her tears did rain,
Kissed his cold lips, until they kissed her own again!

Meanwhile the sentinel down the royal park
Groped his way homeward, stumbling in the dark,
Uncertain of himself and all about;
For the low branches were as hands thrust out,
But whether to urge faster, or delay,
Since they both clutched and pushed, he could not say;
Nor, so irregular his heart's wild beat,
Whether he ran, or dragged his lagging feet.
When, half a league being over, he was near
His poor, mean hut, there broke upon his ear,
As from a child who wakes in dreams of pain,
And, while its parents listen, sleeps again,
A cry like *Father!* Whence, and whose, the cry?
Was it from out the hut, or in the sky?

What if some robber with the boy had fled?
What—dreadful thought! what if the boy were dead?
He reached the door in haste, and found it barred,
As when at set of sun he went on guard,
Shutting the lad in from all nightly harms,
As safe as in the loving mother arms
Which could no longer fold him: all was fast,
No footstep since his own that night had passed
Across the threshold, no man had been there.
'Twas still within, and cold, and dark, and bare;
Bare, but not dark; for, opening now the door,
The fitful moon, late hidden, out once more
Thrust its sharp crescent through the starless gloom
Like a long scymetar, and smote the room
With pitiless brightness, and himself with dread,
Poor, childless man—for there his child was dead!
He spake not, wept not, stirred not; one might say,
Till that first awful moment passed away,
He was not, but some dead man in his place
Stood, with a deathless sorrow in its face!
Then—for a heart so stricken as was his,
So suddenly set upon by agonies,
Must find as sudden a relief, or break—
He wept a little for his own sad sake,
And for the boy that lay there without breath,
Whom he so freely sacrificed to Death.
Thereafter kneeling softly by the bed,
Face buried, and hands wrung above his head,
He said what prayer came to him, and be sure
The prayers of all men at such times are pure.
At last he rose, and lifting to his heart
Its precious burden—limbs that dropped apart,
Hands that no longer clasped him, little feet
That nevermore would run his own to meet,
Wrapping his cloak round all with loving care,

To shield it from the dew and the cold air,
He staggered slowly out in the black night.
Nowhere was that strange woman now in sight
To take the child ; but at the palace gate
The king stood waiting him—reprieved of Fate.
"What was it, soldier?" "God preserve the King!
'Twas nothing." "Tell me, quickly." "A small thing,
Not worth your hearing. In the park I found
A lonely woman sitting on the ground,
Wailing her husband, who had done her wrong,
Whose house she had forsaken, but not long;
For I made peace between them, dried the tears,
And added some, I hope, to their now happy years."
"What bear you there?" "A child I was to bring—"
He paused a moment—"It is mine, O King!"
"I followed, and know all. So young to die,
Poor thing, for me! You should be King, not I.
You shall be my Vizier, shake not your head,
I swear it shall be so. Be comforted.
For this dead child of yours, who met my doom,
I will have built for him a costly tomb
Of divers marbles, glorious to behold,
With many a rich device inlaid of gold,
Ivory and precious stones, and thereupon
Blazoned the name and story of your son,
And yours, Vizier, of whom shall history tell
That never King but one had such a Sentinel."

——o——

THE BALLAD OF CRECY.

What man-at-arms, or knight
Of doughty deeds in fight,
What King whose dauntless might
Still lives in story,

Deserves such fame as one
Who, when his sight was gone,
Fought till he fell—King John,
Bohemia's glory?

That fatal August day
The French and English lay
Drawn up in dread array,
With bows and lances.
Determined then to try
Which host could bravest die,
Which host would soonest fly,
England's or France's.

The morning light revealed
On Crecy's famous field,
Armed with his spear and shield,
This fearless foeman,
Who, with his old blind eyes,
Will for his French allies
Do battle till he dies,
And fly from no man.

His bridle rein he tied
To a good knight's at his side,
Among the French to ride,
That saw astounded
Who with their foremost pressed,
His shield before his breast,
His long spear set in rest—
The trumpet sounded!

Full tilt against their foes,
Where thickest fell the blows,
And war cries mingling rose,
"St. George!" "St. Denys!"

Driven by the trumpet's blare
Where most the English dare,
And where the French despair,
He there and then is.

Up, down, he rode, and thrust,
Unhorsed, knights rolled in the dust,
Whom he encounters must
Go down or fly him :
All round the bloody field
Spears rattle on his shield,
But none can make him yield ;
Few venture nigh him.

Here, there, he rides until
His horse perforce stands still :
He spurs it, but it will
No longer mind him ;
It cannot stir for fright,
So desperate now the fight,
Death on the left, the right,
Before, behind him.

But this, so blind was he,
The old King could not see ;
An he had seen, pardie !
His soul delighting
Had faster rained down blows
Upon his puny foes,
And in the dark death-throes
Had gone out fighting !

When the last rout was done,
And when the English won,
They found the brave King John,
Who fought so lately,

Stone dead, his old blind eyes
Up-looking to the skies,
As he again would rise,
And battle greatly!

They bore him to his rest,
His shield upon his breast,
Where blazoned was his crest,
Three ostrich feathers;
Under, in gold, was seen
The royal words, "ICH DIEN,"
Which most Kings now think mean,
Save in foul weathers.

Not so the Black Prince thought,
Who then at Crecy fought,
And old John's valor caught,
And was victorious.
"Who serve like him," quoth he,
"Commend themselves to me;
Such royal servants be
Forever glorious!"

——o——

ROME.

"Roma, Roma, Roma!
Non è più come era prima."

STILL the City stands:
Fallen away
From its old renown,
The wonder and the terror of the Lands!
Temple and tower gone down,

Nothing left to fall
But weeds upon the wall;
All decay—
Utterly desolate!
Haunted by the ghost of its dead state,
Memory of its men who ruled like gods,
Memory of the gods who ruled its men,
Dreaming in despair of what was then,
Flamens, augurs, lictors with their rods,
Legions on their marches
Through triumphal arches,
Cæsar in his car
With the spoils of war,
From Carthage, from Egypt, from all the realms afar,
And, drooping in his train,
Proud Kings overthrown,
Their sceptres now his own,
And palest Queens discrowned, superb in their disdain
Of Cæsar marching home
Victorious to Rome!
Who on her Seven Hills
Sits, Mistress of the World
Which she with carnage fills;
Hated of men, but to the gods austere
Dear,
For does not mightiest Jove protect, defend,
And his eagle send
To perch upon her standards? Look above,
There where his million altar-smokes are curled—
The Capitolian Jove!
And Mars, Mars,
He of the shield and spear—
How dear
To him and his this Rome of never-ending wars!
Hidden in the secret shrine,

(Stately Juno, come not here,
Chaste Diana, disappear,
These are none of thine,)
Where they wreathe the roses,
Where they pour the wine,
Who on that couch reposes,
With arms that twine and twine?
Venus Aphrodite,
Goddess of the Sea,
She is the most mighty,
And the sweetest, she.
Venus, Venus, Venus!
Thou alone of all the Powers
Dost from sorrow screen us,
Thy power alone in all the hours
Lets nothing come between us,
Who adore thee, Venus!
Nothing part
Heart from heart
In thy bliss of blisses,
But our delaying kisses!

Horror! Who are these?
Shapes, or shadows rather,
Which like the Night do gather,
From where? For what? To seize!
The Fates! The Fates!
The Hun is at the gates!

Still the City stands:
Fallen away
From its old renown,
The wonder and the terror of the Lands!
Temple and tower gone down,

Nothing left to fall
But weeds upon the wall;
All decay—
Utterly desolate!

——o——

CÆSAR.

"Render, therefore, unto Cæsar the things which are Cæsar's."

CÆSAR is fallen! Shout!
Shout that his sword is broken, lost his crown!
Shout that his braggart hosts are put to rout!
His empire has gone down!
Exult as wildly as ye would have wailed
If Cæsar had prevailed!
That yesterday you feared him,
Whom you to-day despise,
Forget, deny;
But be no more deceived by kingly lies,
For what he was to all your kings endeared him,
As what they are finds favor in your eyes.
Ah, why, why
For such as these, and he, will ye still live and die?

Be just—just!
What has he done your rulers would not do?
What do they care for you,
Ye peoples, who in princes put your trust?
What has he done, I say, they have not done?
Made blood like water run
In the dense streets his dreadful cannon swept,
Where France above her slaughtered children wept?
It is a way they have who wear the crown,

Your good king shot his loving subjects down;
But, though submissive, brave,
They gathered up their dead,
And, while they bore them to their honored grave,
Compelled him to look on with white, uncovered head!
If this, our Cæsar, strode through guilt to power,
If in the blood he spilt he built his throne,
He did not stand alone,
For France was with him in that desperate hour;
For though she might not welcome the strong hand
That steered her suddenly from the dangerous shore,
Whereon, full driven, she had been wrecked before,
And brought her safe to land,
She let the helm within his hand remain;
For rent by furious factions,
And weary of distractions,
She wanted peace again,
Demanded peace, the wealth that she had lost,
And her old greatness, at whatever cost.
Remember what he found her,
And what she was when her first Cæsar fell,
With Europe armed around her,
And none to wish her well;
How with their bayonets dripping with her blood,
Its kings brought back the kings who had oppressed her,
But never once redressed her,
And all pronounced it good!
Too weak, they felt, to chain
Her giant limbs again,
That with the world had wrestled, and might yet,
They drugged her till she slept,
And then upon her crept,
And o'er her cast a net.
She struggled, but in vain;
But she did not forget.

And he did not forget!
And when, a stormy wooer,
That would no longer sue her,
He leaped into her arms,
It was that he might free her,
And that the world might see her
In her recovered charms,
No trace of tears, no fear of tribulations,
Most beautiful and powerful, the queen of all the nations!
This her Cæsar made her,
And this at last betrayed her,
For this has brought upon her the conquering Invader!

Cæsar is fallen! Shout!
Shout till your throats are hoarse, and stunned your ears,
Fire your loud cannon, hang your banners out,
But leave me to my tears.
Not o'er this fallen Cæsar do I weep,
Nor for the thousands whom to death he led,
Nor for your thousands in the same dark sleep,
I weep not for the dead.
I weep for the unutterable blindness
That makes a Cæsar possible to-day,
That will not let the nations live in kindness,
And die the natural way.
What though ye have one Cæsar overthrown?
Ye have set up another of your own.
What is it, pray, to us?
What is it to the Race,
Whether the Gaul or Pruss,
The Latin or the Russ,
Is now in Cæsar's place?
It matters not a jot,
They love us—love us not!
They trust us, when they must,

They use us, when they will,
They grind us to the dust,
They cheat, they rob, they kill!
Exult who may. For me, I must deplore,
I must lament, and pray
That God will bring the day
When Cæsar is no more!

ABRAHAM LINCOLN.

A HORATIAN ODE.

NOT as when some great Captain falls
In battle, where his Country calls,
Beyond the struggling lines
That push his dread designs

To doom, by some stray ball struck dead:
Or, in the last charge, at the head
Of his determined men,
Who *must* be victors then.

Nor as when sink the civic great,
The safer pillars of the State,
Whose calm, mature, wise words
Suppress the need of swords.

With no such tears as e'er were shed
Above the noblest of our dead
Do we to-day deplore
The Man that is no more.

Our sorrow hath a wider scope,
Too strange for fear, too vast for hope,
A wonder, blind and dumb,
That waits—what is to come!

Not more astounded had we been
If Madness, that dark night, unseen,
Had in our chambers crept,
And murdered while we slept!

We woke to find a mourning earth,
Our Lares shivered on the hearth,
The roof-tree fallen, all
That could affright, appall!

Such thunderbolts, in other lands,
Have smitten the rod from royal hands,
But spared, with us, till now,
Each laurelled Cæsar's brow.

No Cæsar he whom we lament,
A Man without a precedent,
Sent, it would seem, to do
His work, and perish, too.

Not by the weary cares of State,
The endless tasks, which will not wait,
Which, often done in vain,
Must yet be done again:

Not in the dark, wild tide of war,
Which rose so high, and rolled so far,
Sweeping from sea to sea
In awful anarchy:

Four fateful years of mortal strife,
Which slowly drained the nation's life,
(Yet for each drop that ran
There sprang an armèd man!)

Not then; but when, by measures meet,
By victory, and by defeat,
By courage, patience, skill,
The people's fixed "*We will!*"

Had pierced, had crushed Rebellion dead,
Without a hand, without a head,
At last, when all was well,
He fell, O how he fell!

The time, the place, the stealing shape,
The coward shot, the swift escape,
The wife, the widow's scream—
It is a hideous Dream!

A dream? What means this pageant, then?
These multitudes of solemn men,
Who speak not when they meet,
But throng the silent street?

The flags half-mast that late so high
Flaunted at each new victory?
(The stars no brightness shed,
But bloody looks the red!)

The black festoons that stretch for miles,
And turn the streets to funeral aisles?
(No house too poor to show
The nation's badge of woe.)

The cannon's sudden, sullen boom,
The bells that toll of death and doom,
    The rolling of the drums,
    The dreadful car that comes?

Cursed be the hand that fired the shot,
The frenzied brain that hatched the plot,
    Thy country's Father slain
    Be thee, thou worse than Cain!

Tyrants have fallen by such as thou,
And good hath followed—may it now!
    (God lets bad instruments
    Produce the best events.)

But he, the man we mourn to-day,
No tyrant was: so mild a sway
    In one such weight who bore
    Was never known before.

Cool should he be, of balanced powers,
The ruler of a race like ours,
    Impatient, headstrong, wild,
    The Man to guide the Child.

And this *he* was, who most unfit
(So hard the sense of God to hit,)
    Did seem to fill his place.
    With such a homely face,

Such rustic manners, speech uncouth,
(That somehow blundered out the truth,)
    Untried, untrained to bear
    The more than kingly care.

Ay! And his genius put to scorn
The proudest in the purple born,
Whose wisdom never grew
To what, untaught, he knew,

The People, of whom he was one.
No gentleman, like Washington,
(Whose bones, methinks, make room,
To have him in their tomb!)

A laboring man, with horny hands,
Who swung the axe, who tilled his lands,
Who shrank from nothing new,
But did as poor men do.

One of the People! Born to be
Their curious epitome;
To share yet rise above
Their shifting hate and love.

Common his mind, (it seemed so then,)
His thoughts the thoughts of other men:
Plain were his words, and poor,
But now they will endure!

No hasty fool, of stubborn will,
But prudent, cautious, pliant still;
Who since his work was good
Would do it as he could.

Doubting, was not ashamed to doubt,
And, lacking prescience, went without:
Often appeared to halt,
And was, of course, at fault;

Heard all opinions, nothing loath,
And, loving both sides, angered both:
Was—*not* like Justice, blind,
But, watchful, clement, kind.

No hero this of Roman mould,
Nor like our stately sires of old:
Perhaps he was not great,
But he preserved the State!

O honest face, which all men knew!
O tender heart, but known to few!
O wonder of the age,
Cut off by tragic rage!

Peace! Let the long procession come,
For hark, the mournful, muffled drum,
The trumpet's wail afar,
And see, the awful car!

Peace! Let the sad procession go,
While cannon boom and bells toll slow.
And go, thou sacred car,
Bearing our woe afar!

Go, darkly borne, from State to State,
Whose loyal, sorrowing cities wait
To honor all they can
The dust of that good man.

Go, grandly borne, with such a train
As greatest kings might die to gain.
The just, the wise, the brave,
Attend thee to the grave.

And you, the soldiers of our wars,
Bronzed veterans, grim with noble scars,
Salute him once again,
Your late commander—slain!

Yes, let your tears indignant fall,
But leave your muskets on the wall;
Your country needs you now
Beside the forge—the plough.

(When Justice shall unsheathe her brand,
If Mercy may not stay her hand,
Nor would we have it so,
She must direct the blow.)

And you, amid the master-race,
Who seem so strangely out of place,
Know ye who cometh? He
Who hath declared ye free.

Bow while the body passes—nay,
Fall on your knees, and weep, and pray!
Weep, weep—I would ye might—
Your poor black faces white!

And, children, you must come in bands,
With garlands in your little hands,
Of blue and white and red,
To strew before the dead.

So sweetly, sadly, sternly goes
The Fallen to his last repose.
Beneath no mighty dome,
But in his modest home;

The churchyard where his children rest,
The quiet spot that suits him best,
    There shall his grave be made,
    And there his bones be laid.

And there his countrymen shall come,
With memory proud, with pity dumb,
    And strangers far and near,
    For many and many a year.

For many a year and many an age,
While History on her ample page
    The virtues shall enroll
    On that Paternal Soul.

——o——

THE CHILDREN OF ISIS.

Typhon and Osiris
Children were of Isis,
Brothers and Gods, twin-born, the rulers of her land,
Which prospered, nothing loth,
Under both,
For each the sceptre held with equal hand.

Now Typhon and Osiris
With their great Mother, Isis,
Dwelt,—in the cities one, and one in the broad plains,
Whereon a subject race,
Dusk of face,
Was bondsman unto him in ancient chains.

Said Typhon once to Isis:
"This brother mine, Osiris,

Does wrong to keep this people so long beneath his yoke.
They fetch him corn and oil,
For him they toil,
While idle all the year he sits." So Typhon spoke.

To Typhon then spake Isis:
"My son he is, Osiris,
As thou my son, both loved, but neither less nor more.
If his these bondsmen born,
Their oil and corn—
Who built your palaces that line the shore?

If not the tribe," said Isis,
"That labors for Osiris,
Barbaric, a much better, as nearer Us than these.
All day they turn your wheels,
And your proud keels
They lay, and plough for you the dangerous Seas.

Typhon and Osiris,"
Said the sad goddess Isis,
"Children of mine, unnatural, unwise as men,—no more!
Let each still fill his throne,
And rule his own:
There must be peace between you as before."

To Typhon and Osiris
The solemn voice of Isis
Was as a wind unheeded—no sooner come than gone.
Speaking their own rash words,
They drew their swords,
And, calling each his millions, led them on.

"O Typhon! O Osiris!"
Cried out their Mother Isis,

But neither heard her warning, for each with desperate hand
Struck at the other's heart,
No one could part;
So war and waste and want were in the land.

In all the years of Isis
And Typhon and Osiris
Never such dreadful battle, such courage, such despair;
Brothers with brothers fighting,
In blood delighting,
Razed cities, temples sacked, death everywhere!

So Typhon and Osiris
Before the troubled Isis
Fought four dark years together, each bloodier than the last,
Till stronger Typhon's swords
And cunning words
Prevailed, and pale Osiris fell aghast.

Then Typhon slew Osiris
Before the weeping Isis,
And after he was dead by night the body stole;
Whereat who followed him
Limb from limb
Dismembered--hoping so to slay the soul.

Thus Typhon rent Osiris,
To the great grief of Isis,
And thus his mangled body was scattered through the land.
One had his crownèd head,
And one instead
His swordless hand—but rings were on the hand.

So Typhon hid Osiris
Away from sorrowing Isis,
Who straight began her journeys, North, South, and East, and West.
O Mother most undone!
Where is thy Son?
Where the Dead One whose tomb is in thy breast?

Up and down went Isis
Where Typhon and Osiris
Had dwelt before their trouble, the cities and the plains;
But in no pyramid
His bones were hid,
Nor where his bondsmen wept—without their chains.

To and fro went Isis
To find the dead Osiris,
Along her one great river, and over all the land.
She could not find his head,
Nor crown instead,
His hand, nor the rich rings were on his hand!

The spirit of Osiris
Came in a dream to Isis,
Saying, "O mighty Goddess! Why is your heart so sore?
Why do you weep so, Mother?
Because my brother,
Typhon, has hid my body? Weep no more.

Immortal Mother, Isis,
I am thy Son Osiris,
Twin-born,—the king with Typhon, who rules the land alone.
His men have statues made
Where I am laid,
A piece of me in each, one by his throne."

She woke, the wiser Isis,
To seek and find Osiris,
And found, as he had promised, the idols tall and grim,
His shape in every place,
With Typhon's face!
But was Osiris there? A piece of him.

After her dear Osiris
The stern and wrathful Isis
Before the men of Typhon, who trembled at her ire,
Strode up and down the lands,
With her strong hands
Their idols brake, and cast them in the fire.

And now his Mother, Isis,
The limbs of lost Osiris
Found—in every statue of him some precious part;
His head by Typhon's throne;
Beneath a stone
His hand; elsewhere, and last of all, his heart!

The body of Osiris
His Goddess-Mother, Isis,
Laid reverent on her altar, and bowed her sacred head;
Prayed to some Power Unknown,
Some awful Throne,
Then rose and kissed the cold lips of her dead.

The soul of great Osiris
Came back again to Isis;
The mouth with breath is warm, and dares to touch her own;
He stretches out his hands;
He stands—stands!
He is himself once more, and on his throne.

"Eternal Mother, Isis,"
Began the God Osiris,
"Where is my brother Typhon?" And Typhon, "I am here."
He wept, "O brother! brother!
O Mother! Mother!"
And Isis wept—Osiris not a tear.

"Typhon," said Osiris,
"And thou, our Mother Isis,
What was the wrong among us? But righted if it be,
(It must be,) name it not,
It is forgot
By Typhon and Osiris, and, mightiest Isis, Thee!"

——o——

"Why stand ye gazing up into heaven?"
Acts i. 11.

WHY stand ye gazing into Heaven?
What seek ye there? What hope to find
Besides the clouds, which the cold wind
Drives round the world from Morn to Even?
The wan moon, ploughed with ancient scars,
The gracious sun, the alien stars,
The all-embracing Space?
Ye look for God?
Have ye beheld him there?
You, or your fathers in their prime?
Or any man, at any time,
The wise, the good, the fair?
Who has beheld—I will not say his face,
But where his feet have trod?

What have your straining eyes
Discovered in the skies?
Why not look down the Sea?
'Tis deep, and most creative; What eludes
In the upper solitudes,
Still lurking in the lower wastes may be.
Ye look for God, ye tell me. Tell me this—
How know ye that He is?
Because your fathers told ye so, and they
Because, of old, their fathers told them so;
As it is now, so was it long ago,
And will be when the years have passed away.

Nothing can come from nothing. Well, what then?
The Earth, with all its men,
The little insect burrowing in the sod,
Sun, planet, star,
All things that are,
Must have been made by God.
Why made by Him? Who saw them made?
Who saw the deep foundations laid?
The Hands that built the wall?
Why made at all?
Why not Eternal, tell me? Not because
It must created be.
If so Eternal He,
But why Eternal?—why not also This?
Why must the All be His?
It was, and is, and is—because it was!

There is no God then? Nay,
You say it, and not I;
I do but say
We have not yet beheld this God on High:
Not knowing that He is, we live and die.

If we know nothing of Him, yet we feel.
We feel love's kisses sweet,
The wine that trips our feet,
The murderous thrust of steel:
Gladness about the heart when the sun breaks,
Or the soft moon is floating up the skies,
Delight in the wild sea, in tranquil lakes,
In every bird that flies;
And hot tears in our eyes,
When love, the best of earth, its last kiss over—dies!
But He whom we name God, and grope so for above,
Whose arm, we fear, is Power, whose heart, we hope, is Love,
On the worlds below Him,
In the dust before Him,
We may adore Him,
We cannot know Him,
If, indeed, He be, to bless or curse,
And be not this tremendous Universe!

"Higher than your arrows fly,
Deeper than your plummets fall,
Is the Deepest, the Most High,
Is the All in All!"

——o——

WILLIAM SHAKESPEARE.

(*April* 23, 1564.)

SHE sat in her eternal house,
The sovereign mother of mankind;
Before her was the peopled world,
The hollow night behind.

"Below my feet the thunders break,
Above my head the stars rejoice;
But man, although he babbles much,
Has never found a voice.

Ten thousand years have come and gone,
And not an hour of any day
But he has dumbly looked to me
The things he could not say.

It shall be so no more," she said.
And then, revolving in her mind,
She thought: "I will create a child
Shall speak for all his kind."

It was the spring-time of the year,
And lo, where Avon's waters flow,
The child, her darling, came on earth
Three hundred years ago.

There was no portent in the sky,
No cry, like Pan's, along the seas,
Nor hovered round his baby mouth
The swarm of classic bees.

What other children were he was,
If more, 't was not to mortal ken;
The being likest to mankind
Made him the man of men.

They gossiped, after he was dead,
An idle tale of stealing deer;
One thinks he was a lawyer's clerk;
But nothing now is clear,

Save that he married, in his youth,
  A maid, his elder; went to town;
Wrote plays; made money; and at last
  Came back, and settled down,

A prosperous man, among his kin,
  In Stratford, where his bones repose.
And this—what can be less? is all
  The world of Shakespeare knows.

It irks us that we know no more,
  For where we love we would know all;
What would be small in common men
  In great is never small.

Their daily habits, how they looked,
  The color of their eyes and hair,
Their prayers, their oaths, the wine they drank,
  The clothes they used to wear,

Trifles like these declare the men,
  And should survive them—nay, they must;
We'll find them somewhere; if it needs,
  We'll rake among their dust!

Not Shakespeare's! He hath left his curse
  On him disturbs it: let it rest,
The mightiest that ever Death
  Laid in the earth's dark breast.

Not to himself did he belong,
  Nor does his life belong to us;
Enough he *was;* give up the search
  If he were thus, or thus.

Before he came his like was not,
  Nor left he heirs to share his powers;
The mighty Mother sent him here,
  To be her voice and ours.

To be her oracle to man;
  To be what man may be to her;
Between the Maker and the made
  The best interpreter.

The hearts of all men beat in his,
  Alike in pleasure and in pain;
And he contained their myriad minds,
  Mankind in heart and brain.

Shakespeare! What shapes are conjured up
  By that one word! They come and go,
More real, shadows though they be,
  Than many a man we know.

Hamlet, the Dane, unhappy Prince
  Who most enjoys when suffering most:
His soul is haunted by itself—
  There needs no other Ghost.

The Thane, whose murderous fancy sees
  The dagger painted in the air;
The guilty King, who stands appalled
  When Banquo fills his chair.

Lear in the tempest, old and crazed,
  "Blow winds. Spit fire, singe my white head!"
Or, sadder, watching for the breath
  Of dear Cordelia—dead!

The much-abused, relentless Jew,
  Grave Prospero, in his magic isle,
And she who captived Anthony,
  The serpent of old Nile.

Imperial forms, heroic souls,
  Greek, Roman, masters of the world,
Kings, queens, the soldier, scholar, priest,
  The courtier, sleek and curled ;

He knew and drew all ranks of men,
  And did such life to them impart
They grow not old, immortal types,
  The lords of Life and Art!

Their sovereign he, as she was his,
  The awful Mother of the Race,
Who, hid from all her children's eyes,
  Unveiled to him her face ;

Spake to him till her speech was known,
  Through him till man had learned it; then
Enthroned him in her Heavenly House,
  The most Supreme of Men!

——o——

ADSUM.

(*December* 23–24, 1863.)

I.

THE Angel came by night,
  (Such angels still come down,)
And like a winter cloud
  Passed over London town ;

Along its lonesome streets,
  Where Want had ceased to weep,
Until it reached a house
  Where a great man lay asleep :
The man of all his time
  Who knew the most of men,
The soundest head and heart,
  The sharpest, kindest pen.
It paused beside his bed,
  And whispered in his ear;
He never turned his head,
  But answered, "I am here."

II.

Into the night they went.
  At morning, side by side,
They gained the sacred Place
  Where the greatest Dead abide.
Where grand, old Homer sits
  In godlike state benign;
Where broods in endless thought
  The awful Florentine;
Where sweet Cervantes walks,
  A smile on his grave face;
Where gossips quaint Montaigne,
  The wisest of his race;
Where Goethe looks through all
  With that calm eye of his;
Where—little seen but Light—
  The only Shakespeare is!
When the new Spirit came,
  They asked him, drawing near,
"Art thou become like us?"
  He answered, "I am here."

VATES PATRIÆ.

(*November* 3, 1794.)

THERE came a Woman in the night,
  When winds were whist, and moonlight smiled,
Where in his mother's arms, who slept,
    There lay a new-born child.

She gazed at him with loving looks,
  And while her hand upon his head
She laid, in blessing and in power,
    In slow, deep words she said :

"This child is mine. Of all my sons
  Are none like what the lad shall be ;
Though these are wise, and those are strong,
    And all are dear to me.

Beyond their arts of peace and war
  The gift that unto him belongs,
To see my face, to read my thoughts,
    To learn my silent songs.

The elder sisters of my race
  Shall taunt no more that I am dumb ;
Hereafter I shall sing through him,
    In ages yet to come."

She stooped, and kissed his baby mouth,
  Whence came a breath of melody,
As from the closed leaves of a rose
    The murmur of a bee.

Thus did she consecrate the child,
His more than mother from that hour,
Albeit at first he knew her not,
Nor guessed his sleeping power.

But not the less she hovered near,
And touched his spirit unawares;
Burned in the red of morning skies,
And breathed in evening airs.

Unfelt in his, her guiding hand
Withdrew him from the halls of men,
To where her secret bowers were built,
In wood, and grove, and glen.

Sometimes he caught a transient glimpse
Of her broad robe, that swept before,
Deep in the heart of ancient woods,
Or by the sounding shore.

One prosperous day he chanced to see
(Be sure 't was in a lonely place)
Her glance of pride, that sought his own,
At last her noble face.

Not as it fronts her children now,
With clouded brows, and looks of ire,
And eyes that would be blind with tears
But for their quenchless fire!

But happy, gracious, beautiful,
And more imperial than a queen;
A Woman of majestic mould,
And most maternal mien.

And he was happy. For in her
  ("For he," she said, "shall read my mind,")
He saw the glory of the earth,
    The hope of human kind.

Thenceforth, wherever he might walk,
  Through forest aisles, or by the sea;
Where floats the flower-like butterfly,
    And hums the drowsy bee;

By rock-ribbed hills, and pensive vales
  That stretch in light and shade between,
And by the soft-complaining brooks
    That make the meadows green:

He felt her presence everywhere,
  To-day was glad, to-morrow grave;
And what she gave to him in thought,
    To us in song he gave:

In stately songs, in solemn hymns,
  (Few are so clear, and none so high,)
That mirrored her, in calm and storm,
    As mountain lakes the sky.

And evermore one shape appeared,
  To comfort now, and now command,
A bearded Man, with many scars,
    Who bore a battle-brand.

And she was filled with serious joy,
  To know her poet followed him;
Not losing heart, nor bating hope,
    When others' faith was dim.

And as the years went slowly by,
  And she grew stronger and more wise,
Stretching her hands o'er broader lands,
    And grander destinies;

And he, our poet, poured his hymns,
  Serene, prophetic, sad, as each
Became a part of her renown,
    And of his native speech;

She wove, by turns, a wreath for him,
  The business of her idle hours;
And here were sprigs of mountain pine,
    And there were prairie flowers.

And now, even in her sorest need,
  Pale, bleeding, faint in every limb,
She still remembers what he is,
    And comes to honor him.

For hers, not ours, the songs we bring,
  The flowers, the music, and the light;
And 'tis her hand that lays the wreath
    On his gray head to-night!

AT GADSHILL.

(*June* 9, 1870.)

GADSHILL is famous. What of old
  To the world's poet made it dear,
Whether what country gossips told,
  Or stolen hours of cheer

Spent there with men of kindred mind,
Less, yet the largest of mankind,

We know not, and we need not care:
  Enough that Shakespeare loved the place,
And settled in possession there
  The merriest of his race,
Falstaff, whose thirsty spirit still
Haunts all the taverns at Gadshill.

Could Shakespeare, with prophetic eyes,
  Who were to follow him have seen,
And be, if not so great and wise,
  As what man since hath been?
Yet wise and great in smaller ways,
The lords of life of coming days,

He would have chosen out of all
  Dickens, as knowing, loving men,
And let on him the mantle fall
  That was to vanish then!
Long lost, late found, now lost once more—
Ah, who that mantle shall restore?

Sacred to all but Shakespeare's shade,
  And to his ghosts of crownless kings
Abandoned, wretched queens betrayed,
  And high, heroic things,
Is Stratford; let no mortal dare
Disturb its hushed and reverent air.

But Gadshill, whither Falstaff went
  From Eastcheap, (glad to hasten back,)
Though plundered, still on plunder bent,
  Puffed out with lies and sack,

What spot of English earth so fit
For one with more than Falstaff's wit?

Nay, Shakespeare's self was not his peer
  In that humane and happy art
To wake at once the smile and tear,
  And captive hold the heart.
Make room, then, Shakespeare! This is he
Has taken the throne of mirth from thee.

The world of kings and queens is thine,
  Thou hast the soldier's, scholar's ear,
England and Rome, Greece, "Troy divine,"
  Hamlet, Othello, Lear:
Small elves that dance on yellow sands,
And all the spells of fairy lands.

This common work-day world of ours,
  Our little lives of joy and care,
Green lanes, where children gather flowers,
  And London's murky air,
Thieves, paupers, women of the town,
And the black Thames in which they drown;

These were the things that Dickens knew,
  Before his sight like dreams they passed.
If saddened, he was gladdened, too,
  For sorrow should not last.
Happy must be his heart and mind
Whose task it is to help his kind.

Healthy his nature was, above
  All shallow griefs and sympathies;
What others hated he could love,
  And what they loved despise.

His mirth was harder to be borne
Than Thackeray's sadness, Byron's scorn.

He taught the virtues, first and last,
  He taught us manhood, more and more,
The simple courage that stands fast,
  The patience of the poor;
Love for all creatures, great and small,
And trust in Something over all.

This gave him more than royal sway;
  The benefactor of the race,
He would have wiped with smiles away
  The tears from every face.
They drop to-day from many an eye,
He draws them, but he cannot dry.

The hand is still that held his pen,
  His eyes are shut, but not in sleep;
Weeping around his bed are men
  Who do not often weep.
Laughter no more the house shall fill,
For Death is master at Gadshill.

——o——

THE COUNTRY LIFE.

NOT what we would, but what we must,
    Makes up the sum of living;
Heaven is both more and less than just
    In taking and in giving.
Swords cleave to hands that sought the plough,
And laurels miss the soldier's brow.

Me, whom the city holds, whose feet
Have worn its stony highways,
Familiar with its loneliest street—
Its ways were never my ways.
My cradle was beside the sea,
And there, I hope, my grave will be.

Old homestead! In that old, gray town,
Thy vane is seaward blowing,
Thy slip of garden stretches down
To where the tide is flowing:
Below they lie, their sails all furled,
The ships that go about the world.

Dearer that little country house,
Inland, with pines beside it;
Some peach-trees, with unfruitful boughs,
A well, with weeds to hide it:
No flowers, or only such as rise
Self-sown, poor things, which all despise.

Dear country home! Can I forget
The least of thy sweet trifles?
The window-vines that clamber yet,
Whose blooms the bee still rifles?
The roadside blackberries, growing ripe,
And in the woods the Indian Pipe?

Happy the man who tills his field,
Content with rustic labor;
Earth does to him her fulness yield,
Hap what may to his neighbor.
Well days, sound nights, O can there be
A life more rational and free?

Dear country life of child and man!
For both the best, the strongest,
That with the earliest race began,
And hast outlived the longest.
Their cities perished long ago;
Who the first farmers were we know.

Perhaps our Babels too will fall,
If so, no lamentations,
For Mother Earth will shelter all,
And feed the unborn nations;
Yes, and the swords that menace now
Will then be beaten to the plough.

——o——

AN INVOCATION.

I.

BEFORE THE SHRINE.

WHAT and whence this life of ours?
Is it Life, and Death at last?
Or a dream that binds us fast
In the heavy midnight hours?
Shadow of a vanished day,
Or a coming, gone astray
In the sleep of the High Powers?
Great Ones, surely, such ye be,
Hear, and, hearing, answer me.
Answer me, O answer me!

(*Wide their lips were, and their eyes,*
That benignant looked, and wise;
But, false or true, no answer fell,
Silent was the Oracle.)

II.

BEFORE THE STATUE OF ISIS.

AND this dread thing which men call Death?
  Like but longer than all Sleep,
  Shrouded eyes, that fail to weep,
Lips that kiss not, without breath,
  Feet that run no more to ill,
  Hands that nor caress, nor kill!
  Tell me, is it something done?
  Or, sadder, something more begun?
Give me what the Goddess saith,
Powerful over Life and Death.
Life and Death! O Life and Death!

(Mighty did the Mother stand,
With her foot on sea and land,
Brow uplifted to the skies,
With their secret in her eyes.
What she saw and said that day,
None of her pale priests could say:
They lay like dead men. If there fell
Answer from her lips, 'twas well:
But what it was no tongue can tell.)

——o——

A CATCH.

ONCE the head is gray,
  And the heart is dead,
There's no more to do,
  Make the man a bed
Six foot under ground,
There he'll slumber sound.

Golden was my hair,
  And my heart did beat
To the viol's voice
  Like the dancers' feet.
Not colder now his blood
Who died before the flood.

Fair, and fond, and false,
  Mother, wife, and maid,
Never lived a man
  They have not betrayed.
None shall 'scape my mirth
But old Mother Earth.

Safely housed with her,
  With no company
But my brother Worm,
  Who will feed on me,
I shall slumber sound,
Deep down under ground.

——o——

THE KING IS COLD.

RAKE the embers, blow the coals,
  Kindle at once a roaring fire.
  Here's some paper. 'Tis nothing, Sire.
Light it. (They've saved a thousand souls!)
Run for fagots, you scurvy knaves,
  There are plenty out in the public square,
  You know they fry the heretics there:
(But God remembers their nameless graves!)
Fly, fly, or the King may die!
  Ugh! his royal feet are like snow,

And the cold is mounting up to his heart,
    (But that was frozen long ago!)
Rascals, varlets, do as you're told—
        The King is cold.

His bed of state is a grand affair,
    With sheets of satin and pillows of down,
    And close beside it stands the crown;
But that won't keep him from dying there.
His hands are wrinkled, his hair is gray,
    And his ancient blood is sluggish and thin;
    When he was young it was hot with sin,
But that is over this many a day.
Under these sheets of satin and lace
    He slept in the arms of his concubines;
Now they rouse with the Prince instead,
    Drinking the maddest, merriest wines.
It's pleasant to hear such catches trolled,
        Now the King is cold.

What shall I do with his Majesty now?
    For, thanks to my potion, the man is dead.
    Suppose I bolster him up in bed,
And fix the crown again on his brow?
That would be merry! But then the Prince
    Would tumble it down, I know, in a trice:
    It would puzzle the Devil to name a vice
That would make his excellent Highness wince.
But hark, he's coming, I know his step:
    He's stealing to see if his wishes are true.
Ah, Sire, may your father's end be yours.
    (With just such a son to murder you!)
Peace to the dead! Let the bells be tolled,
        The King is cold!

THE MESSENGER AT NIGHT.

A FACE at the window,
  A tap on the pane;
Who is it that wants me
  To-night in the rain?

I have lighted my chamber,
  And brought out my wine,
For a score of good fellows
  Were coming to dine.

The dastards have failed me,
  And sent in the rain
The man at the window,
  To tap on the pane.

I hear the rain patter,
  I hear the wind blow;
I hate the wild weather,
  And yet I must go.

I could moan like the night wind,
  And weep like the rain,
But the Thing at the window
  Is tapping again.

It beckons, I follow.
  Good-by to the light.
I am going, O whither?
  Out into the Night!

OUT TO SEA.

THE wind is blowing east,
  And the waves are running free;
Let's hoist the sail at once,
  And stand out to sea,
    (You and me.)
  I am growing more and more
  A-weary of the shore;
  It was never so before—
    Out to sea!

The wind is blowing east,
  How it swells the straining sail!
A little further out
  We shall have a jolly gale.
    (Cling to me.)
  The waves are running high,
  And the gulls, how they fly!
  We shall only see the sky
    Out to sea!

The wind is blowing east
  From the dark and bloody shore,
Where flash a million swords,
  And the dreadful cannon roar.
    (Woe is me!)
  There's a curse upon the land,
  (Is that blood upon my hand?)
  What *can* we do but stand
    Out to sea?

A GREEK SONG.

DEMETRIUS to his men,
In the sun's setting light:
"Go, brave ones, to the water,
And eat your bread to-night.

But nephew dear, Lamprakes,
Come sit beside me here;
Gird on my arms and use them,
No kin of mine should fear.

Come, take my sword, brave comrades,
(I think ye find it red,)
And cut me down green branches,
And spread them for my bed.

For now I feel death coming,
And I must shortly die;
Make wide my tomb, remember,
And let its roof be high.

Give me room to load my musket,
And stand erect to fight.
Be sure you leave a window,
And leave it on the right,

To entice the merry swallows
To bring the spring that way,
And the nightingale to warble
In the good month of May."

WANDERING along a waste
Where once a city stood,
    I saw a ruined tomb,
    And in that tomb an urn :

A sacred, funeral urn,
Without a name, or date,
    And in its hollow depth
    A little human dust.

"Whose dust is here," I asked,
"In this forgotten urn ?
    And where this waste now lies
    What city rose of old ?"

None knows ; its name is lost ;
It was, and is no more.
    Gone like a wind that blew
    A thousand years ago.

Its melancholy end
Will be the end of all ;
    For as it passed away
    The Universe will pass.

Its sole memorial
Some ruined World like ours ;
    A solitary urn
    Full of the dust of men.

HEAD, OR HEART.

THE loving songs you sing to me
  With such a subtle art,
My poet, are they from the head,
  Or are they from the heart?

"From somewhere in the skies,
  It may be near, or far,
  From cloud, or moon, or star,
A misty Spirit flies,
  When summer nights are deep,
  And all are fast asleep,
The Spirit of whom the flowers,
    In the long, dim hours,
Dream, with their lips apart,
    Who gives, as he goes,
    To lily and rose
      With rapture dumb,
A kiss, that slips in the heart,
Where, when the morn is come,
      We find it as dew,
  Pure, perfect, divine.
Such are these songs of mine."

Not from your heart, then, as you said,
False one, your songs, but from your head.

"Deep down beneath the sea,
  Whose dreadful waves are whirled
  About the roots of the world,
Where death and darkness be,

A little creature lurks,
Who upwards works, and works;
Thorough the waters vast,
Thorough the waters green,
Up, up, until at last
The light of day is seen,
When lo, it has builded an isle
Above the seas,
Whereon the heavens smile,
And summer the whole year through
Hangs fruit on the trees,
And the isle is one great vine.
Such are these songs of mine."

And if your songs, so fine your art,
Are from the head, and from the heart,
I wonder now whence this is?
You answer me—with kisses!

——o——

DRIFTING.

WELL, summer at last is over,
Gone like a long, sweet dream,
And I am slowly waking,
As I drift along the stream.

This *dolce far niente*
Has been too much for me;
Nothing done on my picture,
Except that doubtful tree.

I went to the glen with Gervase,
And sketched one afternoon,
And would have made sunset studies,
But for the witching moon.

The moon did all the mischief.
  The moment I see it shine,
With a pretty woman beside me,
  My heart's no longer mine.

But have I really lost it?
  Or has it slipped away,
Like a child beguiled by summer,
  Who will come home tired with play?

I wonder if I am feeling
  The passion of my life?
Do I love that woman, Alice,
  Enough to call her *wife?*

I think so, but I know not,
  I only know 'tis sweet
To lie, as I am lying,
  In sunset, at her feet;

Watching her face, as, thoughtful,
  She leans upon her hand,
(Is it herself, or *me*, now,
  She seeks to understand?)

While overhead the swallows
  Fly home, with twittering cries,
And through the distant tree-tops
  The moon begins to rise.

If we could only stay so,
  In such a happy dream,
I would not for worlds awaken,
  But drift along with the stream!

THE PROUD LOVER.

I NEVER yet could understand
  How men could love in vain;
I hold it weak and wrong to love,
  And not be loved again.
For me, I must have heart for heart,
Deny me that, and we must part.

There be who love, or think they love,
  Without return for years;
They waste their days in fruitless sighs,
  Their nights in hopeless tears.
Not such am I, my heart is free,
I love not her who loves not me.

——o——

I KNOW a little rose,
  And O, but I were blest
Could I but be the drop of dew
  That lies upon her breast.

But I dare not look so high,
  Nor die a death so sweet;
It is enough for me to be
  The dust about her feet!

——o——

THE DYING LOVER.

THE grass that is under me now
  Will soon be over me, Sweet;
When you walk this way again
  I shall not hear your feet.

You may walk this way again,
  And shed your tears like dew;
They will be no more to me then
  Than mine are now to you!

———o———

UNDER THE ROSE.

SHE wears a rose in her hair,
  At the twilight's dreamy close:
Her face is fair, how fair
    Under the rose.

I steal like a shadow there,
  As she sits in rapt repose,
And whisper my loving prayer
    Under the rose.

She takes the rose from her hair,
  And her color comes and goes,
And I—a lover will dare
    Under the rose!

———o———

EVEN-SONG.

YOU must have an even-song?
You must try to make it, then,
For to-night my thoughts are dumb;
Not a tuneful word will come
From my tongue, or from my pen.
'Tis the hour when all things sleep,
And the flowers are steeped in dew;
Thoughts are deep, but words are few,

For, like thought, they lie too deep.
Silence suits the season best;
Birds are silent in the nest;
Harken, not a note is heard
From the throat of any bird,
Save the distant nightingale,
And her music is a wail.
Better silence till the morrow
Than that mighty dirge of sorrow.
Let *our* singing, then, go by,
Since the prelude is a sigh;
Yet, since you have waited long,
Take this kiss for even-song!

UNDER THE TREES.

WHEN the summer days are bright and long,
And the little birds pipe a merry song,
'Tis sweet in the shady woods to lie,
And gaze at the leaves and the twinkling sky,
Drinking the while the rare, cool breeze,
Under the trees, under the trees.

When winter comes, and the days are dim,
And the wind is singing a mournful hymn,
'Tis sweet in the faded woods to stray,
And tread the dead leaves into the clay,
Thinking of all life's mysteries
Under the trees, under the trees.

Summer or winter, day or night,
The woods are an ever-new delight;

They give us peace, and they make us strong,
Such wonderful balms to them belong:
So, living or dying, I'll take mine ease
Under the trees, under the trees.

———o———

It is a winter night,
And the stilly earth is white
With the blowing of the lilies of the snow;
Once it was as red
With the roses summer shed,
But the roses fled with summer long ago.

We sang a merry tune,
In the jolly days of June,
And we danced adown the garden in the light:
Now December's come,
And our hearts are dark and dumb,
As we huddle o'er the embers here to-night.

———o———

LEAVES.

What is life, and what are we?
Only leaves upon a tree,
Green to-day, to-morrow sear,
Then we are no longer here.

Others, fair and brave as we,
Grew of old upon the tree;
Now they crumble in the mould,
With their histories untold.

So shall we: it is our lot
Thus to die and be forgot.
By and by the tree will fall,
And Oblivion cover all.

——o——

COURAGE AND PATIENCE.

LIFE is sad, because we know it,
  Death, because we know it not;
But we will not fret or murmur,
  Every man must bear his lot.
Coward hearts, who shrink and fly,
Are not fit to live or die.

Knowing life, we should not fear it,
  Neither death, for that's unknown;
Courage, patience, these are virtues
  Which for many sins atone.
Who has these—and have not I?
He is fit to live and die.

——o——

TO BAYARD TAYLOR.

(*On his Fortieth Birthday.*)

"WHOM the gods love die young," we have been told,
And wise of some the saying seems to be,
Of others foolish; as it is of thee,
Who proven hast whom the gods love live old.
For have not forty seasons o'er thee rolled,
The worst propitious, setting like a sea
Toward the haven of Prosperity,
Now full in sight, so fair the wind doth hold?
Hast thou not Fame, the poet's chief desire,

A wife whom thou dost love, who loves thee well,
A child in whom your differing natures blend,
And friends, troops of them, who respect, admire?
(How deeply *one* it suits not now to tell,)
Such lives are long, and have a perfect end.

—o—

TO EDMUND CLARENCE STEDMAN.

(*With Shakespeare's Sonnets.*)

HAD we been living in the antique days,
With him, whose young but cunning fingers penned
These sugared sonnets to his strange-sweet friend,
I dare be sworn we would have won the bays.
Why not? We could have turned in amorous phrase
Fancies like these, where love and friendship blend,
(Or were they writ for some more private end?)
And this, we see, remembered is with praise.
Yes, there's a luck in most things, and in none
More than in being born at the right time;
It boots not what the labor to be done,
Or feats of arms, or art, or building rhyme.
Not that the heavens the little can make great,
But many a man has lived an age too late.

—o—

TO JAMES LORIMER GRAHAM, JR.

(*With Shakespeare's Sonnets.*)

WHAT can I give him, who so much hath given,
That princely heart, so over-kind to me,
Who, richly guerdoned both of earth and heaven,
Holds for his friends his heritage in fee?

No costly trinket of the golden ore,
Nor precious jewel of the distant Ind.
Ay me! These are not hoarded in my store,
Who have no coffers but my grateful mind.
What gift then—nothing? Stay, this Book of Song
May show my poverty and thy desert,
Steeped, as it is, in love, and love's sweet wrong,
Red with the blood that ran through Shakespeare's heart.
Read it once more, and, fancy soaring free,
Think, if thou canst, that I am singing Thee.

——o——

COLONEL FREDERICK TAYLOR.

(*Gettysburg, July* 3, 1863.)

MANY the ways that lead to death, but few
Grandly, and only one is glory's gate,
Standing wherever freemen dare their fate,
Determined, as thou wert, to die—or do.
This hast thou passed, young Soldier, storming through
The fiery darkness round it, not too late
To know the invaders beaten from thy State,
Ah, why too soon to rout them and pursue?
But some must fall as thou hast fallen; some
Remain to fight and fall another day:
And some go down in peace to their long rest.
If 't were not now, it would be still to come,
And whether now, or when thy hairs were gray,
Were fittest for thee, God alone knows best.

TO JERVIS McENTEE, ARTIST.

JERVIS, my friend, I envy you the art
Which you profess, and which possesses you,
To mimic Nature; unto her so true,
Your pictures are what she is to the heart,
The mystery of which it is a part,
That gladdens when we crush the vernal dew,
And saddens when leaves fall and flowers are few,
Nor quite forsakes us in the busy mart
Whence she is banished, save in slips of sky
That swim in mist, or drip in dreary rain,
No glimpse of peaks far off, nor forests nigh,
Only dark streets, strange forms, a barren pain;
Till to my wall I turn a longing eye,
When you restore me mountains, woods again.

FLORENCE NIGHTINGALE.

ENGLAND, if Time from out the Book of Fame
Should blot the desperate valor of thy men
In the Crimea, an Englishwoman's name,
As sweet as ever came from poet's pen,
Would still defy him—Florence Nightingale!
Honor to that fair girl, whose pitying heart
Led her across the sea, to ease the smart
Of soldier wounds, and hush the soldier's wail.
Men can be great when great occasions call:
In little duties women find their spheres,

The narrow cares that cluster round the hearth ;
But this dear woman wipes a woman's tears,
And wears the crown of womanhood for all.
Happy the land that gave such goodness birth.

——o——

TO A FRIEND.

(*With a Vase.*)

POET, take this little vase,
From a lover of the race,
Given to hold, a funeral jar,
The ashes of thy loved cigar.
If for that it seems too fine,
Fill it to the brim with wine,
And drink, in love, to me and mine,
As I drain to thee and thine.
Ashes, though, may suit it best,
(There's a plenty in my breast ;)
Fill it, then, in summer hours,
With the ashes of thy flowers,
Roses, such as on it blow,
Or lilies, like its ground of snow.

——o——

IN MEMORIAM.

I AM followed by a spirit,
  In my sorrow and my mirth ;
'T is the spirit of an infant,
  Dying almost at its birth,
Unlamented, yet how dear,
Since, unseen, I know 't is near.

Would, if only for a moment,
  As I feel it, I could see,
In the light of heavenly beauty,
  Sitting on its father's knee :
It would dry this hopeless tear,
Dropping now, it is so near!

——o——

WHAT shall I sing, and how,
Of what I suffer now?
To nature trust, or art,
The burden of my heart?

'T is three weeks now, but *three*,
Since he was here with me :
The dreadful time has flown,
And now I am alone.

I left him in the morn,
(Not knowing how forlorn,)
There in his little bed,
Weak, sick, but O *not* dead!

When I came back at noon,
(Too late, and yet so soon,)
They met me on the stairs,
Like Judgment unawares!

I stopped. "Your Will is dead!"
"It cannot be," I said.
It *could*, it was—ah, why?
What had he done to die?

I knelt beside his bed,
I kissed his royal head,
His hand, his feet, his arm—
The body yet was warm!

I wept! But did I weep?
Or was my grief too deep?
I only know I cursed;
Pray Heaven that was the worst!

And shall I sing of this?
Or of the dark abyss
In which I grope apart,
Hugging my broken heart?

Not now, whatever I may
In some far distant day;
Enough what here appears,
Drowned in these bitter tears!

——o——

THE Christmas-time drew slowly near,
  The happy days we loved to see;
  Thrice had we had a Christmas-tree,
The evergreen of all the year.

"What have you brought me?" asked the boy
  When I came home at night; and I
  Made some, I know not what, reply,
The promise of a future toy.

"You must not ask me any more,"
  I said at last; "but wait and see,
  When Christmas comes, your Christmas-tree,
For you shall have it as before."

We meant to have a tiny one,
  With pendent toys, and lighted boughs;
  But darkness fell upon the house,
For Death, in passing, took my son.

Nathless he had his Christmas-tree,
  For pines within the graveyard stand,
  Above his bed of yellow sand,
Beside the moaning of the sea.

——o——

I SIT in my lonesome chamber
  This stilly, winter night,
In the midst of quaint old volumes,
  With the cheery fire in sight.

In the darkened room behind me
  My darling lies asleep,
Worn out with constant weeping,
  'Tis now my turn to weep.

What do I weep for? Nothing.
  Or a very common thing;
That the little boy I loved so,
  Like a dove has taken wing.

He used to sleep beside us,
  In reach of his mother's hand;
They have moved his bed, ah, whither?
  They have made him one in the sand!

Why didn't they make mine, also?
  I'm sure I want to go:
But no, I must live for his mother,
  For she needs me still, I know.

For her I must bear my sorrow,
  Nor weep, when she can see;
She grieves too much already,
  To waste a sigh for me.

———o———

You think, I see it by your looks,
That I am buried in my books,
Wherein, as when he lived, I find
An easy solace for my mind.

It is not so. I try, indeed,
What charmed me once again to read;
Page after page I turn in vain,
They leave no meaning in my brain.

I see the words; they come and go,
In dark procession, sad and slow,
Like mourners at a funeral,
I know who lies beneath the pall!

I dally with my books, and why?
Read you the reason in my eye.
Because I would do more than weep;
Grief, even for him, may be too deep.

Had *I* been taken, what would *he*,
Dear heart, be doing now for me?
His few tears dried, (the blow being new
We'll grant he sheds a tear or two,)

He would have smiled as heretofore,
And soon have talked of me no more;
Like other little orphan boys,
He would be playing with his toys.

Should I, a child of larger growth,
(You know you called us children, both,)
Be, in my grief, less wise than he?
Or you be harder, love, with me?

Then chide not, as you have to-day,
For poring o'er my books, but say,
"His ways remind me of the boy's;
For see, he's playing with his toys."

——o——

WHAT shall we do when those we love
Are gone to their seraphic rest?
Since we must live, what life is best
Before the clearer eyes above?

Shall we recall them as they were,
The day, the hour, the dreadful blow
That, dealt in darkness, laid them low,
The coffin and the sepulchre?

Or shall we rather (say, we can,)
Be what we used to be of old?
Work, one for love, and one for gold,
The tender woman, worldly man?

Shall we be jealous if the heart
Lets go a moment of its dead?
Mistrust it, and revile the head,
And say to all but Death, "*Depart?*"

Or shall we willing be to take
What good we may in common things,
Blue skies, the sea, a bird that sings,
And other hearts that do not break?

What God approves, methinks, I know
 (If aught we do approved can be,)
 But since my child was taken from me,
My only pleasure is in woe :

My tortured heart, my frenzied head,
 For when, as now, a smile appears,
 I would be drowned in endless tears,
Or, happier, with my darling—dead!

———o———

WE sat by the cheerless fireside,
 Mother, and you, and I;
All thinking of our darling,
 And sad enough to die.

He lay in his little coffin,
 In the room adjoining ours,
A Christmas wreath on his bosom,
 His brow in a band of flowers.

"We bury the boy to-morrow,"
 I said, or seemed to say;
"Would I could keep it from coming
 By lengthening out to-day!

Why can't I sit by the fireside,
 As I am sitting now,
And feel my gray hairs thinning,
 And the wrinkles on my brow?

God keep him there in his coffin
 Till the years have rolled away!
If he *must* be buried to-morrow,
 O let me die to-day!"

———o———

IT looks in at the window,
  Divinely bright and far,
The loving star of Venus,
  Our little Willy's star.

He used to watch its rising,
  As we have done to-night,
Its lustrous, steel-blue twinkle,
  Its steady heart of light.

"O mamma, there is Venus!"
  Methinks I hear him cry,
As he leads us to the window,
  To watch his brighter eye.

And once we saw him kneeling
  Before it, in his chair,
Folding his hands together,
  And making some sweet prayer.

What did he ask you, Venus?
  To take his soul away?
Or, feeling he must leave us,
  Perhaps he prayed to stay.

God knows; *you* cannot tell us,
  And *he* is gone afar;
And we are left in sorrow,
  To gaze upon his star!

———o———

WHAT shall I do next summer,
  What will become of me
When I draw near my cottage,
  Beside the solemn sea?

Along the dusty roadside
  I shall not see him run,
To greet his loving father,
  So proud to meet his son.

No longer in the distance
  I'll strain my eager eyes,
To catch him at the window,
  And mark his sweet surprise.

The gate how can I enter?
  How bear to touch the door
That opens in the chambers
  Where he is seen no more?

When last I crossed the threshold
  (I'm glad I did not take
His dear dead body thither,)
  I thought my heart would break.

"My son was here last summer,
  He sat in yonder chair;
And there, beside the window,
  I kissed his golden hair!"

With every sweet remembrance
  There came a burst of tears;
There is but one such tempest
  In all our stormy years.

I kissed the chair he sat in,
  The spot his feet had trod;
I clutched the empty darkness
  To pluck him back from God.

O ruined heart and hearth-stone!
  What will become of me,
In my deserted dwelling
  Beside the dreadful sea?

WHEN first he died there was no day
  That was not saddened by my tears.
  "And 't will be thus," I said, "for years;
His memory cannot fade away."

That first wild burst of grief is o'er,
  The spring is sealed of wretchedness;
  Not that I love my darling less,
But love, or think of, others more.

They move me as they could not then,
  My brain at least, if not my heart;
  And so I try to act my part
As patiently as lesser men.

Pale fathers pass me in the street,
  Whose little sons, like mine, are dead;
  I see it in the drooping head,
And in the wandering of the feet.

THE dreary winter days are past,
The cloudy sky, the bitter blast:
    Gone is the snow, the sleet
    That glazed each rugged street.

All things proclaim that Spring is near,
Rejoicing in the wakened Year:
    Even *I*, whose tears are shed
    Above the Winter dead.

Darker than now my death can be,
In that it took my boy from me,
    My heart it did not wring
    Like this first breath of Spring.

What though the clouds were thick o'erhead,
And earth was iron to my tread,
    Rains poured, snows whirled, winds blew,
    And my great grief was new?

'T was still—if not a solace, yet
Something akin that laid regret:
    It hushed my useless moan
    To think I was alone.

When drove the snow, the thought would rise,
"It does not blind his little eyes!"
    When winds were sharp I smiled,
    "They cannot stab my child!"

Now Spring is come, I sigh and say,
"He cannot see this sunny day,
    Nor feel this balmy air
    That longs to kiss his hair!"

The tender spirit of the hour
That stirs the sap, and paints the flower,
    Enfolding land and sea,
    And quickening even me,

So stings my soul, I hold my breath,
And try to break the dream of death,
    And stagger on his track
    Until I snatch him back!

Great God! If *he* should feel it there,
(Where, *where*—some angel tell me where?)
    And struggle so for *me*,
    How terrible 't would be!

——o——

OUT of the deeps of heaven
  A bird has flown to my door,
As twice in the ripening summers
  Its mates have flown before.

Why it has flown to my dwelling
  Nor it nor I may know;
And only the silent angels
  Can tell when it shall go.

That it will not straightway vanish,
  But fold its wings with me,
And sing in the greenest branches
  Till the axe is laid to the tree,

Is the prayer of my love and terror,
  For my soul is sore distrest,
Lest I wake some dreadful morning,
  And find but its empty nest!

LATER POEMS.

AN OLD MAN'S SONG OF MAY.

CAN it be that Spring is come?
  So the Calendar doth say:
March has blustered off, I know,
And wild April soon must go,
  Then, O then it will be May!

'Twas a merry month to me
  Long ago, when I was young.
I have dreams of childish hours,
In the meadows picking flowers,
  And of songs the robins sung.

Does the robin still remain?
  One, I mean, that loves and grieves?
And—supposing that I could
Join the Children in the Wood,
  Would it cover me with leaves?

Flowers, I see, can still be bought,
  And who will may buy, not I:
I want more than these poor flowers,
I demand the dews, the showers,
  Wind, and trees, and summer sky.

Why not say, you poor old man,
  You demand what is no more?

Were it May, twice over May,
You would still be sad to-day,
For you are not as before.

May is only for the young,
Chill December suits you best:
Fallen leaves, not flowers, for you,
You have nothing left to do:
Make your bed, and take your rest.

AN OLD MAN'S NEW-YEAR'S SONG.

I WILL not stir abroad to-day,
But find at home what cheer I may.
Old men like me are out of date:
Who wants to see a grizzled pate?
If silver hairs were locks of gold,
I might be as I was of old;
For then my dead would all be here,
And that would make a happy Year.

The old man now, the young man then,
Are we the same, or different men?
One sits at home with slippered feet,
The other braves the driving sleet:
His light heart suns itself with wine,
It will not warm this heart of mine:
One sees the bridal, one the bier,
And each, in his own way, the Year.

Where are the friends I used to know,
Ned, Fred, not many years ago,
Whose glass clinked mine amid the din
Of *Old Year out and New Year in?*

"Dead rhymes with Ned," the Master said,
Himself among the Masters dead:
Alack, and drear, and fear, and tear,
Methinks, all sad words rhyme with Year.

Some one, perhaps, will care for me
When I no longer hear or see.
I hope my little man of ten,
When he shall take my place with men,
Will think about me in the grave,
If only for the gifts I gave,
And say, "If father was but here,
It would be such a happy Year!"

Peace, old man, peace! And cease this song,
Which does the merry season wrong.
You have the sweetness of regret,
The friendships you remember yet,
You have what time will not destroy,
The love of your remembering boy:
These surely are enough to cheer
The morning of the saddest Year.

THE VANISHED MAY.

WHY is it that when Spring is come,
  The first sweet touch of Spring,
That something all the Winter dumb
  Begins in me to sing?
Begins, perforce, this sunny day
To solemnize the darkened May?

Why the bird sings I know, I see
  Its journeys through the air;

There is a nest in yonder tree,
  Its little ones are there.
Thy song, sweet bird, is not like mine,
But one unending Valentine.

I wander through the woods, and mark,
  Above, below, around,
The tribes that live on leaf and bark,
  And burrow in the ground;
If Life be happiness, I guess
The world is full of Happiness.

Why is it, then, that I am sad?
  What have I done to-day,
When every creature else is glad,
  To lose the joy of May?
Why ask what have I lost? In truth,
What is the saddest loss but Youth?

My youth has gone, and what remains?
  The woods, the clouds, the sea,
The wild March winds, the April rains—
  But what are these to me?
When head and heart alike are gray,
What can restore the vanished May?

——o——

A NEW YEAR'S SONG.

THE world is full of mystery,
  Which no one understands:
What is before our eyes we see,
  The work of unseen hands;
But whence, and when, and why they wrought,
Escapes the grasp of human thought.

There was a time when we were not,
  And there will be again
When we must cease, and be forgot,
  With all our joy and pain.
Gone like the wind, or like the snow,
That fell a thousand years ago.

We live as if we should not die,
  Blindly, but wisely, too;
For if we knew Death always nigh,
  What would we say, or do,
But fold our hands, and close our eyes,
And care no more who lives or dies?

If Death to each man in his turn
  Is coming, soon or late,
Be ours the soldier's unconcern,
  And his courageous fate;
Better to perish in the strife
Than to preserve the coward's life.

Before my hearth-fire pondering long,
  As 't were a bivouac,
I heard last night this solemn song,
  Which I have summoned back.
It seems my sombre mood to cheer,
And is my greeting to the Year.

New Year, if you were bringing Youth,
  As you are bringing Age,
I would not have it back, in sooth;
  I have no strength to wage
Lost battles over. Let them be,
Bury your dead, O Memory!

You can bring nothing will surprise,
And nothing will dismay,
No tears again in these old eyes,
No darkness in my day.
You might bring light and smiles instead,
If you could give me back my dead.

I have beheld your kin, New Year,
Full fifty times, and none
That was so happy, and so dear,
I wept when it was done.
Why should we weep when years depart,
And leave their ashes in the heart?

Good-by, since you are gone, Old Year,
And my past life, good-by!
I shed no tear upon your bier,
For it is well to die.
New Year, your worst will be my best—
What can an old man want but rest?

——o——

MAY-DAY.

If I were asked the season,
I could not tell to-day;
I should say it still was Winter—
The Calendar says May.

If this, indeed, be May-day,
I must be growing old,
For nothing I was used to
Do I to-day behold.

On May-day in New England,
  In that old town of ours,
We rose before the daybreak,
  And went and gathered flowers.

If there are woods in Hingham
  I have forgot; I know
That there were woods in Seekonk
  Some forty years ago.

And thither went the children,
  For there the wild flowers grew;
They plucked them up by handfuls,
  With fingers wet with dew.

And then in pretty baskets,
  With little sprigs of green
They placed them, and stole homeward,
  And hoped they were not seen.

Along the roads and by-ways
  The merry creatures crept,
And round their sweethearts' houses,
  While still their sweethearts slept.

The baskets on their windows
  They hung, and stole away;
And no one knew who did it,
  Or, knowing, none would say.

It spoiled her simple pleasure
  If any maiden knew
Who sent her her May basket—
  She had to guess out who.

Ah, those indeed were May-days,
  But *this*, this dreary day,
The Calendar's mistaken—
  'Tis not the first of May!

Why, if it were, my lady,
  I would have gone in time,
And made you your May basket,
  If only one of rhyme!

But I haven't done it, darling,
  For the words that I have sung
Are only recollections
  Of May when I was young.

UP IN THE TREES.

Would we were there, in the woods together,
Two little birds in the mid-summer weather,
Out of the winter, away from sorrow,
With—think of it—never a thought of the morrow!
Up in the trees, whose branches are swinging,
They sit in the soft airs, singing, singing
A song in which youth and passion are blended,
That is always beginning, and never ended!

Look at them there now, sitting, sitting
Where owls are hooting, and bats are flitting:
One is singing, the other is sleeping,
While the Lady Moon through the leaves is peeping!
And now look at us, whose years are doubled,
We have missed so much, and have been so troubled,
Would we were there in the woods together,
Two happy birds in the mid-summer weather!

AN OLD SONG REVERSED.

"THERE are gains for all our losses."
  So I said when I was young.
If I sang that song again,
'T would not be with that refrain,
  Which but suits an idle tongue.

Youth has gone, and hope gone with it,
  Gone the strong desire for fame.
Laurels are not for the old.
Take them, lads. Give Senex gold.
  What's an everlasting name?

When my life was in its summer
  One fair woman liked my looks:
Now that Time has driven his plough
In deep furrows on my brow,
  I'm no more in her good books.

"There are gains for all our losses?"
  Grave beside the wintry sea,
Where my child is, and my heart,
For they would not live apart,
  What has been your gain to me?

No, the words I sang were idle,
  And will ever so remain:
Death, and Age, and vanished Youth,
All declare this bitter truth,
  There's a loss for every gain!

SONGS UNSUNG.

Let no poet, great or small,
  Say that he will sing a song;
For Song cometh, if at all,
  Not because we woo it long,
But because it suits its will,
Tired at last of being still.

Every song that has been sung
  Was before it took a voice,
Waiting since the world was young
  For the poet of its choice.
O, if any waiting be,
May they come to-day to me!

I am ready to repeat
  Whatsoever they impart;
Sorrows sent by them are sweet,
  They know how to heal the heart:
Ay, and in the lightest strain
Something serious doth remain.

What are my white hairs, forsooth,
  And the wrinkles on my brow?
I have still the soul of youth,
  Try me, merry Muses, now.
I can still with numbers fleet
Fill the world with dancing feet.

No, I am no longer young,
  Old am I this many a year;

But my songs will yet be sung,
  Though I shall not live to hear.
O my son that is to be,
Sing my songs, and think of me!

——o——

SISTE, VIATOR.

As I was going on my way,
  For every man his way must go,
I met a youth, one sweet spring day,
  Who knew me, or who seemed to know;
Bright as a lover when he stands
  Where *she* is in her bridal trim.
"Stop, crown me." Then with ready hands
  I made a rosy crown for him.

As I was going on my way,
  I did not dare to tarry long,
I met a man one summer day,
  Of noble bearing, tall and strong:
The light of love was in his eyes,
  The spirit of love in every limb.
"Stop, live with me." I thought it wise
  To stop a while and live with him.

As I was going on my way,
  But slower than when I began,
I met a man, one autumn day,
  Ah, such a piteous, poor old man!
I saw his tears, and somehow knew
  The grief that made his eyes so dim.
"Stop, comfort me." What could I do
  But stop and try to comfort him?

Now I am going on my way,
  A chill is creeping over me,
But whether from the winter day,
  Or something that I do not see,
Who knows? I feel it stealing near,
  A fearful presence, ghastly, grim:
"*Stop!*" When that dreadful word I hear,
  I shall lie down in dust with him.

——o——

YOUTH AND AGE.

WHEN I was young there seemed to be
No pleasure in the world for me.
My fellows found it everywhere,
Was none so poor but had his share,
          They took mine, too.
I sought in vain, it was my fate
To be too early, or too late.
The nest was there, the bird was flown,
Ah why? And to what golden zone?
          If Youth but knew!

Why art thou, Youth, so swift, so slow?
Why dost thou let thy pleasures go?
All that they grasp thy hands let fall,
The best they do not grasp at all,
          Do not pursue.
What tingles in my blood like wine?
Those tender eyes that turn to mine,
The soft tears in my eyes that start—
Tell me, what does it mean, my heart?
          If Youth but knew!

Now I am old there seems to be
No pleasure in the world for me,
But vain regrets for what is past,
Because I did not hold it fast,
Because it flew.
That Youth is weak, and Age is strong,
Should be the burden of my song,
And might be in my happier hours,
If autumn leaves were summer flowers,
If Age could do!

Mock not my sighs, and my white hair,
O Youth, so foolish and so fair!
Remember, life is not all June,
The lean and slippered pantaloon
Awaits thee, too.
Be wise, delay not, oh make haste,
Go, steal your arms around her waist,
The rosebud mouth begins to blow,
Stoop down, and kiss it—so, boy, so!
If Age could do!

Dum vivimus, the wise men say,
And you can do it, as well as they;
So live and love, then, while you can,
Nor sigh, like me, when you are a man,
"If Youth but knew!"
Far better be where Folly dwells,
And shake with him your jangling bells,
Than hear belated Wisdom come,
And beat upon the muffled drum,
"*If Age could do!*"

IRREPARABLE.

THE sorrow of all sorrows
  Was never sung or said,
Though many a poet borrows
  The mourning of the dead,
And darkly buries pleasure
In some melodious measure.

The loss of youth is sadness
  To all who think, or feel,
A wound no after gladness
  Can ever wholly heal;
And yet, so many share it,
We learn at last to bear it.

The faltering and the failing
  Of friends is sadder still,
For friends grown foes, assailing,
  Know when and where to kill;
But souls themselves sustaining,
Have still a friend remaining.

The death of those who love us,
  And those we love, is sore;
But think they are above us,
  Or think they are no more,
We bear the blows that sever,
We cannot weep forever!

The sorrow of all sorrows
  Is deeper than all these,

And all that anguish borrows,
  Upon its bended knees;
No tears nor prayers relieve it,
No loving vows deceive it.

It is one day to waken
  And find that love is flown,
And cannot be o'ertaken,
  And we are left alone:
No wo that can be spoken,
No heart that can be broken!

No wish for love's returning,
  Or something in its stead;
No missing it, and yearning
  As for the dearer dead:
No yesterday, no morrow,
But everlasting sorrow.

———o———

THE TWO ANCHORS.

It was a gallant sailor man,
  Had just come home from sea,
And as I passed him in the town
  He sang "Ahoy!" to me.
I stopped, and saw I knew the man,
  Had known him from a boy;
And so I answered sailor-like,
  "Avast!" to his "Ahoy!"
I made a song for him one day,
  His ship was then in sight,
"The little anchor on the left,
  The great one on the right."

I gave his hand a hearty grip.
  "So you are back again?
They say you have been pirating
  Upon the Spanish Main.
Or was it some rich Indiaman
  You robbed of all her pearls?
Of course you have been breaking hearts
  Of poor Kanaka girls!"
"Wherever I have been," he said,
  "I kept my ship in sight,
'The little anchor on the left,
  The great one on the right.'"

"I heard last night that you were in,
  I walked the wharves to-day,
But saw no ship that looked like yours.
  Where does the good ship lay?
I want to go on board of her."
  "And so you shall," said he;
"But there are many things to do
  When one comes home from sea.
You know the song you made for me,
  I sing it morn and night,
'The little anchor on the left,
  The great one on the right.'"

"But how's your wife, and little one?"
  "Come home with me," he said.
"Go on, go on; I follow you."
  I followed where he led.
He had a pleasant little house,
  The door was open wide,
And at the door the dearest face,
  A dearer one inside!

He hugged his wife and child, he sang,
His spirits were so light,
"The little anchor on the left,
The great one on the right."

'Twas supper-time, and we sat down,
The sailor's wife and child,
And he and I; he looked at them,
And looked at me, and smiled.
"I think of this when I am tossed
Upon the stormy foam,
And though a thousand leagues away,
Am anchored here at home."
Then, giving each a kiss, he said,
"I see in dreams at night
This little anchor on my left,
This great one on my right!"

——o——

TOO OLD FOR KISSES.

My uncle Philip, hale old man,
Has children by the dozen;
Tom, Ned, and Jack, and Kate and Ann—
How many call me "Cousin?"
Good boys and girls, the best was Bess,
I bore her on my shoulder;
A little bud of loveliness
That never should grow older!
Her eyes had such a pleading way,
They seemed to say, "Don't strike me."
Then, growing bold another day,
"I mean to make you like me."

I liked my cousin, early, late,
  Who liked not little misses :
She used to meet me at the gate,
  Just old enough for kisses!

This was, I think, three years ago,
  Before I went to college:
I learned but one thing—how to row,
  A healthy sort of knowledge.
When I was plucked, (we won the race,)
  And all was at an end there,
I thought of Uncle Philip's place,
  And every country friend there.
My cousin met me at the gate,
  She looked five, ten years older,
A tall young woman, still, sedate,
  With manners coyer, colder.
She gave her hand with stately pride.
  "Why, what a greeting this is!
You used to kiss me." She replied,
  "I am too old for kisses."

I loved—I love my Cousin Bess,
  She's always in my mind now;
A full-blown bud of loveliness,
  The rose of womankind now!
She must have suitors, old and young
  Must bow their heads before her;
Vows must be made, and songs be sung
  By many a mad adorer.
But I must win her: she must give
  To me her youth and beauty;
And I—to love her while I live
  Will be my happy duty.

For she will love me soon or late,
And be my bliss of blisses,
Will come to meet me at the gate,
Nor be too old for kisses!

THE LADY'S GIFT.

"O GIVE me something, Lady,
For I have given my heart,
A trifle to replace it,
When we are far apart."
She drew from out her bosom
A rose-bud wet with dew,
And gave it to him, saying,
"Here's something, Sir, for you."
"I take it, and will keep it,
For never lady wore
A flower so pure and perfect,
But you must give me more."

"I have no more to give, Sir,
A simple maid like me,
Who has nor birth nor fortune,
What should she have?" said she.
"But you have gold," he answered.
"No lady in the land
So rich a dower." "What is it?"
"The ring upon your hand."
She slipped from off her finger
The little ring she wore.
"I take it, and will wear it,
But you must give me more."

"What more have I to give you?
  Why give you anything?
You had my rose before, Sir,
  And now you have my ring."
"You have forgotten one thing."
  "I do not understand."
"The dew goes with the rose-bud,
  And with the ring the hand."
She gave her hand, he took it,
  And kissed it o'er and o'er:
"I give myself to you, love,
  I cannot give you more."

THE MARRIAGE KNOT.

I KNOW a bright and beauteous May,
  Who knows I love her well;
But if she loves, or will some day,
  I cannot make her tell.
She sings the songs I write for her,
  Of tender hearts betrayed;
But not the one that I prefer,
  About a country maid.
The hour when I its burden hear
  Will never be forgot:
"O stay not long, but come, my dear,
  And knit our marriage knot!"

It is about a country maid—
  I see her in my mind;
She is not of her love afraid,
  And cannot be unkind.

She knits, and sings with many a sigh,
  And, as her needles glide,
She wishes, and she wonders why
  He is not at her side.
" He promised he would meet me here,
  Upon this very spot:
O stay not long, but come, my dear,
  And knit our marriage knot!"

My lady will not sing the song.
  "Why not?" I say. And she,
Tossing her head, "It is too long."
  And I, "Too short, may be."
She has her little wilful ways,
  But I persist, and then,
"It is not maidenly," she says,
  "For maids to sigh for men."
"But men must sigh for maids, I fear,
  I know it is my lot,
Until you whisper, 'Come, my dear,
  And knit our marriage knot!'"

Why is my little one so coy?
  Why does she use me so?
I am no fond and foolish boy
  To lightly come and go.
A man who loves, I know my heart,
  And will know hers ere long,
For, certes, I will not depart
  Until she sings my song.
She learned it all, as you shall hear,
  No word has she forgot.
"Begin, my dearest." "Come, my dear,
  And knit our marriage knot!"

PHILLIS.

"PHILLIS, to what can I compare
The golden glory of your hair?
Your cheek—was never cheek so fair,
Tell me if those be blushes there,
    Or roses dropt on lilies?
Close, an you will, your eyes divine,
Still through their lids I feel them shine:
You will some day to me incline,
No distant day you must be mine;
    Then why not now, O, Phillis?"
Phillis, without frown or smile,
Sat and knotted all the while.

"You are a fair one, Phillis; but who knows
Whether the lily and the rose,
(Methinks your color comes and goes,)
Your golden tresses, and all those
    Bewildering charms and graces,
Who, save your maid—why do you start?
Knows what is nature, what is art?
Do you ever keep the two apart?
What have you given me for my heart
    But patched and painted faces?"
Phillis, with a frown and smile,
Sat and knotted all the while.

"Your waiting-woman, Mistress Prue,
Has more and deeper wit than you:
She knows precisely what to do
When Matt and Diggory come to woo,
    And how to hold her lovers.

Now you—I have a mind to see
What pretty Prue will say to me
(She is a buxom wench, pardie,)
'Twill not be 'fie!' and 'la, let be!'
    That angry flush discovers."
Phillis, with a frown, not smile,
Sat and knotted all the while.

"Phillis, you love me, you confessed
When I began my silly jest;
The guarded secrets of your breast
Slipped out, your heart among the rest,
    Your heart that now so still is,
A little bird, that fluttered then
For fear that I, like lighter men—
Your nod says 'Yes.' But tell me when,
Or I must summon Prue again—
    When shall it be, O Phillis?"
Phillis, with a happy smile,
Sat and knotted all the while.

——o——

THE NECKLACE OF PEARLS.

He met her in the garden,
  A bright and beauteous maid,
Who, grown at once a woman,
  Was not of love afraid:
She loved, and could not help it,
  Her heart went out to his,
And as he stooped to kiss her
  She rose to meet his kiss.

He kissed her in the garden,
  And—was it what he said,

Or the shadow of the roses
  That made her cheeks so red?
Her bosom rising, falling,
  With new and strange delight,
The string of pearls upon it
  Was not so white, so white.

He drew her down the garden,
  He would not hear her "No,"
She must go if she loved him
  Who loved her, loved her so:
They must go pluck the roses
  And listen to the dove:
The dove was wooing, wooing,
  As he was her—for love.

He led her down the garden,
  And while her arms were round
The neck she, parting, clung to,
  She saw upon the ground
The string that held her necklace,
  With not a pearl thereon:
The slender string was broken,
  And all the pearls were gone.

Then up and down the garden
  She wandered with dismay,
And wondered where her pearls were,
  And how they slipt away:
They nestled in her bosom
  One little hour ago,
Before they plucked the roses,
  And her tears began to flow.

So round and round the garden
  She went with peering eyes:

O is not that the necklace
  That shining yonder lies?
'Tis but a string of dew-drops
  The wind has broken there,
Or the tears that she is shedding
  That make her look more fair.

Still round and round the garden
  She hunted high and low,
In the red hearts of the roses,
  The lily's breast of snow:
The thorns they pricked her fingers,
  Her fingers bled and bled,
But her heart was bleeding faster—
  O why was she not dead?

For she must leave the garden
  And meet her mother's eye,
Who will perceive she sorrows,
  And ask the reason why;
And she must meet her father,
  Who, as she hangs her head,
Will miss the priceless necklace,
  And wish that she were dead.

——o——

THE FLOWER OF LOVE LIES BLEEDING.

I MET a little maid one day,
  All in the bright May weather;
She danced, and brushed the dew away
  As lightly as a feather.
She had a ballad in her hand
  That she had just been reading,
But was too young to understand

That ditty of a distant land,
  "The flower of love lies bleeding."

She tripped across the meadow grass,
  To where a brook was flowing,
Across the brook like wind did pass,
  Wherever flowers were growing
Like some bewildered child she flew,
  Whom fairies were misleading:
"Whose butterfly," I said, "are you?
And what sweet thing do you pursue?"
  "The flower of love lies bleeding.

I've found the wild rose in the hedge,
  And found the tiger-lily,
The blue flag by the water's edge,
  The dancing daffodilly,
King-cups and pansies, every flower
  Except the one I'm needing;
Perhaps it grows in some dark bower,
And opens at a later hour,
  This flower of love lies bleeding."

"I wouldn't look for it," I said,
  "For you can do without it.
There's no such flower." She shook her head.
  "But I have read about it!"
I talked to her of bee and bird,
  But she was all unheeding:
Her tender heart was strangely stirred,
She harped on that unhappy word,
  "The flower of love lies bleeding!"

"My child," I sighed, and dropped a tear,
  "I would no longer mind it;

You'll find it some day, never fear,
  For all of us must find it.
I found it many a year ago,
  With one of gentle breeding;
You and the little lad you know,
I see why you are weeping so—
  Your flower of love lies bleeding!"

——o——

WISHING AND HAVING.

If to wish and to have were one, my dear,
  You would be sitting now
With not a care in your tender heart,
  Not a wrinkle upon your brow.
The clock of time would go back with you
  All the years you have been my wife,
Till its golden hands had pointed out
  The happiest hour of your life:
I would stop them at that immortal hour,
  The clock should no longer run:
You could not be sad, and sick, and old—
  If to wish and to have were one.

You are not here in the winter, my love,
  The snow is not whirling down,
You are in the heart of the summer woods,
  In your dear old sea-side town;
A patter of little feet in the leaves,
  A beautiful boy at your side;
He is gathering flowers in the shady nooks—
  It was but a dream that he died!
Keep hold of his hands, and sing to him,
  No mother under the sun

Has such a seraphic child as yours—
  If to wish and to have are one.

Methinks I am with you there, dear wife,
  In that old house by the sea;
I have flown to you as the bluebird flies
  To his mate in the poplar-tree.
A sailor's hammock hangs at the door,
  You swing in it, book in hand;
A boat is standing in for the beach,
  Its keel now grates on the sand:
Your brothers are coming—two manly men,
  Whose lives have only begun:
Their days will be long in the land, dear heart,
  If to wish and to have are one.

If to wish and to have were one, ah me!
  I would not be old and poor,
But a young and prosperous gentleman,
  With never a dun at the door.
There would be no past to bewail, my love,
  There would be no future to dread;
Your brothers would be live men again,
  And my boy would not be dead.
Perhaps it will all come right at last,
  It may be, when all is done,
We shall be together in some good world,
  Where to wish and to have are one.

——o——

THE FOLLOWER.

WE have a youngster in the house,
  A little man of ten,
Who dearest to his mother is
  Of all God's little men.

In-doors and out he clings to her,
He follows up and down;
He steals his slender hand in hers,
He plucks her by the gown.
"Why do you cling to me so, child?
You track me everywhere;
You never let me be alone."
And he, with serious air,
Answered, as closer still he drew,
"My feet were made to follow you."

Two years before the boy was born,
Another child of seven,
Whom Heaven had lent to us awhile,
Went back again to Heaven.
He came to fill his brother's place,
And bless our failing years,
The good God sent him down in love,
To dry our useless tears.
I think so, mother, for I hear
In what the child has said
A meaning that he knows not of,
A message from the dead.
He answered wiser than he knew,
"My feet were made to follow you."

Come here, my child, and sit with me,
Your head upon my breast;
You are the last of all my sons,
And you must be the best.
How much I love you, you may guess
When, grown a man like me,
You sit as I am sitting now,
Your child upon your knee.

Think of me then, and what I said,
  (And practised when I could,)
'Tis something to be great and wise,
  'Tis better to be good.
O, say to all things good and true,
" My feet were made to follow you."

Come here, my wife, and sit by me,
  And place your hand in mine,
(And yours, my child,) while I have you
  'Tis wicked to repine.
We've had our share of sorrows, dear,
  We've had our graves to fill;
But thank the good God overhead,
  We have each other still.
We've nothing in the world beside,
  For we are only three;
Mother and child, *my* wife and child,
  How dear you are to me.
I know, indeed, I always knew,
My feet were made to follow you!

———o———

LOVE'S WILL.

LOVE always looks for love again.
If ever single, it is twain,
And till it finds its counterpart
It bears about an aching heart.
Glory is with itself content,
Wisdom, with what the gods have sent;
But love, whom they look down upon,
Fond fool, will have all things or none.

Who dare deny his high demands,
Let them beware, for he hath hands;
Strong hands hath Love, and swift to slay,
And feet that know themselves the way
To where his parted self may be.
"Go, find, and fetch her unto me,"
He cries, and straightway they are twain.
Love always will have love again.

——o——

THE FILLET.

Love has a fillet on his eyes,
  He sees not with the common ken;
Whom his fine issues touch despise
  The censures of indifferent men.
There is in love an inward sight,
  That not in wit nor wisdom lies;
He walks in everlasting light,
  Despite the fillet on his eyes.

If I love you, and you love me,
  It is for solid reasons, Sweet,
For something other than we see,
  That satisfies, though incomplete;
Or, if not satisfies, is yet
  Not mutable, where so much dies.
Who love, as we, do not regret
  There is a fillet on love's eyes.

A CATCH.

Was ever yet a man,
Since this old world began,
That looked upon a woman bewitched not of her eyes?
Mating, or separating,
Or loving her, or hating,
In all his commerce with her the fool was never wise.

Heigho! It cannot be,
For seeing she is she,
She has him at advantage, in body, and in mind:
Pursuing, or undoing,
She still compels his wooing,
And therefore is it, ladies, that Love is painted blind!

LOVE.

Love is older than his birth.
So a loving poet sung.
How can he be so old, so young,
Born every hour throughout the earth?
Hearts grow cold,
And bells are tolled;
His heart has never ceased to beat,
Still his feet are dancing feet.

Blazing in his strong right hand
Is the hymeneal torch;
He lights the bridegroom from the porch
To where the priests and altars stand;

Leads the maid,
Who, unafraid,
Passes then from maid to wife,
Knows the secret of her life!

Earth hath kings—he kings them all.
Their rich palaces are his.
They were, and are not, but he is.
He sees great empires rise and fall,
Fall and rise,
With equal eyes;
Nothing disturbs his happy reign,
So our kissing lips remain.

When you press your lips to mine,
What care I for Time or Fate?
Death must pass me by, or wait
For a moment less divine.
Heart to heart,
We cannot part;
Henceforth we breathe immortal breath,
Love is mightier than Death.

——o——

AT LAST.

WHEN first the bride and bridegroom wed,
They love their single selves the best;
A sword is in the marriage bed,
Their separate slumbers are not rest.
They quarrel, and make up again,
They give and suffer worlds of pain.
Both right and wrong,
They struggle long,

Till some good day, when they are old,
Some dark day, when the bells are tolled,
Death having taken their best of life,
  They lose themselves, and find each other;
They know that they are husband, wife,
  For, weeping, they are Father, Mother!

——o——

A DIRGE.

Low lies in dust the honored head,
  Cold is the hand that held the sword;
Slowly we bear them to the dead,
  And lay them down without a word.

What is there to be said, or done?
  They are departed, we remain;
Their race is run, their crowns are won,
  They will not come to us again.

Cut off by fate before their prime
  Could harvest half the golden years,
All they could leave they left us—time,
  All we could give we gave them—tears.

Would they were here, or we were there,
  Or both together, heart to heart.
O death in life, we can not bear
  To be so near—and so apart!

A CARCANET.

NOT what the chemists say they be
  Are pearls—they never grew;
They come not from the hollow sea,
  They come from heaven in dew.

Down in the Indian sea it slips,
  Through green and briny whirls,
Where great shells catch it in their lips,
  And kiss it into pearls.

If dew can be so beauteous made,
  O, why not tears, my girl?
Why not your tears? Be not afraid—
  I do but kiss a pearl!

A ROSE SONG.

WHY are red roses red?
  For roses once were white.
Because the loving nightingales
  Sang on their thorns all night,
Sang till the blood they shed
Had dyed the roses red.

Why are white roses white?
  For roses once were red.
Because the sorrowing nightingales
  Wept when the night was fled,
Wept till their tears of light
Had washed the roses white.

Why are the roses sweet?
  For once they had no scent.
Because one day the Queen of Love
  Who to Adonis went
Brushed them with heavenly feet—
That made the roses sweet!

LILIAN.

All men admire you, even I,
Who like you not, pronounce you fair.
Time was I had not passed you by,
You might have caught me with your hair,
That still is beauteous to behold.
If I should liken it to gold,
I should disparage it, and you,
Which, certes, I could never do.

Go, Lilian, go, but ere you leave,
I must an ancient story tell.
Before our father Adam fell,
Before he saw our mother Eve,
He had a wife, whom God the Lord
Made for his mate when He made him;
Tall as he was, and strong of limb,
Of splendid beauty, stern and cold,
Glorious with golden hair, that rolled
Down to her feet. She was so bold
She stung him into savage ire;
Her sharp tongue cut him like a sword,
Wayward as wind, and fierce as fire.
This woman, Lilith, born his wife,
The torment was of Adam's life.

He left her, as you may conceive,
And God created mother Eve.
You think the serpent tempted her,
And she our father, but you err;
It was Lilith in the serpent, she
It was who tempted with her lies,
(As once you might have tempted me,)
And lost them Paradise!
Nor was her vengeance sated then,
For, devil as she was at birth,
She has gone up and down the earth
Tempting till now the sons of men.
She captives with unholy arts:
Who loves her, dies. We know her dead—
There is a hair from out her head
Twisted around their hearts!

O lady of the golden hair!
Lillian, or Lilith, when I die,
When this poor heart has ceased to beat,
They will not find *you* tangled there,
Nor will they find me at your feet,
For, see, I pass you by.
The hair around my heart that day,
If golden once, will then be gray!

——o——

GOING HOME.

I WENT home with Ludmilla,
  As I very often do;
We sat on the grass together—
  But what is that to you?

Beneath the trees we chatted,
  But not a word of love;
As innocent as children,
  Or the birds that sang above.

I squeezed her little fingers,
  That pressed, methought, my own.
"Ludmilla, O Ludmilla,
  If you were only grown!"

At the cheeks of poor Ludmilla,
  Who turned away her head,
You might have lighted a candle,
  They blushed so red, so red!

"What is it, dear Ludmilla,
  What maiden hopes or fears?"
Her answer to my question
  Was a sudden stream of tears.

"Weep not, weep not, Ludmilla,
  Or let your tears be few:
My heart is constant ever,
  And only beats for you."

The moon stole out of the darkness,
  As bright as bright could be;
She smiled when I kissed my darling,
  And wished that she were she.

We'll meet again to morrow,
  And each the promise made:
Then something rustled near us,
  But we were not afraid.

I went home with Ludmilla,
  Not as I used to do,
For I covered her with kisses—
  But what is that to you?

——o——

AT THE WINDOW.

I SAW him through the window,
  When the new moon was in sight,
Come stealing down the garden,
  One balmy summer night.

He tapped upon the window,
  "Give me a kiss," he said;
And straightway I was hidden,
  Like a little mouse, in bed.

One eye above the bed-clothes
  Was, O, so fast asleep;
But the other beneath—it was lucky
  He was not there to peep.

He called again, as eager
  As the stag for cooling brooks,
Or the bee that in the lilies
  For golden honey looks.

The silence of my chamber—
  It almost made me start,
For nothing there betrayed me,
  But the beating of my heart.

He knocked, and called, and called me,
  And his voice, so clear and sweet,
It pulled away the bed-clothes,
  And stood me on my feet!

It drew me to the window.
  "He must be gone," I thought.
I raised the window softly,
  And peeping out was caught.

Was caught and showered with kisses.
  How many did he get?
As many as my blushes,
  For I am blushing yet!

SORROW AND JOY.

TELL me what is sorrow? It is a garden-bed.
  And what is joy? It is a little rose,
    Which in that garden grows.
 I plucked it in my youth so royal red,
 To weave it in a garland for my head;
 It pricked my hand, I let it drop again,
 And now I look and long for it in vain.

Tell me what is sorrow? It is an endless sea.
  And what is joy? It is a little pearl,
    Round which the waters whirl.
 I dived deep down, they gave it up to me,
 To keep it where my costly jewels be;
 It dazzled me, I let it fall again,
 And now I look and long for it in vain.

Tell me what is sorrow? It is a gloomy cage.
And what is joy? It is a little bird,
Whose song therein is heard.
Opening the door, for I was never sage,
I took it from its perch; with sudden rage
It bit me—bit, I let it go again,
And now I look and long for it in vain.

Tell me when my sorrow shall ended, ended be?
And when return the joy that long since fled?
Not till the garden-bed
Restores the rose; not till the endless sea
Restores the pearl; not till the gloomy cage
Restores the bird; not, poor, old man, till age
Which sorrow is itself, is youth again—
And so I look and long for it in vain!

——o——

IN ALSATIA.

HERE is a friend shall fight for thee,
Be thou good fellow, and under ban.
Where have I met thee? Let me see,
But, tush! what matter? A man's a man.
This is a hand has handled sword,
So fill up thy can, and clink with me;
Out with thy troubles, thou hast my word,
Here is a friend shall fight for thee.

Thirty years man-at-arms was I,
Trailed pike in Flanders, rough work there,
Stormed forts, sacked cities—pass that by,
Also the women dragged by the hair.

There must be soldiers, I suppose,
  So long as kings and peoples be.
Marry, sir, 'tis a world of blows,
  But here is a friend shall fight for thee.

"Free lance, freebooter," runs the song,
  Writ by some skulking clerk, I wot.
I never do peaceful burghers wrong,
  Nor kiss a woman, an she would not.
Never take purse, but from the dead,
  That are long past spending, unlike me,
Who seek not your gold, but good instead,
  For here is the friend shall fight for thee.

What knaves be these? No friends of mine.
  I'll parley with them. What want ye here?
The splash on my ruffle? Pshaw! 'tis wine,
  Will draw on ye, dogs, if you dare come near.
Have at ye, then, without a word,
  Man enough yet for two or three.
Old fellow, thou hast one friend—thy sword,
  For this is the friend that fights for thee!

———o———

THE FLOWN BIRD.

THE maple leaves are whirled away,
  The depths of the great pines are stirred;
Night settles on the sullen day,
  As in its nest the mountain bird.
My wandering feet go up and down,
And back and forth, from town to town,
Through the lone woods, and by the sea,
To find the bird that fled from me.

I followed, and I follow yet,
I have forgotten to forget.

My heart goes back, but I go on,
  Through summer heat, and winter snow;
Poor heart, we are no longer one,
  We are divided by our woe.
Go to the nest I built, and call,
She may be hiding, after all,
The empty nest, if that remains,
And leave me in the long, long rains.
My sleeves with tears are always wet,
I have forgotten to forget.

Men know my story, but not me,
  For such fidelity, they say,
Exists not—such a man as he
  Exists not in the world to-day.
If his light bird has flown the nest,
She is no worse than all the rest;
Constant they are not, only good
To bill and coo, and hatch the brood.
He has but one thing to regret,
He has forgotten to forget.

All day I see the ravens fly,
  I hear the sea-birds scream all night;
The moon goes up and down the sky,
  And the sun comes in ghostly light.
Leaves whirl, white flakes about me blow—
Are they spring blossoms, or the snow?
Only my hair! Good-bye, my heart,
The time has come for us to part.
Be still, you will be happy yet,
For Death remembers to forget!

THE RIVALS.

A KING of a most royal line
  Stood at his gates, as History saith:
He stretched his hand, he made the sign
  To put a captive there to death.

As those who can no further fly
  Turn sharp and grasp the deadly swords,
So the poor wretch about to die
  Abused the king with bitter words.

"What does he say?" the king began,
  To whom his jargon was unknown.
His Vizier, a kind-hearted man,
  Who knew that language like his own,

Answered him, "'O my lord!' he cries,
  'Who stay their hasty hands from blood—
God made for such men Paradise.
  He loves, He will defend the good.'"

The King's great heart was touched at this.
  "The captive's blood shall not be shed."
Then—for a serpent needs must hiss—
  A rival of the Vizier said:

"It is not decorous that we
  Whose blood comes down from noble springs—
No matter what the end may be,
  We should speak truth before our kings.

The man who kneels respited here
  Abused our gracious, clement lord:
There was no blessing, O Vizier,
  There was a curse in every word."

Sternly to him the king: "I see,
  You speak the truth, no doubt; but still
His falsehood better pleaseth me,
  For he meant good, and you mean ill.

If I should punish, as I might,
  (Be thankful that I am not just)
Your head, when I commanded 'Smite!'
  Would roll before me in the dust."

——o——

THE VOICE OF EARTH.

THE Caliph Omar came one summer day
Where one of the great House of Ommeyeh
Was to be borne within the sepulcher,
And, straight commanding not a man should stir,
Went down among the tombs with a loud cry,
And left them wondering there. An hour passed by,
And his attendants waited. Then he came,
Like one whose head is bowed with grief or shame.
Red were his eyes with tears he could not check,
And the great veins were swollen on his neck.
"Commander of the Faithful," then they said,
"What has so long detained you with the dead?"
"I sought their tombs who dearest were," said he,
"Saluted all, but none saluted me.
I turned my back upon them to depart,
And from the Earth a voice that smote my heart

Cried out: 'Omar, why dost not ask of me
Where are the arms, that they salute not thee?'
'What is become of them?' And Earth replied:
'The bands that tied them once have been untied.
The hand, the wrist, the arm, the shoulder-blade,
All now are separated, all decayed.'
Turning my back in terror to depart,
Again the dreadful voice that shook my heart.
Earth called to me once more: 'Omar, Omar!
Why dost not ask me where the bodies are?'
'What is become of them?' And Earth replied:
'What once were bodies lie on every side.
The shoulders parted from the ribs, and they
From the backbone, the hip bones dropped away,
The two thigh bones, the knees, the legs, the feet,
All have departed, never more to meet.'
I turned me for the third time to depart.
Again the same dark voice that crushed my heart:
'Attend to me, Omar. Hast thou no shroud
That wears not out?' And I, with spirit bowed:
'O, what will not wear out?' Earth answered: 'These—
The fear and love of God and his decrees.'"

———o———

SAINT AND SINNER.

A CERTAIN holy anchorite
Who for himself a cave had made,
Comfortless, in the waste Thebaid,
Where, like a wild beast in his den,
He passed a long life far from men,
Untroubled by the hateful sight
Of woman—this old man austere
Fasted, and scourged himself, and prayed,

Renouncing all the world holds dear;
His sole thought being, day and night,
How to find favor in God's eyes,
And thereby enter Paradise.

He led this life threescore and ten
Starved years, puffed up with sanctity.
"Who more a saint?" he thought, and then
Prayed God to show him what saint he
Should emulate to holier be;
Thinking, no doubt, like many now,
Who kneel self-righteously, and pray,
That God would stoop from Heaven, and say:
"There is none holier than thou."

That night God's Angel came to him,
(The sun at noonday would be dim
By the great light that filled the place,)
And said: "If thou in sanctity,
And in the growth of heavenly grace,
Would'st all surpass, thou must do more
Than fast, and scourge thyself, and pray.
Thou must be like, or strive to be,
A certain man; a poet he,
For he upon a pipe doth play,
And sing and beg from door to door."

He heard in great astonishment,
Arose, and took his staff, and went
Wandering the neighboring country round
To find this poet; whom, when found
(He sat a-piping in the sun,
And sang what songs came in his head,)
He questioned earnestly, and said:
"I pray thee, brother, tell me now

What good and great work thou hast done?
What path that holy men have trod,
What fast, what penance, or what vow
Makes thee acceptable to God?"

Ashamed to be so questioned, he
Hung down his head as he replied:
"O, father, do not scoff at me;
I know no good work I have done,
And, as for praying, well-a-day,
I so unworthy am to pray,
That, sinner, I have never tried.
I go from door to door and play,
(You caught me piping in the sun,)
Cheering the simple people there,
Who something for my hunger spare."

The holy man insisted: "Nay,
But in the midst of thy ill life,
(For it is ill, as thou dost say,)
Perhaps some good work thou hast done."
The singer then: "I know of none."

Within the hermit's mind a strife
Now rose—the Angel—who could tell
Whether it were from Heaven or Hell?
"How hast thou," to the poet then,
"Become the beggar that thou art?
Hast thou thy worldly substance spent
In riotous living—women, wine,
Like most that idle craft of thine
Who follow Hellward, sinful men?"

To whom the other, pained at heart,
But not a whit ashamed: "It went

Another way. 'Twas thus. I found
A poor, pale woman, running round
Hither and thither, sick, distraught,
(It pains me to recall it yet,)
Her husband, children had been sold
In slavery to pay a debt.
But she was comely to behold,
So certain sons of Belial sought
Her ruin, whom may God condemn!
Her, weeping, to my hut I brought,
And there protected her from them.
I gave her all that I possessed,
Went with her to the city where
Her wretched husband had been sold,
And her young children; found them there
And brought them back. You guess the rest,
For they are happy as of old.
But what of that? In Heaven's name
What man would not have done the same?"

The hermit, smitten to the heart
At the sad tale of that poor wife,
Wept bitterly, saying: "For my part,
I have not done, in all my life
I thought so holy, so much good.
And thou art so misunderstood,
And yet thou makest no complaint;
And men, because I fast and pray,
While thou upon thy pipe dost play,
They call thee Sinner, and me Saint!"

BRAHMA'S ANSWER.

ONCE when the days were ages,
And the old Earth was young,
The high gods and the sages
From Nature's golden pages
Her open secrets wrung.
Each questioned each to know
When came the Heavens above, and whence the Earth below.

Indra, the endless giver
Of every gracious thing
The gods to him deliver,
Whose bounty is the river
Of which they are the spring,
Indra, with anxious heart,
Ventures with Vivochuno where Brahma is apart.

"Brahma! Supremest Being!
By whom the worlds are made,
Where we are blind, all-seeing,
Stable, where we are fleeing,
Of Life and Death afraid,
Instruct us, for mankind,
What is the body, Brahma! O Brahma, what the mind?"

Hearing as though he heard not,
So perfect was his rest,
So vast the Soul that erred not,
So wise the lips that stirred not,
His hand upon his breast
He laid, whereat his face
Was mirrored in the river that girt that holy Place.

They questioned each the other
What Brahma's answer meant.
Said Vivochuno, "Brother,
Through Brahma the great Mother
Hath spoken her intent,
Man ends as he began—
The shadow on the water is all there is of Man."

"The Earth with woe is cumbered,
And no man understands:
They see their days are numbered
By one that never slumbered,
Nor stayed his dreadful hands,
I see with Brahma's eyes,
The body is the shadow that on the water lies."

Thus Indra, looking deeper,
With Brahma's self possessed.
So dry thine eyes, thou weeper,
And rise again, thou sleeper!
The hand on Brahma's breast
Is his divine assent,
Covering the soul that dies not. This is what Brahma meant.

—o—

HYMNS OF THE MYSTICS.

ROSES I see, the sweetest roses,
As in the cool kiosk I pass,
Tied in a thousand fragrant posies,
And fastened to the roof with grass.

What has bewitched the grass, I wonder?
It is the humblest weed that grows.

How comes it that it sits up yonder
  And on a level with the rose?

"Silence!" The grass said, and in sadness
  Let fall its tears in pearls of dew;
"The generous man robs none of gladness
  And never scorns old friends for new.

I am no rose among the roses,
  And yet there's not a child but knows
That the poor grass that ties these posies
  Is from the Garden of the Rose!"

---o---

THE love I bear you, dearest,
  Would make the prettiest tale,
If I had for a pen to write it
  The bill of a nightingale.

And what should I have for paper?
  I know what would be best:
Each page should be a rose-leaf,
  As snow white as your breast.

And with such pen and paper
  What ink should then be mine?
Tears—when I wrote of my sorrow,
  When I wrote of my pleasure—wine!

---o---

"THE flying of the arrow
    In the air;
  The shifting of the shuttle
    In the loom;

The sinking of the water
  In the sand;
The passing from the cradle
  To the tomb;
Tell me, Sufi, tell me, is it all?

What the bow that shoots us
  Into life?
Where the loom that throws us
  To and fro?
Whose the hands that spills us
  Into death?
What in the making mars us
  Here below?
O tell me, tell me, Sufi, what it is!"

"I see the arrow flying,
  Not what sends it,
The bow that shoots it hither,
  And who bends it;
I see the shuttle shifting,
  Not what throws it,
The weaver who begun it,
  And will close it;
I see the water sinking,
  Not what spills it;
The emptied pitcher filling,
  And who fills it;
But where the arrow flieth,
  And what the loom is weaving,
  And where the water sinketh,
    I do not see at all.
What in the cradle lieth,
And what it is that thinketh,
And what it is that dieth,

The living and the leaving,
I do not know at all.
Perhaps it is not, Hadje,
Perhaps it does but seem :
The shadow of a vanished cloud
On a troubled stream ;
What some Power remembers—the Phantom of its Dream !"

——o——

THEIR names who famous were of old
Are antiquated ; long ago
Camillus, Cæsar, Scipio
Were with forgotten men enrolled.
Augustus, Hadrian, Antonine,
There is an end to all the line.
Where is the hand that grasped the sword ?
The brow that wore the diadem ?
Let the grave answer, if it can ;
Speak, speak, thou dust that once was man !
The hollow grave returns no word,
Oblivion long has buried them.
This fate is theirs, and this alone,
Who in a wondrous way have shone.
For all the rest, who go to death,
As soon as they breathe out their breath,
They are gone—pursuit of them is vain,
And no man speaks of them again.
Since all is dust, then, what remains
That should employ our serious pains ?
Just thoughts, as if the gods were by,
Good deeds, and words which never lie :
A disposition that receives,
Accepts what happens, and believes

The hidden spring from which it flows,
The distant sea to which it goes,
Though by no mortal understood,
Is necessary, wise, and good.
Great names have perished; this survives,
And shapes the issue of our lives.

---o---

TRUST not fortune. She will be
Everything but true to thee.
False and fickle all her life,
The old dame has been the wife
Of a thousand bridegrooms—none
Mourned a day when he was gone.
She delights to desolate,
Very bitter is her hate;
And she hates most when she knows
There are those who scorn her, those
Who rejoice in better things
Than the baubles that she brings,
Conqueror's laurel, crown of kings!
To reject these and be wise
Is a folly in her eyes;
To be good is worse than this,
Since it shows her what she is,
And that she is baffled, too;
For what is there she can do
To the good and to the wise,
Who her earthly dross despise,
For their hearts are in the skies,
Where their heavenly treasure lies!

---o---

MEN seek retreats, and some retire
To country houses; mountains these
Affect, and those the shore of seas:
Thou, too, dost such things much desire.
This is a mark of common men,
Which thou, desiring, shouldst refuse.
There is for thee, when thou shalt choose,
Deeper retirement. Have it, then.
Retire into thyself; nowhere
With greater quiet, lesser care
Than in his own soul man can be,
The seat of all tranquillity;
For rest is nothing else, I find,
Than the good ordering of the mind.
Give, then, thyself to this retreat
Constantly, and thyself renew;
And let thy principles be few,
But like the earth beneath thy feet
Solid, and like the Heaven serene,
For these will keep thy spirit clean.
It will return not as it went,
But free from every discontent.

Desire of the thing called Fame,
The petty wish to leave a name,
Perhaps torments thee. It should not.
See how soon all things are forgot,
Things that are mean and things sublime.
The chaos of unending time
Stretches before thee and behind:
Behold it with a stable mind.
Know that applause is empty; know
That who pretend to give thee praise
Hold not the same mind many days;
And for the praise that flatters so,

Think of the narrowness of the space
That circumscribes it. For the earth,
The whole earth, is a point, and small
The nook that is thy dwelling-place;
And few are in it; and from birth
They hasten deathward, one and all.
Who are these men, and what their ways,
That thou shouldst hanker for their praise?

What, then, remains? This there remains,
This territory of thine own.
Retire into it, be alone,
Dismiss what now disturbs, or pains;
Be strong—you may, be free—you can,
And look at all things like a man;
For know that things, or great or small,
Do never touch the soul at all.
And know that all which thou dost see
Changes and will no longer be.
Nothing endures, O Lord, but Thee!

———o———

WHAT harmonious is with thee,
O Universe! is so with me,
Nothing too early, or too late,
That is at thy appointed date.
Everything is fruit to me,
  Which thy seasons, Nature, bring:
All things from thee, and all in thee,
  To thee returneth everything.
"Dear city of Cecropia,"
  The poet said its streets who trod:
Wilt thou not say—be wise and say—
  "Dear city of the living God!"

———o———

THOUGH thou shouldst live a thousand years,
Whatever fate gives,
Or what refuses,
Let this support thee in thy fears,
Let this console thee in thy tears,
Man loses but the life he lives,
And only lives the life he loses.
Longest and shortest are but one:
The present is the same to all;
The past is done with and forgot;
The future is not yet begun;
Nothing from either can befall,
For none can lose what he has not.
All things from all Eternity
Come round and round the whirling spheres;
It makes no difference if we see
The same things for a hundred years,
Or for a million. They are here.
Who longest lives, who shortest dies,
Loses the same sweet earth and skies,
For they remain—we disappear.

———o———

PAIN and pleasure both decay,
Wealth and poverty depart;
Wisdom makes a longer stay,
Therefore, be thou wise, my heart.

Land remains not, nor do they
Who the lands to-day control.
Kings and princes pass away,
Therefore, be thou fixed, my soul.

If by hatred, love, or pride
  Thou art shaken, thou art wrong;
Only one thing will abide,
  Only goodness can be strong.

---o---

THE whole of this great world, I say,
  From the first to the last born,
Since it passes swift away,
  Is not worth a barley-corn.

To some better world than this
  Hie thee—open wide the door
To some chamber—such there is—
  Whence thou shalt depart no more.

---o---

WHEN the drum of sickness beats
  The change o' th' watch, and we are old,
Farewell youth, and all its sweets,
  Fires gone out that leave us cold!

Hairs are white that once were black,
  Each of fate the message saith;
And the bending of the back
  Salutation is to death.

---o---

TO bear what is, to be resigned,
The mark is of a noble mind.

Stir not thy hand, or foot, or heart,
Be not disturbed, for Destiny
Is more attached, O man, to thee
    Than to thyself thou art!
If patience had but been thy guest,
  Thy destined portion would have come,
And like a lover on thy breast
  Have flung itself, and kissed thee dumb!

———o———

WHY should man struggle early, late,
When all he is is fixed by Fate?

For everything that comes and goes,
Goes, comes at its appointed date.

The wind is measured as it blows,
The grains of sand have each their weight.

Only the fool can say he chose
The woman that is now his mate.

And so with friends and so with foes,
The rising and the falling State.

'Tis idle to support, oppose,
To open or to shut the gate.

What is we see; but no one knows
What was, or will be, small or great.

Nothing is certain but the close,
And that is hid from us by Fate.

———o———

OLD Bishop Ivo met one day,
  As he went up and down the lands,
A stern, sad woman on her way,
  With fire and water in her hands;
In this hand water, that hand fire,
And she was filled with holy ire.

"What mean those symbols, Mother, tell?
  And whither go you?" She replies:
"To quench with this the flames of Hell,
  With this to burn up Paradise.
Fear, hope must nevermore be known,
But man serve God through love alone."

———o———

THE carver thought, the carver wrought,
  There was a rapture in his mood;
He saw Our Lady in his thought,
  And wrought upon the sandal wood.
His hand would not obey his will,
It faltered and forgot its skill.
"No one will say who sees that face,
'Hail, Mary Mother, full of grace!'"

He dropped his tools, he bowed his head,
  He heard a voice that somewhere spoke:
"Go, burn the sandal-wood," it said,
  "And work upon that block of oak.
What one holds not the other may,
The image may be there to-day."
It was, and all who saw her face
Said, "Mary Mother, full of grace!"

———o———

THERE was of old a Moslem saint
 Named Rabia. On her bed she lay
Pale, sick, but uttered no complaint.
 "Send for the holy men to pray."
And two were sent. The first drew near:
"The prayers of no man are sincere
Who does not bow beneath the rod,
And bear the chastening strokes of God."
Whereto the second, more severe:
"The prayers of no man are sincere
Who does not in the rod rejoice,
And make the strokes he bears his choice."
Then she, who felt that in such pain
The love of self did still remain,
Answered: "No prayers can be sincere
 When they from whose wrung hearts they fall
Are not as I am, lying here,
 Who long since have forgotten all.
Dear Lord of Love! There is no pain."
So Rabia, and was well again.

———o———

SAID IBN ABI WAKKOO, whose strong bow
Laid from afar the Prophet's foemen low,
So sure his arrows in their deadly flight,
Was smitten in his age with loss of sight.
As he was led to Mecca, on the way
The men he passed entreated him to pray
To God for them. Whereat his nephew spake,
Feeling great pity for his blindness' sake:
"Uncle, to-day make one thing clear to me.
Thou prayest for others, and God heareth thee;
Why dost thou, then, remain in this thy night?
Why not implore Him to restore thy sight?"

"Son of my brother," with a smile he said,
And laid his hand upon the stripling's head,
"If I see not, God sees, and His decree
Is dearer than the eyes with which I used to see."

———o———

THERE came to Nushervan, surnamed the Just,
A certain man, a courtier, with the dust
Of travel on him, and with heart elate.
"I hear," he said, "that God (His Name be Great!)
Has taken from the world your mortal foe,"
Naming a king whom death had then laid low.
"And did you hear," the Sultan made reply,
"That I am overlooked, and not to die?
I have no room for exultation, friend,
For, like my rival's life, my life must end."
The courtier slunk away, abashed and sad,
For he had learned that good news may be bad.

———o———

LET me a simple tale repeat,
As Sadi wrote it. Thus it ran:
His servants, at a hunting seat,
Were roasting game for Nushervan,
And, as they had no salt there, one
Was sent unto a village near
To fetch some. Ere the man could run,
The Sultan called him back. "Come here.
Take it at a fair price, and see
There is no force, lest there should be
A precedent established so,
Which might the village overthrow."

They asked what damage could ensue
From such a trifle. Whereupon
He answered: "When the race was new
Oppressions were but small and few;
But as the years went on and on
Every new comer added more,
And each was larger than before,
Till what was small had grown so great
It toppled o'er on many a State,
And crushed the people unto dust.
We must be just." And from that day,
Sadi, I think, goes on to say,
They surnamed Nushervan the Just.

———o———

He needs a guide no longer
  When he hath found the way
That leads already to the Friend;
  He cannot go astray.

He need not search for ladders
  To climb with feet and hands,
When on the topmost dome of heaven
  His soul already stands.

No messenger nor letter
  He needs, when he at rest
Lies folded close in favor
  Upon the Sultan's breast.
Rumi, thou needest nothing more,
  For what thou hast is best.

———o———

" How many, many centuries,
When Death's long sleep has closed my eyes,
Mankind will walk above my head,
And I shall never hear their tread.
My kingdom as it came will go,
  Another will possess my lands;
They passed from hand to hand, and so
  Will pass from mine to other hands."

This verse was written long ago
Upon the crown of Kai Khosro.

———o———

WALKING along the shore one morn,
  A holy man by chance I found,
Who by a tiger had been torn,
  And had no salve to heal his wound.
Long time he suffered grievous pain,
  But not the less to the Most High
  He offered thanks. They asked him why?
For answer he thanked God again;
And then to them: " That I am in
  No greater peril than you see,
  That what has overtaken me
Is but misfortune—and not sin."

———o———

"SHALL we, O Master," Ke Loo said,
" Still serve the spirits of the dead?"
" To serve the dead why should we strive,
Who could not serve them when alive?"

"Tell me what death is," said Ke Loo.
  To whom again Confucius saith:
"While life we do not, cannot know,
  What can we hope to know of death?"
And further, since he still would seek:
"Ke Loo, I do not care to speak."

"If you, the Master, speak not, then,
What shall your scholars say to men?"
"Does Heaven speak?" the sage replied,
And as he spoke his spirit sighed:
"The seasons run their endless ways,
  The days go by with tireless wing,
And all things come in all the days,
  But Heaven—does Heaven say anything?"

THOMAS MOORE.

(*May* 28, 1879.)

A LORD of lyric song was born
  A hundred years ago to-day;
Loved of that race that long has worn
  The shamrock for the bay.

He sung of wine, and sung of flowers,
  Of woman's smile, and woman's tear,
Light songs, that suit our lighter hours,
  But O, how bright and dear!

Who will may build the epic verse,
  And, Atlas-like, its weight sustain;
Or solemn tragedies rehearse
  In high, heroic strain.

So be it. But when all is done,
  The heart demands for happy days
The lyrics of Anacreon,
  And Sappho's tender lays.

Soft souls with these are satisfied.
  He loved them, but exacted more,
For his the lash that Horace plied,
  The sword Harmodius wore.

Where art thou, Brian, and thy knights,
  So dreaded by the flying Dane?
And thou, Con of the Hundred Fights?
  Your spirits are not slain!

Strike for us, as ye did of yore,
  Be with us, we shall conquer still,
Though Irish kings are crowned no more
  On Tara's holy hill.

Perhaps he was not hero born,
  Like those he sung—Heaven only knows;
He had the rose without the thorn,
  But he deserved the rose.

For underneath its odorous light
  His heart was warm, his soul was strong;
He kept his love of Country bright,
  And sung her sweetest song.

Therefore her sons have gathered here
  To honor him, as few before,
And blazon on his hundredth year
  The fame of Thomas Moore.

SALVE, REGINA.

THE race of greatness never dies.
Here, there, its fiery children rise,
Perform their splendid parts,
And captive take our hearts.

Men, women of heroic mould
Have overcome us from of old;
Crowns waited then, as now,
For every royal brow.

The victor in the Olympian Games—
His name among the proudest names
Was handed deathless down:
To him the olive crown.

And they, the poets, grave and sage,
Stern masters of the tragic stage,
Who moved by art austere
To pity, love, and fear—

To these was given the laurel crown,
Whose lightest leaf conferred renown
That through the ages fled
Still circles each gray head.

But greener laurels cluster now,
World-gathered, on his spacious brow,
In his supremest Place,
Greatest of their great race—

Shakespeare! Honor to him, and her
Who stands his grand interpreter,
Stepped out of his broad page
Upon the living stage.

The unseen hands that shape our fate
Moulded her strongly, made her great,
And gave her for her dower
Abundant life and power.

To her the sister Muses came,
Proffered their masks, and promised fame;
She chose the tragic—rose
To its imperial woes.

What queen unqueened is here? What wife,
Whose long bright years of loving life
Are suddenly darkened? Fate
Has crushed, but left her great.

Abandoned for a younger face,
She sees another fill her place,
Be more than she has been—
Most wretched wife and queen!

O royal sufferer! Patient heart!
Lay down thy burdens and depart;
"Mine eyes grow dim. Farewell."
They ring her passing-bell.

And thine, thy knell shall soon be rung,
Lady, the valor of whose tongue,
That did not urge in vain,
Stung the irresolute Thane

To bloody thoughts and deeds of death,
The evil genius of Macbeth;
    But thy strong will must break,
    And thy poor heart must ache.

Sleeping, she sleeps not; night betrays
The secret that consumes her days.
    Behold her where she stands,
    And rubs her guilty hands.

From darkness, by the midnight fire,
Withered and weird, in wild attire,
    Starts spectral on the scene
    The stern, old gipsy queen.

She croons her simple cradle song,
She will redress his ancient wrong—
    The rightful heir come back
    With Murder on his track.

Commanding, crouching, dangerous, kind,
Confusion in her darkened mind,
    The pathos of her years
    Compels the soul to tears.

Bring laurels! Go, ye tragic Three,
And strip the sacred laurel-tree,
    And at her feet lay down
    Here, now, a triple crown.

Salve, Regina! Art and Song,
Dismissed by thee, shall miss thee long,
    And keep thy memory green,
    Our most illustrious Queen.

DIES NATALIS CHRISTI.

Not as of old they came,
With harp and flute, and the shrill sistrum's ring,
Before the chariot of their dusky king,
What time the Sun a-flame
From winter's gloomy solstice did appear,
To light the torches of the coming Year;
With whom the priests, with banner and with shrine,
Past shapes colossal, Sphinx and Pyramid,
And what therein is hid,
The dust of early kings, or lore divine,
Following the morn in slow procession while
The sacred singers clap their hands
Where great Osiris' statue stands,
Who, lost, is found, and guards again the Nile,
Marking the rhythm of that rejoicing chorus
Wherewith they celebrate the birth of Horus,
The son of god Osiris, the happy infant Horus!

Nor as the Magi went,
Before the dawn of Day,
And clomb the mountains from whose steep ascent
They caught the earliest ray,
In robes as spotless as their own desire,
Who silver censers bore, where burned the Sacred Fire.
Lo, in his ivory car,
Like some white cloud inlaid with morning's gold,
The haughty Persian monarch borne in state,
On whom his nobles wait,
Fierce satraps tamed of old,
Mounted upon their camels whose trappings blaze afar.

The summit reached, all faces toward the East,
Puts on his wreathed tiara the High-Priest,
And standing reverent there,
Welcomes the rising sun with incense and with prayer.
"Glory to Ormuzd!" all the Magi sing;
"The Just Judge! The All-Seeing!
The Centre of all Being!
The Universal King!
To Mithras, salutation!
The Never-Sleeping, Most-Exalted One,
Who from the golden watch-tower of the sun
Beholds his fair creation!
Created and Creator,
Mithras, Mediator,
Between the Good and Ill, perpetual Mediator!"

Nor as the sterner race,
Who, many gods adoring, most adored
The strong and cruel master of the sword,
Dread Mars, who drove their legions o'er the earth,
Consented for a space
To stoop to harmless mirth.
Rank, like the robe it wore, was laid aside,
Master and slave changed places,
And slaves, with happy faces,
Went strutting round the streets in sudden pride,
Each with the freedman's cap upon his head,
Aping patrician airs, and richly garmented.
The slave was master now,
The master waited on his slave,
What he demanded gave,
Brought wine when he commanded, and chaplets for his brow.
Gifts were exchanged, they loved who late had hated,
The useless sword was sheathed, old feuds were ended,

Prisoners were liberated,
And labor was suspended:
The lowest lorded like the best,
Enjoyed his scurril jest,
Nor was imperial Cæsar's self offended.
Equal, as in the years of old,
When gracious Saturn ruled mankind,
And Earth, untilled, brought forth the yellow corn,
And all the gods were of one mind,
Before the evil days were born,
The happy Age of Gold!
To Saturn's temple all repair,
"O Father Saturn, hear our prayer!
Hear, and help, and bring again
The old Saturnian reign,
Gracious Father Saturn, the glad Saturnian reign!"

With other rites the Wise Men of the East,
Prophet, and King, and Priest,
Girded their loins, and hasted from afar,
Led by the light of that auspicious Star
From Sabæan altars to Jerusalem,
Where Herod asked of them,
"Whence are ye come, and why?"
And spirits not their own their tongues unloose:
"Where is He who is born King of the Jews?
We have beheld His planet in the sky,
And come to worship Him."
Then Herod, troubled, called the Sanhedrim:
"Where shall this Child be born, this King appear?"
"From Bethlehem, in Judæa,
A Governor shall come, as seers foretell,
To rule my chosen people, Israel."
The Wise Men tarry not; for now the Day
Draws down the West, and in the darkening East

Hovers the watchful Star whose light increased
To guide them on their way.
They followed where it led,
Till o'er the Infant's head,
Who wrapt in swaddling bands in a manger lay,
It stood, and filled the place—
Or was it from His face
That more than Light that turned the Night to Day?
They knelt. The holy Child
Stretched out His hands, and smiled,
And took their gifts, gold, frankincense, and myrrh:
Love, awe, divine surprise
Were in His mother's eyes,
As if again the Angel spake to her.
The shepherds ran to see
What the great light might be,
Leaving their flocks untended on the plain,
And what the heavenly song,
So sweet, so clear, so strong,
Of which they did but catch the glad refrain,
Not heard on earth till then,
"Good-will and peace to men!
Glory to God on high! Good-will and peace to men!"

This is the Child foretold
By seers and prophets old;
Of whom, in the beginning, it was said,
The Woman's seed shall bruise the Serpent's head.
Nor was the gracious promise once forgot,
Though man remembered not;
For when the tribes of Israel went astray,
Bowing to other gods that could not save,
Their young men captive, and their strong men slain,
Disconsolate they turned to Him again,
He did not turn away,

But, full of mercy, still the promise gave,
            The Comforter to them.
There shall come forth a rod on Jesse's stem,
  A branch from out his roots. And He shall be
To those who dwell in darkness a great light,
            A spirit of counsel and might
  That shall subdue, enlighten, and set free.
            And Earth, rejoiced, shall see,
Outgrown its ancient hate, that love is best,
  Nor to the weak the strong be terrible;
  Together then the wolf and lamb shall dwell,
The leopard and the kid lie down to rest,
  And a little child shall lead them. This is He.
And He shall judge the nations, and rebuke
            The warring sons of men;
  Swords shall be beaten into plowshares then,
The murderous spear into the pruning-hook;
  Nor sword nor spear uplifted as before,
            For War shall be no more!
        Zion, awake, arise, unloose thy bands!
Arise, put on thy strength, be not cast down!
Put on thy beautiful garments and thy crown,
            And stretch thy sceptred hands
            Above the subject lands,
            Revered, beloved of them,
No captive but a Queen, supreme Jerusalem!
The City of God on Earth! Divine Jerusalem!

            Not like a king He came,
  With princes and the powerful of the Earth
        Gathered around his Virgin Mother's bed,
        While priestly hands are laid upon His head,
  And heralds through the land proclaim His birth,
        And all the happy people shout His name.
            Only the Wise Men knew,

The Wise Men and the shepherds kneeling round,
Immanuel was found,
The Prince of Peace, who should the Kings of Earth subdue!
These, and the host above,
Who sang the hymn of love,
That rose triumphant then,
"Good-will and peace to men!
God has come down on Earth! Good-will and peace to men!"

——o——

THE MASQUE OF THE THREE KINGS.

I.

[*Before the Inn at Bethlehem. The Shepherds.*]

First Shepherd.

WHAT men be these in brave array!
And who be they that follow them?
They ride before the break of day,
And soon will halt at Bethlehem.

Second Shepherd.

I know them not, but I can see
That they are strangers, and, I guess,
Of noble lineage. They should be
Kings, or the sons of kings—no less.

Third Shepherd.

It may be they have gone astray,
And did not mean to come this way.
I will accost them at the gate,
Hear what they say, and set them straight.
[*Enter the three Kings.*
Hail, Masters, hail!

First King.

And who be ye
That meet us here? We looked to meet
The elders who should wash our feet
And offer hospitality;
Not shepherd swains, with homely looks,
Whose only sceptres are their crooks.

First Shepherd.

True, we are shepherds, nor the first
This city on the hill hath nursed;
For once the Flower of Jesse's Stem
Tended his flocks at Bethlehem.
Thence were we honored in the Past,
And henceforth shall be honored more
Than ever shepherds were before,
For we have seen it all at last.

Second King.

What mean ye, shepherds?

Second Shepherd.

Hear, O King!
Give ear unto a wondrous thing.
We sat and watched our flocks last night,
When suddenly the heavens were bright,
As though a thousand mornings shone.
Amid that Light we saw a Throne,
But not Who sat thereon. Below
We saw the angels come and go,
Glorious and gracious to behold,
With shining wings and harps of gold.
They touched their harps, and sung a song,

So low and sweet, so loud and strong,
One might live on it his whole life long.
We knew not half the angels sung,
For it was in an unknown tongue;
But the refrain thereof was plain,
(O, may it never cease again!)
"Glory to God!" it ran, and then,
"Good will on earth, and peace to men!"

Third King.

And this was all?

Third Shepherd.

A Star now stood
Above the heavenly multitude,
Higher than the highest ever trod,
But far below the feet of God.
A moment stood, then settled down
And rested over Bethlehem town,
Whereto there came, as rumor saith,
Along the road from Nazareth,
A man and woman, travelling slow.
They reach the Inn, but find the door
Fastened. There is no room for more.
Where shall the way-worn travellers go?
Only the stable-floor remains,
A stall for chamber, straw for bed,
Where he may rest his weary head,
And she endure her mother-pains.

This is the stable. Enter ye
And greet the Holy Family.

II.

[*In the Stable. Joseph, Mary, the Child Jesus, and the Three Kings.*]

Joseph.

Pray who are ye that thus molest
Poor travellers in their nightly rest?

First King.

Sir, take it not amiss that we
Have come unbidden unto thee,
From the depth of distant lands,
Over mountains, over sands,
Seeking a Child, whose birth, foretold
By seers and oracles of old,
Has long been sought, and promised near.
We followed his Star, and it led us here.

Joseph.

But who are ye, whose looks declare
That not of common folk ye are?
For, peering at ye closely now,
I see a crown on every brow.

First King.

I am Balthazar. My race,
Strong in war and swift in chase,
Was the first of old to trace
Motions of the stars in Space—
What surrounds the Sun's broad track,
Mystery of the Zodiac.
These things to know, not Heaven to dare,
Nor its jealous Power to share,

Did Nimrod build his tower on high.
Of his imperious seed am I,
King of Chaldea, Balthazar,
Who have sought thee from afar,
Following thy Child's bright Star,
Bringing, as a king may bring,
A present worthy of a king,
("King of Jews" they say He is,
But Herod likes it not, I wis,)
This censer, such the Magi swing
In my temple, fetched from thence,
Filled with precious frankincense.

Second King.

I Melchior am, whose kingdom stands
Beyond the swart Egyptian lands,
Under the glare of burning skies,
Nubia, which barren sands enclose,
Save where the lordly current flows
Of Nilus, and my mountains rise
Along the rim of the Red Sea.
Such treasuries no king save me
Had ever. Gold from base to crown,
There is not a river but washes it down!
I fetch thee gold. This wedge behold.

Joseph.

Ah, that is something like, now—gold!

Third King.

I am Caspar. Your wise king,
Solomon o' th' Magic Ring,
Hearing of my rocky shores,
Rich in gold and silver ores,

Sent his ships across the seas,
That they should laden be with these,
So his workmen might adorn
His great Temple, wall and floor;
And what precious stones are worn
On the High Priest's breastplate, where
They flash out their imprisoned fire
On the purple stuffs of Tyre
Which are the curtains. Furthermore,
Tusks of ivory white as milk,
And curious, broidered robes of silk,
For his concubines to wear,
Making fairer what was fair.
These I do not offer, sir;
But instead a box of myrrh.

Joseph.

That, too, is something; for they say
Its healing properties are sure.
Moreover, if it fails to cure,
It leads to death the easiest way.
Nay, still is potent; for when death
Has robbed a man of his last breath,
And shut the doorways of the head,
We use it to embalm the dead.

Mary.

The pain is ended
Before the morn:
By none attended,
The child was born.
He lies asleep in these arms of mine,
In this poor stable, among the kine.

If what was spoken
  Should not be true,
My heart is broken,
  My Son, for you:
For never till now, since the world begun,
Has a virgin mother borne a son.

But my soul rejoices,
  For, hark, I hear
The heavenly Voices,
  Far off and near.
They sing in my soul as they sing in the sky—
Lord, what a happy mother am I.

No great king's daughter
  So happy is
When they have brought her
  Her child to kiss;
No matter from whom his lineage springs,
For thou, my Son, art the King of kings!

First King.

He stretches out his little hand,
Like one accustomed to command;
He lifts three fingers. There must be
A sacred mystery in Three.

Second King.

But the night is going,
The cock is crowing,
The beasts are stirring in the stall;
We must away
Before the day,
Lest Herod should discover all.

For he is crafty, and I fear
His messenger has dogged us here.

[*Exeunt the Three Kings.*

[ENTER SATHANAS.

Sathanas.

The kings have gone, with all their train,
But not to Herod's court again.
He will be very wroth with them,
And all the folk in Bethlehem;
For he determined has to slay
All children that are born to-day.
Weep, Rachel, for your children slain!
But *one* shall live. It suits me not
This Child should perish with the rest;
Though death upon his mother's breast,
Methinks, were better than the lot
Which I perceive is his. For he
Hath been delivered unto me
To work my will on. Child, prepare,
For I shall tempt thee everywhere—
The heavy burden thou must bear,
The awful doubt that follows thy prayer.
I bring not incense, gold, nor myrrh,
For I am not thy worshipper;
But, not to be behind these Kings,
So lavish with their offerings,
I have torn from Eden's Tree
A slip, and planted it for thee,
On the hill of Calvary.
Thou shalt be nailed upon it there,
By Roman soldiers, high in the air,
With a crown of thorns for a diadem,
And die in sight of Jerusalem.

The Child Jesus.

Get thee behind me, Satan—so.
I know thee, and myself I know.
What thou hast threatened will befall;
A part thou seest, but not all—
Else thou wouldst worship. Nay, thou dost,
And worshipping thou art not lost;
Saved by Him thou hast withstood,
For thou art Evil—He is Good.

——o——

A CHRISTMAS CAROL.

Of all the merry days of old,
  When merry days did most abound,
When cups were drained, and catches trolled,
  And hearty healths went round,
The best was Christmas, all the rest
But ushers to this royal Guest.

Before he came, from out the wood
  The log was dragged with noisy mirth;
With last year's brand the baron stood
  Beside the blazing hearth:
Bring in the Yule log! Light it—more—
Now let the wide old chimney roar!

Within the hall, with ivy hung,
  They gather, laughing, high and low;
And maids are kissed, if they be young,
  Beneath the mistletoe.
If Care appears each thirsty soul
Will drown it in the wassail bowl.

He comes—he's here! Let dinner wait
  Until the silver trumpets sound.
The boar's head is borne in in state,
  With rosemary garlands crowned.
They sing—how does the burden go?
Qui estis in convivio.

What suited feudal days and men
  Suits not a later day and race;
Rank has abased itself since then,
  Gone is the pride of place.
Except when nature makes them so,
There is no longer high and low.

Put off the crown, put up the sword,
  Abhorrent to the heart and mind;
His equal spirit has restored
  The manhood of mankind.
Wisely we celebrate His birth,
The benefactor of the Earth.

Wisely and gladly. What was best
  Of that old Christmas time is here:
The merry heart, the ready jest,
  The hospitable cheer.
Welcome to all, the rich, the poor,
Welcome the beggar at the door.

But merrier be; the children hear,
  They must not hear a sigh to-day;
Dear hearts, they must not see a tear,
  But laugh, and romp, and play.
Gayly the Christmas Eve began
With many a little maid and man.

Looked forward to for days before,
  And dreamed about at night, it comes;
They gather at the guarded door,
  And their hearts beat like drums.
The door is now flung back, they see,
O sight of sights—the Christmas Tree!

Green as if wet with summer dew,
  And fairies there did late carouse,
Loaded with toys as if they grew
  On its enchanted boughs,
And lighted candles—what can be
More beauteous than the Christmas Tree?

The children of the poor that night
  Hang up their stockings by the bed,
For Santa Claus will surely light
  Upon the roof o'erhead,
And stealing in the chamber share
His gifts among the sleepers there.

Be merrier, merrier, young and old,
  Let nothing cloud this happy day.
Chime, bells, as if ye never tolled!
  And golden moments stay!
Fold, fold your wings, delay your flight,
Prolong this hallowed day and night.

Beneath the cross, beneath the spire,
  Wherever Christian people meet,
Around the cheerful household fire,
  Along the crowded street,
Blessing has fallen, and prayers forgot
Have risen from hearts that knew it not.

Prepare the feast. Unlock the bin,
  Bring out to-night the generous wine;
Bring flowers, and have the children in
  When you sit down to dine.
Prepare yourselves, put on your best,
To honor every Christmas guest.

The dinner waits, and so do we;
  Your arm—this way—find each his place;
The smile on every lip shall be
  Received as silent grace.
Be seated all, draw up, and then
Fall to like valiant trenchermen.

This turkey is a royal one,
  A king on this alone might dine;
The wine—but taste it—bright the sun
  That ripened this good wine:
A little for the children, Dear,
For Christmas comes but once a year.

John, Master George will take some wine;
  Be careful of that lady's dress;
Mother, the children think it fine,
  Behold their happiness!
Fill up, for bumpers now I call,
"A health to all! God bless us all!"

We are happy. Would that every heart
  In this great city, all the poor
Who herd together, hide apart,
  The wronged, the evil-doer,
The desperate who shun the light,
O would that these were so to-night!

For they are men; the worst are men,
  And they must live, and they must die.
Look kindly down upon them, then,
  Our Father, and be nigh.
Thy hand is strong to help, to save,
Thou art their Judge beyond the grave!

Be pitiful: they must be fed:
  O entertain these guests of thine!
Give these, thy hungry children, bread,
  Their water turn to wine!
Make them as happy as Thou art,
O Love Divine! Paternal Heart!

A WEDDING UNDER THE DIRECTORY.

In the French Republic, second year,
    About the first of May,
    A wedding party went on their way
  Under the newly budded trees
  In the Garden of the Tuileries,
That was crowded far and near;
    And old, and young,
    They chatted and sung,
For the wind was mild, and the weather was clear.
This newly wedded groom and bride
Strolled slowly homeward side by side,
He holding her reticule and fan,
And counting himself a happy man,
She thinking herself a happy wife,
And Buddal the brightest season of life.
O, she was fair in her long white dress
  Of silk, or satin—who cares which now?

With her yellow curls low down on her brow,
Under her flowing bridal veil,
That made her look just a trifle pale,
Pure as the rose-bud in her breast,
(Ah, little bird, to have such a nest
A picture of perfect loveliness!

What do you think of your Aucassin,
O beautiful Nicolette?
He is brave without, and good within,
And he will never forget.
Life is rosy with him to-day,
As he struts along with your big bouquet,
And his jaunty hat—no cockade there!
(Does he think of the 13th Vendimaire?
No, he lives, so he was away,
Or was *not* in the Rue St. Honoré!)
Do you guess what songs are singing within
The half-turned head of your Aucassin?
Hearken, and you will hear
In your inner ear:
"*Ma mie,*
Ma douce amie,
Réponds à mes amours.
Fidèle
A cette belle
Je t'aimerai toujours."

What do you think of your Nicolette,
O Citoyen Aucassin?
Without a coy rose-bud coquette,
She's as chaste as a lily within!
The sprays above her are not so sweet,
Nor the day so debonair,
As she with her delicate, noiseless feet

Tripping from stair to stair.
You lucky fellow, you have on your arm
A loving, confiding, perfect charm!
"*Tra la! tra la!*" her light heart goes
As she trips and skips on the tip of her toes.
Her slippers were made by Bourdon: her hair
Was dressed by Léonard—*Peste!* Why do you smile?
I know his style,
And, as Buffon says, the style is the man,
The Citoyenne's is *à la Persane.*
Do you know what pretty chansonette
Runs through the head of your Nicolette?
"*Je le veux; car c'est la raison*
Que je sois maître en ma maison."
(That elderly person looking this way
Wrote that *vieille ronde gauloise*—Beaumarchais.
He is lifting his hat. "*Merci, M'sieu.*")
Such is the song she is singing to you:
But deeper down, where her feelings are,
She is crooning the dirge of the queen of Navarre,
(See that she does it never!)
"*Je n'ay plus ny père, ny mère,*
Ny sœur, ny frère."
Here she sighs,
And looks in your eyes,
And hopes you will love her forever!

What do you think of the happy pair,
O saucy, pert Dorine?
You only think that you are fair,
And you know you love to be seen.
You have no heart, but plenty of art,
And you flatter yourself that you are smart—
Don't be so quick,
It is my vile English—"*Tu est chic!*"

You are wearing a love of a hat, Dorine,
And what dainty satin shoes!
Whose miniature is that, Dorine,
On your little white neck?
Do you run at his beck?
But remember you still have something to lose.
She heeds me not—she is lost, not won,
And is singing a song of Villon:
"Dictes moy, ou ne en quel pays
Est Flora la belle Romaine,
Archipiada, ne Thais
Qui fut sa cousine germaine?"

(*He sings.*)

"Malbrough s'en va-t-en guerre,
Mironton, mironton, mirontaine;
Malbrough s'en va-t-en guerre,
Ne sait quand reviendra,"
And Nicolette hummed the refrain,
And Dorine went "*Tra-la-la.*"

(*His friend warns him.*)

"What are you doing, and why so gay,
Georges Cadoudal? A word in your ear.
Barras and Carnot have seen you here,
Mon cher camarade at Savenay!
O General Cadoudal, fly with your wife,
Madame, beseech him to save his life!
I warn you, *ami*, have nothing to do
With Pichegru;
For he is as rash as you are brave,
Or you will fall in the Place de Grève,
Riddled with bullets!" "We'll change the strain,"
Said Cadoudal, "with a new refrain:

'Général Cadoudal est mort,
Mironton, mironton, mirontaine;
Général Cadoudal est mort,
Est mort et enterré.'"
"*Fi donc,*" Dorine said. "*Mais il est fort.*"
And he was, on that terrible day.

—o—

TWO KINGS.

"*Two kings are dead.*"—THOMAS GOFFE.

I SAW, but whether it was in a dream,
Where Present, Future, Past
Blend and bewilder us, and strange things seem
Familiar—while they last;

Or in the flesh, as walking in the street
We see a friend or foe—
Who knows? I saw a man with faltering feet
Who down a hill did go.

The bleak and barren hill like iron rang
Beneath his fitful tread;
The trees had shed their leaves, and no bird sang—
The birds were flown, or dead.

The time of the year was autumn, and the hour
The last that leaves the light;
For in the sullen West like a great flower
Day faded into Night.

What could be more forlorn than that hill-side,
    Where, through the withered leaves,
That wrinkled, bent old creature walked and sighed,
    That mournfulest of eves?

The grief that looked out of his hollow eyes
    Refused to be consoled
By tears, that still would come, with heavy sighs—
    Piteous in one so old!

He wrung his trembling hands, and tore his hair,
    Then stood as carved in stone,
And stared behind him—there was no one there,
    For he was all alone.

"Why are you here in such a woful plight?
    Why do you turn your head,
And stare so backward through the glimmering light?"
    "Because my Kings are dead."

"Clearly," I thought, "his wits have gone astray."
    And then to him I said,
"*Your* Kings—what Kings? There are none here to-day—"
    "Because the Kings are dead."

I thought it best to humor this old man,
    Who like another Lear
Went wandering down the hill-side, weak and wan,
    As if his end were near.

"Tell me about them, Sire, for I perceive
    That you are kingly, too.
I will go downward with you, by your leave."
    He smiled, and said, "You do."

I scanned him closer, and, to my surprise,
He was not as before;
There was a wild light in his laughing eyes,
And he was old no more!

"O Prince! O King!" he cried; but not to me
His greeting was addressed,
Nor any person there whom I could see.
"My master, and my guest!

Most beautiful art thou of all thy race,
Most gracious and benign;
The right to rule is in thy royal face,
And in those lips of thine.

No robe is rich enough for thee to wear,
What earthly robe could be?
The bright abundance of thy golden hair
Is crown enough for thee.

All things that thou dost look on are made fair.
The eagle's eye sees far;
But thy soft eye sees farther—everywhere
It lights upon a star.

The feet of the mountain does are swift in flight—
Off like the wind they go;
Thou art before them on the mountain height,
And thou art first below.

This to the eye thou art; but to the heart
Whose pulses beat with thine,
Who can declare what happiness thou art?
Declare, O Heart of mine!

Dear is the pressure of a woman's hand,
And woman's lips are sweet;
Weak men by her caresses are unmanned,
And grovel at her feet.

But she is not the best of all good things,
For, when I am with thee,
I love thee better, O my King of Kings!
And dost not thou love me?

His presence honors my poor house again,
I give him of my best;
Who would not give his all to entertain
So beautiful a guest?"

"I do not see the King you speak of, Sire."
The old man shook his head:
"Nor I, for I have lost my heart's desire,
My dear, young King is dead!"

"But where, pray, tell me, have they buried him?"
"I know not, but I guess
That somewhere in a chamber, hushed and dim,
He lies in loveliness.

Wrapped in a purple pall, as if asleep,
His hands upon his breast;
And fair, sad women watch, but do not weep,
Lest they disturb his rest.

Right royally his brother filled his place,
And glorious to behold
Was his tall form, broad chest, and bearded face,
And his great crown of gold.

No yellow locks for him, he wears the crown,
And can the helmet wear;
He bears a sword that smites his foemen down,
Who angers him, beware!

For this great King is swift as he is stern,
Nor pity knows, nor fear;
He can see thousands fall, and cities burn,
And never shed a tear.

But war delights him not, for he is wise,
And knows that peace is best.
There is a kindly humor in his eyes,
And he can laugh and jest.

What his dead brother only had begun,
(What rare beginnings those!)
Taken up by his strong will, was straightway done,
Cities and ramparts rose.

This masterful great man, who was my King,
And who was full of cares,
Had time to hear his merry minstrels sing,
And hear his people's prayers.

But he is gone, the strong, the good, the just,
And gone his golden crown;
His sceptre and his sword are in the dust,
His kingdom has gone down.

Low lies that mighty form that filled the throne,
Low lies that royal head;
The race is ended: I am here alone
Because the King is dead!"

"Thou strange old man," I said, "if man thou art,
    That growest so thin and pale,
I feel a chillness creeping round my heart
    At thy accursèd tale.

Who art thou? Speak!" He spoke not—was not there,
    If ever there, had flown,
And left me talking to the empty air,
    On the dark hill alone!

"I am the man whom I have seen," I said,
    "I have my story told;
I have a wrinkled face and a gray head,
    And I am growing old.

I have outlived my youth, that was so dear,
    Seen manhood pass away,
And now have reached the autumn of my year,
    The evening of my day.

For lo, in the far West, so lately red,
    There is no spark of light;
Darkness below, and darkness overhead—
    Alone, alone at night!"

TO THE MEMORY OF KEATS.

(*On coming into possession of his copy of "The Rogue: or Guzman de Alfarache." London*, 1634.)

GREAT Father mine, deceased ere I was born,
And in a classic land renowned of old;
Thy life was happy, but thy death forlorn,
Buried in violets and Roman mold.

Thou hast the Laurel, Master of my soul!
Thy name, thou saidst, was writ in water—No,
For while clouds float on high, and billows roll,
Thy name shall worshipped be. Will mine be so?
I kiss thy words as I would kiss thy face,
And put thy book most reverently away.
Girt by thy peers, thou hast an honored place,
Among the kingliest—Byron, Wordsworth, Gray.
If tears will fill mine eyes, am I to blame?
"O smile away the shades, for this is fame!"

——o——

ABRAHAM LINCOLN.

THIS man whose homely face you look upon,
Was one of Nature's masterful, great men;
Born with strong arms, that unfought battles won;
Direct of speech, and cunning with the pen.
Chosen for large designs, he had the art
Of winning with his humor, and he went
Straight to his mark, which was the human heart;
Wise, too, for what he could not break he bent.
Upon his back a more than Atlas-load,
The burden of the Commonwealth, was laid;
He stooped, and rose up to it, though the road
Shot suddenly downwards, not a whit dismayed.
Hold, warriors, councilors, kings! All now give place
To this dear benefactor of the Race.

——o——

THE VICTORIES OF PEACE.

SOLDIERS! Brave men that gather here to-day,
Veterans, ye know what war is—none so well,
For you have faced, in many a fatal fray,
The stern arbitrament of shot and shell;

Have seen your comrades, brothers, as they fell,
Struck out of life, or maimed for life. Ye know,
Better than civic song like mine can tell,
Red battle-fields where thousands are laid low,
The last victorious charge, the final overthrow!

Peace hath her victories no less renowned
Than war, and they more lasting are, and true;
With olive-leaves, not laurels, they are crowned,
And simple tasks and pleasures they pursue.
We owe these victories to men like you.
Strength such as yours, when nations are betrayed,
Springs on the foemen—certain to subdue.
Upon the deep foundations war has laid
Peace builds her durable home, and is no more dismayed.

To you and your courageous deeds we owe
That this our dear Republic is not dead,
Crushed like the Commonwealths of long ago,
For which in vain their sturdy children bled.
I see your camps, I hear your martial tread
As you go tramping southward. You know best
What followed, as the long months slowly fled,
Drawn battles, victories that were not pressed,
The thousands Carnage stamped in Earth's maternal breast!

Peril and death awaited you afar,
Heart-ache and apprehension were our lot;
We bore at home the burden of the war
Which never for a moment was forgot.
We looked and sighed for letters—that came not,
Imagined all dark reasons for delay,
Struck down, perchance, by some stray picket shot,
Or in the sick bed, where life ebbed away:
We prayed, we wept, we died a thousand deaths each day!

But this is ended—ended! What was then
Has vanished like a nightmare, and no more
The slaughter of our best and bravest men,
Our sires, our sons, our brothers, we deplore;
For now, on firmer basis than before,
The up-builded structures of the State remain.
The winds may blow thereon, the waves may roar
And batter against the pillars—but in vain;
War, baffled, beaten so, will not return again.

Peace hath her victories no less renowned
Than war. Her ways are wider; they embrace
More than a thousand city walls surround—
She folds to her impartial heart the Race,
To what shall I compare her perfect face,
Benignant, gracious, calm? No Goddess, she,
Sky-born, superior to time and space,
But human, Woman—Mother, whom to see
Strengthens their hearts and arms, and keeps her children
free.

Pursue the wings of morning as she flies
Across the broad and peaceful Continent,
Under the endless arch of summer skies,
To where the evening makes her slow descent,
Reddening the headlands of the firmament,
And the long wave that welters from Japan;
Tell me if the blue heavens were ever bent
Above a happier realm since time began?
God gave the Old World to kings—He kept the New for
Man!

Soldiers! The peaceful victories of home
Outweigh the deadly victories of war;
No column consecrates them, no proud dome,
They cost no blood, they heal without a scar.

By these the sinews of the nation are
Strengthened, not strained, but kept inviolate,
To grapple with foes at home, and foes afar;
For, soldiers, these preserve, perpetuate
The glory you restored—the greatness of the State!

HISTORY.

THE Vision of a Woman comes to me,
As I am walking in the crowded street;
Of more than mortal mold she seems to be,
And bears the dust of empires on her feet.
Gathering below her generations meet,
And Time before her strict tribunal stands.
She sits, impartial, on the judgment seat,
And holds an iron tablet in her hands;
Around her are the scribes who write what she commands.

Back to the dim beginnings of the race,
The far-off, primitive days, she turns her eyes;
She has but to will, and suddenly time and place
Are brought to doom before her. They arise
From unremembered graves, with bitter cries,
Because their evil deeds are known at last,
Their foul abominations, based on lies;
Ashes in vain upon their heads they cast:
We harden our hearts against the unpardonable Past!

Whence came, and when, the families of men
That sparsely peopled earth when she was young?
Who can declare the immeasurable *when*,
The inconceivable, infinite *whence* they sprung?
Much-knowing History answers not, and the tongue

Of her elder sister, Fable, charms no more:
Gone is the high descent to which they clung,
Children of gods whom mortal mothers bore;
They came not after their gods, but thousands of years before.

They left no history, but lived and died
Like the wild animals round them which they slew;
The woods and streams their ravenous wants supplied,
To hunger and to thirst were all they knew.
The skins of beasts about their loins they drew,
And made themselves rude weapons out of stone,
Sharp arrow-heads and lances, to subdue
Their fellow savages, waylaid alone:
From these beginnings Man and War and Woe have grown.

By slow degrees their dull wits were aware
Of ways less dangerous: they somehow found
They need not track the wild beasts to their lair,
And slay them for their flesh, for in the ground
A power was that brought forth the grains around,
The taste whereof was good: they made them plows
Of flint and bone, which they to hurdles bound
With willow withes, and twigs of forest boughs;
Tame creatures they yoke thereto that break the sods they browse.

Others of these are shepherds, whose live wealth
Whitens the land for leagues, a watchful band,
Near whom the gaunt wolves, baffled, prowl by stealth;
Their tents of skins that summer suns have tanned
Are pitched where rivers fertilize the land;
Young children part the curtains, and look out,
Or, gamboling where their tethered playmates stand,

The petted lambs, or kids, they laugh and shout :
Nomadic tribes are these, whom horsemen put to rout.

Before all these are Shadows, born of fear
And hope, that slowly put on Shapes unknown :
They seem to threaten, and they domineer,
Huge, uncouth images of wood and stone,
Set up in templed places, groves that none
Dare violate, and few dare penetrate,
Save those, austere, who wait on them alone,
Gray-bearded, reverend men whose words are fate :
In the stead of their gods they judge the people at the
gate.

The will of these high gods they all declare,
What power behind each hideous symbol lies :
Their wrath must be appeased by priestly prayer,
Their mutable favor bought by sacrifice.
Lo, where the smokes of their burnt offerings rise
Grateful to their craving palates,—kindle more!
They scrutinize the world with sleepless eyes,
And harken to the suppliants who implore ;
They punish those who scoff, but they bless those who
adore !

If they have might, they do not put it forth
To succor their worshippers, nor heed their tears ;
For still in every corner of the earth
Are swift, dark horsemen, armed with bows and spears,
Whose sudden war-cries ring in the startled ears
Of the shepherds and husbandmen whom they surround,
Harry and pillage, and enslave for years :
Happier are they whose life-blood stains the ground
Than those they drag away, men, women, children—
bound !

To guard against these woeful tribulations
Tribes band themselves together, one by one,
Until the growing multitudes are nations.
Then chiefs they choose, and kings: from sire to son
Their lordly lines in clear succession run.
The rustic tills his pastures as before,
And drives his herds home when the day is done;
The merchant, bolder, sails from shore to shore:
Protected, they forget the perilous days of yore.

Artificers come, and industries begin.
The potter turns his wheel, and molds his clay;
Matron and maid at whirring distaffs spin,
Twisting long threads of flax; and all the day
The weaver plies his shuttle, and whiles away
The peaceful hours with songs of battles past;
Strong spear-heads and sharp swords wherewith to slay,
And armor-plates, are hammered out or cast;
Tents lessen, structures rise, and cities are at last.

If men are plundered when the tribes are small,
Slaughtered, enslaved, given over to stripes and blows,
Greater calamities on nations fall,
For hatred in the heart of greatness grows;
All powerful peoples are begotten foes;
Their kings suspect each other, but pretend
Credence of what their lying lips disclose;
Friendly a king may be, but not a friend,
For he seeks by forcible means to gain a peaceable end.

The whirlwind of a thousand battle-storms
Bursts on my sight, interminable cloud
Over all ages, lands, where terrible forms—
Deep Darkness in the darkness—struggle and crowd;
Furrows below as though mankind were plowed,

Great armies grappling in the death-embrace,
To whom, unheard, the thunder calls aloud,
Under whom, unfelt, the earthquake rocks the base
Of the imperturbable Earth, which breeds this savage race!

The Vision of a Man—if he were Man—
Who such prodigious armies led to war,
Who Arabia, Libya, India overran,
And, flaming westward like a baleful star,
Across the Asian table-lands his car
Drove to barbaric Thrace, where graven were his
Tremendous deeds on pillars seen afar:
The proud inscription underneath was this:
"Sesostris, King of Kings, Beloved of Ammon is!"

Glimpses of conquerors, imperious ghosts,
That once inhabited tenements of clay;
Glimpses of soldiery, in serried hosts,
And of the encompassed cities where they lay;
Of sharp, incessant attacks, day after day;
Of stout resistance, and night-sallies out;
Of those who sullenly bear their dead away,
And hurriedly strip and bury them—Ah, that shout!
A desperate dash at gates, a stubborn rally—a rout!

Tumultuous ages follow, awful waves
Which the sea of time rolls shoreward more and more;
No longer men, but monsters, soldiers and slaves,
They labor, and fight, and cruel gods adore.
Deserts are where great cities were of yore;
They camp in sight of their ruins, and know it not.
Other cities elsewhere bear the names they bore:
Forgot are old races, new ones are begot,
But there are mighty names that will not be forgot!

Out of the whirling tempest that overwhelms
Kingdoms and empires, ruinous conquerors glare;
The brows of some are bright with brazen helms,
Dinted with blows; their diadems others wear;
Purple their robes are, and their swords are bare,
And all drip blood! They menace Man again;
Cambyses, Alexander, Cæsar dare
The world to arms against them; Tamerlane
Comes with his Tartar horde and thousands of captives slain!

And is this all? These surgings to and fro
Of sanguinary forces, are they all?
Enormous rivers of doom they flow and flow
Luridly, darkened by terrors that appall:
Before their fury nations, races fall,
Swept on to annihilation, till at last
Sheer down the steeps of a mighty mountain wall
They plunge—and are no more! Earth stares aghast!
Are these iniquities, then, the substance of the Past?

No! In the Order of the Universe
They are only parts thereof,—the smallest part,
For they have blessed the world they meant to curse,
And have wrested away their sceptres that man's heart
Might govern his lesser brain, and larger art
Than theirs have created, to themselves unknown:
Out of their fertile desolations start
Fresh forms of life that are not overthrown,
Benignant growths of Peace the hands of War had sown.

The would-be conquerors of the Earth were more
Than they conceived: behind their iron hands,
That smote so blindly at the hearts before,
The inscrutable Creator stood—and stands;

The everlasting Spirit of Good commands,
For lo, the hands are folded that so late
Grappled and mangled the still-bleeding lands
Where Turk and Muscovite in deadly hate
Struggled to defend and to seize the long-sought Golden Gate

Where battle-pillars were planted cities rose,
And hid the spot where armies were interred;
Above the graves where mouldering kings repose
The hum of busy multitudes is heard;
Sweet thoughts are whispered, happy hearts are stirred,
And hands are joined with holy marriage rites:
Invisible walls of Law the people gird,
Shutting injustice out; and Art invites
All that is divine in man to her diviner heights.

Four Shapes she hath. The first of these is Sound,
The melody of voice and lute and lyre,
That makes the feet trip and the spirits bound;
A sister Shape sits near, but sits up higher,
Fulfilled of solemn songs and portents dire,
With sudden and tragic endings, long foretold;
Two others, lesser in the sacred quire,
But more esteemed of men, color and mold
Greatness and glory and grace that die not, and grow not old.

Slowly but surely in the shock of wars
The ample victories of Peace are wrought.
They bind up new-made wounds, and heal old scars,
They cherish letters, and encourage thought:
Old, dusty scrolls are to the daylight brought,
And copied by pious hands in convent cells;
Philosophy in learned schools is taught;
Religion summons with sonorous bells,
And up cathedral domes the pealing organ swells!

All this, and all that was, and is, the eyes
Of the Muse of History at a glance behold.
Unshaken is she, whoever lives or dies,
Calm as a marble statue, and as cold;
Ten thousand plausible lies to her are told,
She neither harkens nor heeds, but guides the pen
Whereby the truth is written from of old.
Austere Observer of the ways of men,
What dost thou think of us, and what wilt thou write—
and when?

We stand upon the threshold of great things;
Shall we cross it, and possess them? O, shall we,
Who have not inherited the curse of kings,
Come under their rule hereafter? Shall we be
Among the Commonwealths that once were free,
But soon in Empires sank? Shall Man repeat
His old defeats in us? Or History see
One race in whom all resolute virtues meet,
That will not stand condemned before her judgment seat?

———o———

GUESTS OF THE STATE.

(*July* 4, 1876.)

Victorious in her senate-house she stands,
Mighty among the nations, latest born.
Armed men stood round her cradle, violent hands
Were laid upon her, and her limbs were torn;
Yet she arose, and turned upon her foes,
And, beaten down, arose,
Grim, as who goes to meet
And grapple with Defeat,

And pull Destruction from her iron seat!
When saw the Earth another,
O valorous Daughter of imperious Mother,
Who greatly dared as thou?
Making thy land one wide Thermopylæ,
And the long leagues of sea thy Salamis,
Determined to be free
As the unscaled Heaven is,
Whose calm is in thy eyes, whose stars are on thy brow!

Thy children gathered round thee to defend,
O mother of a race of hardy sons!
Left plows to rust in the furrows, snatched their guns,
And rode hot haste as though to meet a friend,
Who might be nigh his end,
Which *thou* wert not, though often sore beset.
Nor did they fall in vain who fell for thee,
Nor could thy enemies, though its roots they wet
With thy best blood, destroy thy glorious tree,
That on its stem of greatness flowers late.
Hedged with sharp spines it shot up year by year,
As if the planets drew it to their sphere,
The quick earth spouting sap through all its veins,
Till of the days that wait
To see it burst in bloom not one remains,
Not so much as an hour,
For, lo, it is in flower,
Bourgeoned, full blown in an instant! Tree of trees,
The fame whereof has flown across the seas,
Whereat the elder sisters of the race
Have hastened to these walls,
These vast and populous halls,
To look on this Centurial Tree,
And to strike hands with thee,
And see thy happy millions face to face.

First comes, as nearest, an imperial dame,
  Named for that king's fair daughter whom Jove bore
  Through the blue billows to the Cretan shore,
        Where she its queen became.
Parent of many peoples, strong and proud,
  Comes Europe in her purples, peaceful here:
Her great sword sheathed, and rent the battle-cloud
    Wherewith her kings surround her,
    The chains that long have bound her
    Concealed, though clanking loud,
        As stately she draws near.
    Hither Europe, great and mean,
    Half a slave, and half a queen,
    Hear what words are to be spoken,
    What the Present doth foretoken,
    Hear, and understand, and know,
As did our wiser Mother a hundred years ago.

England, our Mother's Mother! Come, and see
A greater England here! O come, and be
    At home with us, your children, for there runs
    The same blood in our veins as in your sons;
The same deep-seated love of Liberty
Beats in our hearts. We speak the same good tongue:
Familiar with all songs your bards have sung,
Those large men, Milton, Shakespeare, both are ours.
Come from the shadow of your minster towers,
  Vast, venerable, from your storied domes,
Where Glory guards the ashes of the Great,
  And your baronial halls, and cottage homes:
Hither, and learn what constitutes a State.
Not royal rulers, who inherit Power,
  Which otherwise they never had attained,
Torn from the world in some disastrous hour
  By violent kings, whose hands with blood were stained.

Nor dukes, nor earls, who trace their pedigrees
Through tortuous lines to some old ancestor,
Who was a yeoman then,
But who became the instrument of these,
And was ennobled, and was man no more :
Not lords, and kings—but men!
England of Sidney, Vane,
What we received from you, receive from us again!

Next come those neighbors twain,
Fair, fickle, courtly France, and sombre Spain.

Shorn of her ancient strength, but potent still,
From her great wall-girt city by the Seine,
Shattered by hard beleaguerment, and wild ire
That sacked and set her palaces on fire,
Pulled down her pillared Column in disdain,
Most apt for all things ill;
From her green vineyards, ripening in the sun
On southern slopes their misted, purple blooms,
From cunning workshops, and from busy looms,
And where her princely painters ply their Art,
Artificer and Artist, both in one,
Tempter and Tempted, Syren of mankind,
Of many minds, but not the stable mind,
Keen wit and stormy heart :
With blare of trumpets and with roll of drums
She comes triumphantly—France comes!

Spain, with a grave sedateness,
That well befits her old renown and greatness,
When she put boldly forth to find a world,
Found it, and pillaged it, and with flags unfurled,
Sailed in her galleons homeward, red with blood,
But wealthy with her spoil; nor did the flood

Engulf her for her cruelties, blessed, not banned,
By him who holds the keys of Peter in his hand!
They came not to bring peace here, but a sword,
Sharp followers of the meek and loving Lord,
Whom priests and monks were riding, and still ride,
Cowls over crowns, and over all the pride
That arrogates to know the will of God,
Holding alike His sceptre and His rod,
Lighting at once the censer, and the fires
Wherein the poor wretch Heresy expires!
Te Deums then, but now—
But thou dost well to bow,
And cross thyself, and mutter *Aves*. We,
Who know not thy temptations, cannot know
What their punishment should be;
But Heaven adjusted vengeance long ago,
When the New World passed from thee!

Three follow. Deadly feud
Two cherished many years;
For one was held in bitter servitude,
And flouted for her tears.

But she has risen victorious, and is crowned
Among the nations, with one foe remaining,
Powerless, except in curses, and complaining,
And spiritual thunders that not now confound,
Controlling, where he can,
The consciences of the living, souls of the dead,
Vicegerent of High God in puny man;
More arrogant than She who sat of old
On her Seven Hills, where altar smokes up-curled,
Hungry for blood and gold,
Sleepless, and ever mailed and helmetèd,
Whose legions scourged the World!

Free Italy comes hither,
Bringing with her
The memory of her glorious, great dominions,
What time her eagles swept with iron pinions
Three Continents, and her conquerors came home,
Followed by fallen kings, the slaves of Rome;
The memory of her patriots and sages,
That burned like watch-fires through the long, dark ages:
Grave senators, stout captains, famous men
Who wielded sword and pen:
Tasso, Boccaccio, the stern Florentine,
With other children of her royal line,
Who govern the soul and heart
With Music, Song, and Art!

Austria, who wears the crowns of divers lands,
Snatched from pale brows in battle by red hands;
Haught mistress of old peoples, Serb and Slave,
Bohemian, Styrian, stalwart Tyrolese,
Whom now she must provoke and now appease;
From where the waters of the Danube lave
Vienna's walls, and winding past Komorn
Flow southward down through Hungary to the sea;
And where her chamois-hunters wind the horn
Along the Rhetian Alps, she comes, elate,
Peaceful, and prosperous, hither. May she be
A civic nation, with a happier fate
Than fell on her at Sadowa! O may she
Be lenient, juster, wiser than before,
Mother, and not Oppressor,
Redresser, not Transgressor,
And her black eagles' talons rend no more!

But who is she comes with her, with such a mountain air,
And singing on her way,

A simple spray of edelweis in her abundant hair,
  A cold light in her bright, blue eyes, like that of
    winter day,
Steady, but sparkling, like her lakes, which Heaven
    stoops down to see,
And sees itself so clearer? Who may the maiden be?
No maiden, but a matron, mother of sturdy men,
  Whose lion spirits Nature with independence fills,
  Walled in with kingdoms, empires, and the everlast-
    ing hills.
Perhaps they have been conquered: but tell us where
    and when.
Not where her Arnold grasped the Austrian spears,
  Nor when the Tuileries gave up its king,
And they were hacked in pieces! All the years
      Have seen them dying, dying,
        But never flying,
  Unless they followed Victory's crimson wing!
As peaceful as the bosom of their lakes,
  As rugged as the Alps which are their home,
  Along whose granite feet their rivers foam,
As dreadful as the thunder when it shakes
Its lightnings over Jura! Heart and hand
Welcome the sole Republic—Switzerland.

      With these come other three,
One kingdom and two empires, all at peace,
  But dreaming of new warfare. Who shall say
  When they may draw their million swords, and slay
The poor, unpitied peoples? What release
  These have from them, and what the end may be?

Six years of doubtful greatness, hardly won,
  Hath *She* possessed, and guarded day and night,
  Forging huge cannon, in her grim delight,

To do (mistaken!) what can not be done.
The weak will band against her when she becomes too strong,
The strong will fall upon her when she becomes too weak,
And none will plead for her who smote them long,
Nor will her children turn the over-smitten cheek.
They sow but ill who sow the seeds of hate,
For while the harvests grow, the reapers wait.
Another Jena may efface Sedan,
And Kaiser (grant it, God!) give place to Man.
She should be greater in good things than they
Who sit on thrones about her, Pope and Czar,
For she was born beneath a better star,
And had good men to guide her on her way.
"Iron and blood" are curses
That hatch out sure reverses:
For Conquest flies from Carnage, which she brings,
Borne down in the lost battle by its tremendous wings!
Be greater than thy neighbors, Germany,
Severe step-mother, whom thy sons forsake
For peace and freedom elsewhere. Glory lies
Not in thine arms, but arts, in what is wise
Among thy thinkers, scholars, who partake
Of a larger nature than belongs to thee.
Better the land whose battles Luther fought
Than that of Frederick, misnamed the Great;
To which the deaf Beethoven, harkening, brought
God's chapel music; for which Goethe thought;
A prosperous People, not a powerful State!

But who is she, woman of northern blood,
With fells of yellow hair and ruddy looks,
Berserker wife, with many an ocean son?
Her robe is hemmed with mountains, fringed with fiords,

With scattered islands sown like pearls thereon,
Rivers therein as plentiful as brooks.
Her feet are in the seas, and arctic birds
Hover and scream about her; on her brow
The shadows of great pine woods: like the flood
Enters, and like the pine stands Sweden now!

Towering above and dwarfing these a Shape
Enormous and portentous. She looks down
And captives with her smile, and with her frown
Destroys, till none escape.
Her head in arctic winters, she looks round,
Westward and eastward, from the wild White Cape,
Across Siberian wastes to Behring Strait.
In the far distance her sharp eyes are glancing
To where her feet are stealthily advancing,
On peoples whom her Cossacks will surround,
On kings they will unking, and temples great
Whose gods they will destroy, or mutilate,
Despite the many hands that smite no more.
Southward, to where the mountain passes lead
To India; from her red Crimean shore,
Where she beheld in rage her children bleed,
Southward, along the waters, till she sees
Minarets and mosques,
Green gardens, cool kiosks,
Seraglios, where the Sultan lolls at ease—
She scarce can keep her hands off, for her hands
Pluck empires from her pathway! She commands
Her myriads, they obey: her shadows darken
Europe, Asia, who to her whispers harken,
Dreading her voice of thunder,
And the foot that tramples them under—
So comes imperious Russia! Giantess
With thin spots in her armor, forged too fast

Of outworn breastplates of old generations,
Her strength enfeebled by sparse populations,
Nomadic in the steppes: if she were less
She would be greater; she has grown too vast.
What does she see within her and without her?
What guards has sovereign Nature set about her?
Above an icy ocean, and below
Innumerable streams that come and go,
Through wildernesses, and unherded plains,
Long mountain ranges, where the snow remains,
And mocks the short-lived summer, penal mines,
Where poor, enslaved, rebellious Poland pines,
Chastising armies on her wide frontiers,
Where, imminent, War appears!
These things, O Russia! are thy weakness, these
Thy hard misfortune; nor can all thy state
Their terrible force abate,
Nor thy great cities, nor thy navied Seas,
Colossal Sister, whom we welcome here
To these high halls in this Centurial Year!

Who is this Woman of majestic mien?
More than woman, less than Queen,
Her long robe trailed with the dust
Of the old, ruined cities wherein she
Sate, abject, head bowed, in dead apathy,
Till some young, cruel hunter, spying, thrust
(Half in anger, half in play,)
His sharp spear at her as he rode that way,
Grazing her heart, till, startled back to life,
She rose, and fled, and hid among the tombs,
Safer where gaunt hyenas were at strife,
Than where men were! O wretched and forlorn!
Why art thou living? O why wert thou born?

Where are the many crowns that thou hast worn,
Discrowned One, and the many sceptres where?
Thy face is furrowed, furrowed, and thy hair
(Still golden) is disheveled! O what dooms
  Have fallen upon thee! O what suns are set!
      Thy far eyes see them yet.
The light of lost dominion lingers there,
  The melancholy evening of regret;
And in thine ears what voices of despair,
  The wailings of thy myriad children slain
By Mede and Roman, Turk and Tartar hordes,
The rush of onset and the din of swords,
  Gengis, and Bajazet, and Tamerlane:
      Weep, Asia, weep again!
      Another in thy place,
So suddenly we did not see thee go;
Thou wert, and here she is! If there was woe,
  There is no trace thereof in her untroubled face.
Who can declare the stature of this Woman,
  The simple light of wonder in her eyes,
  The strange, mysterious gloom that deeper lies,
And whether she be Godlike, or be Human?
    Unhusbanded, and primitive;
    But now, behold, her children live,
Crowding about her knees, the Mother of the Race!
    Tents arise, and flocks are fed,
    And men begin to bury dead.
    O Shepherdess, thy sons depart,
      The tents, the flocks, and where they were;
    Cities gather, and thou art
      No Shepherdess, but Worshipper.
    For round thee exhalations rise,
    Which men, beholding, straightway say,
    "Lo, these are Gods!" and go their way,
    And carve in wood, and mold in clay,

And cut in stone rude images
Hideous thereof, and bow to these,
Thou being their Priestess, both when they
Bring their first-fruits and on the altars lay,
And when their yearling lambs they sacrifice
To Gods that know not of it, nor any thing.
The ruler at the gate is now a king,
Has armèd men and horsemen, and is to battle gone,
Headed and goaded on by thee, O more than Amazon,
Whose once white robe is purple, whose strong right
hand is red—
Heap ashes on thy head,
Thou dark, infuriate Mother, whose children's blood is
shed!
Who shall declare her, from her garment's hem
To the tall towers of her great diadem,
Goddess! Gone again—
For here poor, ruined Asia weeps, and weeps in vain!

With her are certain of her peoples—they
Who dwell in far Cathay;
They, neighboring, who their island empire hold;
They, less remote, more old,
Who live in sacred Ind.

What shall we call
This Curious One, who builded a great wall,
That, rivers crossing, skirting mountain steeps,
Did not keep out but let in the Invader;
Who is what her ancients made her;
Who neither wholly wakes, nor wholly sleeps,
Fool at once and sage,
Childhood of more than patriarchal age?
With twinkling, almond eyes, and little feet,
She totters hither, from her fields of flowers,

From where Pekin uplifts its pictured towers,
And from the markets where her merchants meet
And barter with the world. We close our eyes,
And see her otherwise.
(Perhaps the spell began
With the quaint figures on her painted fan.)
At first she is a Land,
A stretch of plains and mountains, and long rivers,
Down which her inland tribute she delivers
To the sea cities : where a child may stand,
A man may climb, plants are, and shrubs, and trees ;
Arable every where,
No idlers there
In that vast hive-world of industrious bees.
Now she is many persons, many things,
The little and the great ;
The Emperor plowing in the Sacred Field,
What time the New-Year comes in solemn state :
A soldier, with his matchlock, bow, and shield,
Behind the many-bannered dragon wings ;
A bonze, where the high pagodas rise,
And Buddha sits, cross-legged, in rapt repose ;
A husbandman that goes
And sows his fields with wheat,
And gathers in his harvests, dries his tea ;
Hunter, from whom the silver pheasant flies ;
Boatman, whose boat floats downward to the sea ;
Sailor, whose junk is clumsy ; woodman, who
Cuts camphor-trees, and groves of tall bamboo ;
Gardens, where flowers and fruits together grow,
The banyan and pomegranate, and the palm,
And the great water-lily, white as snow ;
Rivers, with low squat bridges ; every where
Women and children ; beardless men, with queues,
In tunics, short wide trowsers, silken shoes,

Some with the peakèd caps of Mandarins;
  Behold the ruby button burning there,
And yonder severed head that ghastly grins;
  Old hill-side tombs, where mourners still repair;
Innumerous Bustle, immemorial Calm—
        And this is China!

She

Who follows quickly—if she woman be—
Is clad in a loose robe, whose flowing folds
  Mold out the shape they cover, and discover
      To the eye of lord and lover,
The strong limbs, girdled waist, the arm that holds
  Her island children, and the breasts that feed.
    Woman and mother, why that manly stride,
    And the two swords at thy side?
  Offended or defended, who must bleed?
Her face is powdered, painted, and her hair,
  Drawn high above her head, with pins of gold
Is fastened: if light olive tints are fair,
  Fair is her oval face, though over-bold.
  Good-humor lights it, frankness and the grace
  Of high-born manner, honor, pride of place:
    But, looking closer, keener, we discern
      Something that can be stern,
Like the dark tempest on her mountain highlands,
The wild typhoons that whirl around her thousand islands!
  Most bounteous here, as in her sea-girt lands,
    Where she stretches forth her hands,
Plucks cocoas and bananas in woods of oak and pine,
        Grapes on every vine,
And walks on gold and silver, and knows her power increased,
Nor fears her nobles longer—the Lady of the East!

What words of what great poet can declare
This woman's fallen greatness, her despair,
The melancholy light in her mild eyes?
She neither lives—nor dies!
First-born of Earth's First Mother, she gave birth
To the infant races, and her dwelling-place
Cradled the young religions: face to face,
Her many gods and children walked the Earth.
(Who could know, when Life began,
Which was God, and which was Man?)
Her mountains are the bases of the sky,
Where the gods brooded, uncreate, eternal,
Celestial and infernal,
Indra every where, and Siva nigh—
Thunder voice that in the summer speaks,
Shadow of the wings that fly,
Arrow in the bended bow!
Did they wander down the mountain peaks,
Through the clouds and everlasting snow?
Or did men clamber up, and fetch them down below?
Who may know
What their heads and hands portend,
What the beasts whereon they ride,
And whether these be deified;
What was in the beginning, and shall be in the end?
What matter? Things like these,
Struggles to ascend the ladder of the air,
Plunges to reach unbottomed mysteries,
Have been thy ruin, India, once so fair,
So powerful, prayerful! Hands that clasp in prayer
Let go the sword and sceptre: thou hast seen
Thine roughly wrested from thee, and hast been
A prey to many spoilers, some thine own.
Timor proclaimed himself thy Emperor;
And Baber conquered, beaten thrice before;
And Nadir took thy glorious Peacock Throne;

And others, Hindoo, Moslem, self-made kings,
Carved out rich kingdoms from thy wide domains,
Had violent, bloody reigns,
And perished (the gods be thanked!) like meaner things,
If meaner, crueler in thy forests be,
Among the wolves and jackals skulking there,
And dreadful tigers roaring in their lair,
Than these foul beasts that so dismembered thee!
O Mortal and Divine!
The largeness of the primitive world is thine!
The everlasting handywork remains,
In the high mountain ranges, the broad plains,
The wastes, and vast, impenetrable woods,
(Oppressive solitudes
Where no man was,) the multitudinous rivers—
The Gods were generous givers,
If from the heavenly summit of Meru,
Beyond all height, they sent the Ganges down.
Or is it, Goddess, from thy mountained crown,
Far-lifted in the inaccessible blue,
Its waters, rising in perpetual snow,
Come in swift torrents, swollen in their flow
By larger rivers, others swelling them,
All veins to this long stem
Of thy great leaf of verdure? Sacred River,
That from Gangotri goest to the Sea,
Past temples, cities, peoples, Holy Stream,
Whom but to hear of, wish for, see, or touch,
Bathe in, or sing old hymns to, day by day,
Whom but to name a hundred leagues away,
Was to atone for all the sins committed
In three past lives, (for Vishnu so permitted,)
O Ganges! would the Powers could re-deliver
Thy virtues lost, or we renew the dream:
We can restore so much,
India, we cannot yet relinquish Thee!

A Vision of a Cloud,
Remote, but floating nearer, looming higher;
Movements therein as if of smothered fire,
And voices that are neither low nor loud.
A Vision of a Shadow, stooping down,
Or rising up: we first behold the feet,
Then the huge, grasping hands; at last the frown
On what should be the face of this Afreet.
A Vision of a Form that lies supine,
Feet in the Indian Ocean, elbow leaning
On a green Atlantic cape, with nothing screening,
Not even a lifted palm-leaf, the fierce shine
Of summer from its blinking, blinded eyes,
The hot sirocco from its desert brain,
Which a great Sea cannot cool: supine it lies—
If chained, it hugs the chain!
Its head is on the mountains, and its hands
Fumble in its long slumber and dull dreams;
They finger cowries in the briny sands,
And dabble in the ooze of shrinking streams.
What happens around it neither hears nor heeds,
Awake or sleeping: over it lizards crawl,
The desert ostrich scampers in its face,
The hippopotamus crushes its river reeds,
Locusts consume, lions tear: it lies through all—
Most brutish of the Race!

A Vision of a River, and a Land
Where no rain falls, which is the river's bed,
Through which it flows from waters far away,
Great lakes, and springs unknown, increasing slow,
Till the midsummer currents, rushing red,
Come overflowing the banks day after day,
Like ocean billows that devour the strand,
Till, lo, there is no land,

Save the cliffs of granite that inclose their flow,
And the waste sands beyond; subsiding then
Till Earth comes up again, and the husbandmen
(Chanting old hymns the while)
Sow their sure crops, which till midwinter be
Green, gladdening the old Nile
As he goes on his gracious journey to the Sea!
Land of strange gods, human, and beast, and bird,
Where animals were sacred and adored,
The great bull Apis being of these the chief;
Pasth, with her woman's breast and lion face,
Maned, with her long arms stretching down her thighs;
Nu, with the ram's head and the curlèd horns;
And Athor, whom a templed crown adorns;
And Mut, the vulture. And the higher Three,
The Goddess-Mother Isis, and her lord,
Divine Osiris, whom dark Typhon slew,
For whom, in her great grief,
(Leading unfathered Horus, weeping, too,)
She wandered up and down, lamenting sore,
Searching for lost Osiris: Libya heard
Her lamentations, and her rainy eyes
Flooded the shuddering Nile from shore to shore,
Till she had found, in many a secret place,
The poor dismembered body (can it be
These are supreme Osiris?) whereat she
Gathered the dear remains that Typhon hid,
And builded over each a Pyramid
In thirty cities, and was queen no more;
For Horus governed in his father's stead,
The crowns of Earth and Heaven on his anointed head!
From out the mists of hoar Antiquity
Straggle uncertain figures, gods or men,
Menes, Athothis, Cheops, and Khafren;
No matter who these last were, what they did,

Save that each raised a monstrous Pyramid
To house his mummy, and they rise to-day
Rifled thereof! And she
Colossal Woman, couchant in the sands,
Who has a lion's body, paws for hands,
(If she was wingèd, like the Theban one,
The wide-spread wings are gone.)
Nations have fallen round her, but she stands,
Dynasties came and went, but she went not,
She saw the Pharaohs and the Shepherd Kings,
Chariots and horsemen in their dread array,
Cambyses, Alexander, Anthony,
The hosts of standards, and the eagle wings,
Whom, to her ruinous sorrow, Egypt drew:
She saw, and she forgot,
Remembered not the old gods, nor the new,
Which were to her as though they had not been;
Remembered not the opulent, great Queen,
Whom riotous misbecomings so became,
Temptress, whom none could tame,
Splendor and Danger, fatal to beguile;
Remembered not the serpent of old Nile,
Nor the Herculean Roman she loved and overthrew!
Half buried in the sand she lies:
She neither questions, nor replies;
And what is coming, what is gone,
Disturbs her not: she looks straight on,
Under the everlasting skies,
In what Eternal Eyes!
Out of all this a Presence comes, and stands
Full-fronted, as who turns upon the Past,
Modern among the ancients, and the last
Of re-born, risen nations: in her hands,
That once so many sceptres held, and rods,
A palm leaf set with jewels: Princess, she,

She has her palaces along the Nile,
Her navies on the Sea;
And in the temples of her fallen gods,
(Not hers, she knows but the One God over all,)
She hears from holy mosques the muezzins call,
"Lo, Allah is Most Great!" And when the dawn
Is drawing near, "Prayer better is than Sleep."
She rides abroad, her curtains are undrawn,
She walks with lifted veil, nor hides her smile,
Nor the sweet, luminous eyes, where languors creep
No more: she is no more Circassian girl,
But Princess, woman with the mother-breast;
No Cleopatra to dissolve the pearl
And take the asp—the East become the West!
Honor to Egypt, honor,
May Allah smile upon her!
He does; for, while on others waning now,
The Prophet's Crescent broadens on her brow.
O prosper, Egypt, prosper! Nor deplore
What was, and might have been,
When thou wert slave and queen:
Hither, and sing "*In Exitu*" no more!

Welcome, a thousand welcomes! Our emotion
Demands a speech we have not: it demands
The unutterable largeness of the Ocean,
The immeasurable broadness of the Lands
That own us masters. Who is he shall speak
This language for us? From what mountain peak?
And in the rhythms of what epic Song,
At once serene and strong?
Welcomes, ten thousand welcomes! It is much,
O Sisters, ye have done in coming here,
For from the hour ye touch

Our peaceful shores, ye are peaceful, equal, dear!
Not with exultations,
O Sister, Mother Nations,
Do we receive your coming; for more than many see
Comes with ye; do ye see it? It is what is to be
Some day among your myriads, who will no more obey,
But, peaceable or warring, will then find out the way
Themselves to govern: if they tolerate
Kaisers, and Kings, and Princelings, as to-day,
It will be because they pity, and are too good to hate.
The New World is teaching the Old World to be free:
This, her acknowledgment from these, is more
Than all that went before.
Henceforth, America, Man looks up to Thee,
Not down at the dead Republics. Rise, arise!
That all men may behold thee. Be not proud,
Be humble and be wise,
And let thy head be bowed
To the Unknown, Supreme One, who on high
Has willed thee not to die!
Be grateful, watchful, brave,
See that among thy children none shall plunder,
Nor rend asunder,
Swift to detect and punish, and strong to shield and save!
Shall the drums beat, trumpets sound,
And the cannon thunder round?
No, these are warlike noises, and must cease;
Not thus, while the whole world from battle rests,
The Commonwealth receives her honored guests;
She celebrates no Triumphs but of Peace.

THE PEARL OF THE PHILIPPINES.

"I HEAR, Relempago, that you
Were once a famous fisherman,
Who at Negros, or Palawan,
Or, maybe, it was at Zèbou,
Found something precious in the sand,
A nugget washed there by the rain,
That slipped from your too eager hand,
And soon as found was lost again.
If it had been a pearl instead,
(Why does your good wife shake her head?)
I could the story understand;
For I have known so many lost,
And once too often to my cost.
I trade in pearls; I buy and sell.
They say I know their value well.
I have seen some large ones in my day,
Have heard of larger—who shall say
How large these unseen pearls have been?
I don't believe in things unseen.
I hear there's one now at Zèbou
That dwarfs a bird's egg, and outshines
The full moon in its purity.
What say you, is the story true?
And what's the pearl called? Let me see—
The Pearl of all the Philippines."
'Twas at Manilla, and the three
Sat in a shaded gallery
That looked upon the river, where
All sorts of sailing boats all day
Went skimming round, like gulls at play,
And made a busy picture there.

The speaker was—what no one knew,
Except a merchant: Jew with Jew,
A Turk with Turks, Parsee, Hindoo,
But still to one religion true,
And that was Trade: a pleasant guest,
Who, knowing many things, knew best
What governs men, for he was one
Whom many trusted, trusting none.
His host, Relempago, who heard
His questions with an inward shock,
Looked up, but answered not a word.
He was a native Tagaloc;
A man that was not past his prime,
And yet was old before his time.
His face was sad, his hair was gray,
His eyes on something far away.
His wife was younger, and less sad;
A Spanish woman, she was clad
As are the Tagal women; fair,
With all her dark abundant hair,
That was a wonder to behold,
Drawn from her face with pins of gold.
"You have not seen it, I perceive,"
Said the pearl merchant; "nor have I.
I'd have to see it to believe,
And then would rather have you by.
There's no such pearl." "You spoke of me,"
After a pause his host began:
"Yes, I was once a fisherman,
And loved, though now I hate, the sea.
'Twas twenty—thirty years ago,
And this good lady by my side
Had not been many moons the bride
Of poor but proud Relempago.
That I was poor she did not care,

She let me love her—loved again.
She comes of the best blood of Spain;
There is no better any where.
You see what *I* am. As I said,
I cast my bread upon the sea,
Or from the sea I drew my bread,
What matter, so it came to me?
We loved, were young, our wants were few:
The happiest pair in all Zèbou!
At last a child, and what before
Seemed happiness was more and more
The thing it seemed, the dream come true.
You smile: I see you never knew
A father's pleasure in a child."
"Pardon, my friend, I never smiled;
I am a father. I have three
Sweet troubles that are dear to me."
"But ours was not a trouble, no,"
Said simple, good Relempago.
"It was the sweetest, dearest child;
So beautiful, so gay, so wild,
And yet so sensitive and shy,
And given to sudden, strange alarms:
I've seen it in its mother's arms,
Bubbling with laughter, stop and sigh.
It was like neither in the face,
For we are dark, and that was fair;
An infant of another race,
That, born not in their dwelling-place,
Left some poor woman childless there!
A bird that to our nest had flown,
A pearl that in our shell had grown,
We cherished it with double care.
It came to us as legend says
(I know not if the tale be true)

Another child in other days
Came hither to depart no more,
Found one bright morning on the shore,
The Infant Jesus of Zèbou."
"So you, too, had," the merchant said,
With just a touch of quiet scorn,
"What shall I say—a Krishna born?
But with no halo round its head.
What did you name the boy?" "A girl,
Not boy, and therefore dearer, sweeter,
We called the infant Margarita,
For was she not our precious Pearl?
You, who have children, as you say,
Can guess how much we loved the child,
Watching her growth from day to day,
Grave if she wept, but if she smiled
Delighted with her. We were told
That we grew young as she grew old.
I used to make long voyages,
Before she came, in distant seas,
But now I never left Zèbou,
For there the great pearl-oysters grew,
(And still may grow, for aught I know,
I speak of twenty years ago.)
Though waves were rough and winds were high,
And fathoms down the sea was dark,
And there was danger from the shark,
I shrank from nothing then, for I
Was young and bold and full of life,
And had at home a loving wife,
A darling child, who ran to me,
Stretching her hands out when I came,
And kissed my cheek, and lisped my name,
And sat for hours upon my knee.
What happier sight was there to see?

What happier life was there to be?
I lived, my little Pearl, in thee!
O, mother! why did I begin?"
He stopped, and closed his eyes with pain,
Either to keep his tears therein,
Or bring that Vision back again.
"You tell him."
"Sir," the lady said,
"My husband bids me tell the tale.
One day the child began to ail;
Its little cheek was first too red,
And then it was too deathly pale.
It burned with fever; inward flame
Consumed it, which no wind could cool;
We bathed it in a mountain pool,
And it was burning all the same.
The next day it was cold—so cold
No fire could warm it. So it lay,
Not crying much, too weak to play,
And looking all the while so old.
So fond, too, of its father, he,
Good man, was more to it than I:
The moment his light step drew nigh
It would no longer stay with me.
I said to him, 'The child will die.'
But he declared it should not be."
"'Tis true," Relempago replied:
"I felt if Margarita died
My heart was broken. And I said,
'She shall not die till I have tried
Once more to save her.' What to do?
Then something put into my head
The Infant Jesus of Zèbou.
'I'll go to him: the Child Divine
Will save this only child of mine.

I will present him with a pearl,
And he will spare my little girl,
The largest pearl that I can find,
The one that shall delight his mind.
The purest, best, I give to you,
O Infant Jesus of Zèbou!'
'Twas morning when I made the vow,
And well do I remember now
How light my heart was as I ran
Down to the sea, a happy man!
All that I passed along the way,
The woods around me and above
The plaintive cooing of the dove,
The rustling of the hidden snake,
The wild ducks swimming in the lake,
The hideous lizards large as men,
Nothing, I think, escaped me then,
And nothing will escape to-day.
I reached the shore, untied my boat,
Sprang in, and was again afloat
Upon the wild and angry sea,
That must give up its pearls to me,
Its pearl of pearls! But where to go?
West of the island of Bojo,
Some six miles off, there was a view
Of the cathedral of Zèbou,
Beneath whose dome the Child Divine
Was waiting for that pearl of mine.
Thither I went, and anchored; there
Dived fathoms down, found rocks and sands,
But no pearl-oysters anywhere,
And so came up with empty hands.
Twice, thrice, and—nothing! 'Cruel sea!
Where hast thou hid thy pearls from me?
But I will have them, nor depart

Until I have them, for my heart
Would break, and my dear child would die.
She shall not die! What was that cry?
Only the eagle's scream on high.
Fear not, Relempago!' Once more,
Down, down, along the rocks and sands
I groped in darkness, tore my hands,
And rose with nothing, as before.
'O Infant Jesus of Zèbou!
I promised a great pearl to you:
Help me to find it.' Down again,
It seemed forever, whirled and whirled;
The deep foundations of the world
Engulfed me and my mortal pain;
But not forever, for the sea
That swallowed would not harbor me.
I rose again, I saw the sun,
I felt my dreadful task was done.
My desperate hands had wrenched away
A great pearl-oyster from its bed,
And brought it to the light of day;
Its ragged shell was dripping red,
They bled so then. But all was well,
For in the hollow of that shell
The pearl, pear-shaped and perfect, lay.
My child was saved. No need to tell
How I rejoiced, and how I flew
To the cathedràl of Zèbou;
For there the Infant Jesus stands,
And holds my pearl up in his hands."
He ended. The pearl merchant said,
"You found your daughter better?" "No,"
The wife of poor Relempago
Replied. "He found his daughter dead."
"'Twas fate," he answered. "No," said she,

"'Twas God. He gave the child to me;
He took the child, and He knew best:
He reached, and took it from my breast,
And in His hand to-day it shines,
The Pearl of all the Philippines!"

——o——

WRATISLAW.

Of all the songs that have been sung,
Of all the tales that have been told,
One never wearies, young or old,
Nor has since this old world was young—
The tale, the song that celebrates
That fiery something in the breast
Which makes man do his worst and best,
And underlies his loves and hates,
The basis of the iron will
That is wrought up at once to kill,
Nor cares whose heart's blood it may spill.
Such strength is grand, no doubt, but still
There is a stronger and a better,
That strikes no blow and knows no fetter,
Yet makes its stubborn sinews bend,
And overcomes it in the end.
The strength of weakness, which above
The angels call the might of love,
And bow to with adoring awe,
As did the little Wratislaw.

Where now the Servian and the Turk,
Born foes, as slave and master are,
Are at their grim old murderous work,
Grappling in most unequal war,

Six hundred years ago, or more,
The land was wasted, as to-day,
Overrun, as when the shore gives way
And the wild waves devour the shore,
By Tartar tribes as wild as they,
The barbarous horde of Genghis Khan,
Who scourged mankind as never man
Before or since, as if he were
Hell-sent to pitch his dark pavilions
Upon the grave of slaughtered millions,
And make the earth a sepulchre!
Down from the steppes of Tartary
His countless thousands swept for years,
His long-haired horsemen with their spears,
His bowmen with their arrows keen;
Such pitiless fiends were never seen
Till then, and worst of all was he,
Destruction's self whose iron tread
Shook kingdoms: peaceful peoples lay
Secure before him in Cathay;
He passed that way and they were dead.
Across the swift, swollen winter rivers,
Across the hot, parched summer sands,
With bended bows and bristling quivers,
And spears and scymetars in their hands,
Rushed Tartar, Mongol, Turkoman,
To do the bidding of Genghis Khan,
Through Russia, Poland, down to where
Morava is; they halted there.
Before they came there was—if not
Perpetual peace, which nowhere reigns,
So darkly Nature shapes our ends—
There still were times when men forgot
They had been foes, and might be friends,
Having the same blood in their veins.

Princes and peoples prospered. Now—
How do we track the savage sea,
When its spent waves no longer roar,
But by their ravage of the shore
Whose once tall cliffs have ceased to be?
Such was the track of Genghis Khan,
Who from his boyhood overran
The lands, and made their rulers bow
To his imperious will, or whim,
As if the world belonged to him.
Temples and towers were trampled down,
Were pillaged, and were set on fire:
Pagoda, mosque, and Christian spire,
The great walled city, little town,
The herdsman's hut, the monarch's hall,
He pillaged and destroyed them all:
Nor stayed the hands of his rough horde
Who put their dwellers to the sword,
The soldier fighting on the wall,
The old, old man with snow-white hair,
Mothers with children at the breast,
Virgins—but let thy curtain fall,
Oblivion, and conceal the rest!
The work of death was never done,
For everywhere along their track
Were flights of vultures; everywhere
The wolves came trooping from their lair,
Came famished, and went glutted back.
The smoke of battle dimmed the sun,
And darkness like a funeral pall
Was on the ruins, all were black
Save when the embers smouldered red:
It was as if the Earth were dead,
And they heaped ashes on her head!
They halted in Morava. Nay,

They were defeated there and then,
By Slavic chiefs and Slavic men,
Warriors more desperate than they,
Whose spears and lances cleft their way
To where their horsemen were at bay,
And horse and rider rolled in dust,
And whose sharp swords with lightning thrust,
Ringing on helmet, armor, shield,
Pierced, clove, until they turned and fled,
And left them masters of the field
Piled with a hundred thousand dead!

This Sir Berka, valiant knight,
Though too old for combat now,
From his castle on the height
Saw, and hungered for the fight,
Saw, but with an anxious brow.
All that day and all the morrow
On his battlements he stood,
Now in joy, and now in sorrow,
Gazing on the distant wood,
In whose depths, like frightened deer,
He saw the Tartars disappear.
Sitting at the old man's side,
But no help to the old man,
Was Ludmilla, once his pride,
Wife of his first-born, his Jan,
Jan, who girt on his good sword,
And pursued the flying horde;
Who returned not with his train,
To the castle gates again,
And who was not with the slain!
She was gazing on his track,
And her heart was sore afeard,
For the Tartars disappeared,

And her husband came not back!
There was yet another one
Clinging to Sir Berka's side,
Wratislaw, his youngest son,
Who his sorrow strove to hide,
For some one must be brave, he saw,
And cheer his father, poor, old man,
Whose heart had gone out after Jan,
And had forgotten Wratislaw.
A piece of childhood, for, in sooth,
One might not call the lad a youth;
The suns of twelve short summers had shed
Their light upon his little head,
Upon the golden locks that shone
With greater glory than their own;
The flowers of twelve short springs had come
And looked upon him, like the sun,
And seen their loveliness outdone
By something in his pensive face:
Perhaps it was his winning grace,
Perhaps its might of martyrdom;
For there was that about the boy,
Young as he was, and slight of frame,
Which only tenderness could tame,
And only death destroy.
Such was the child, and such the fire
That in his fair, frail body burned,
As he beheld the wasted land;
He sighed, but wept not, for his sire
Hated the sight of tears; he turned
And shut them back, and kissed his hand.

There are seasons, hours of dread,
When something must be done or said;
Hearts bear much, but their tense chords

Must be touched, or they will break.
Nature then, for sorrow's sake,
Smites its silence into words.
The woman's heart was here the first
That into lamentation burst,
And thus the pale Ludmilla spake :
" Ah, my hero, ah, my Jan,
Dearest husband, princely man,
Woe to thy poor wife, to me,
Who have lost my sons with thee!
Woe to thy forefathers' land,
Whose bright star hath set with thine ;
It hath now nor head nor hand,
The strongest is as weak as mine.
O, that we have lived to pray
As we must on this dark day,
For we cannot be comforted
But by the thought that thou art dead.
Bitter comfort, dreadful prayer,
Death to thee, to us despair!
But better so, if so it be,
Far better thou wert in thy grave
Than living captive and a slave :
But none can make a slave of thee ;
Slaves die a thousand deaths a day,
Thou hast but one death, Jan, and I,
Thy childless widow, bid thee die,
And I will follow!" "Sister, nay,"
Said Wratislaw, and stole to her,
" There is a better Comforter."

Sir Berka was the last to speak,
And bitter were the words he said,
And piteous were the tears he shed,
For tears would come, and all the same

When brushed away they came and came.
"What have I done, Lord, to arouse
Thine anger on our ancient house?
For thou art angry, sure, with me.
Why are its deep foundations shaken?
Why is its last strong pillar taken?
Why am I thus in age forsaken?
Lord God! what have I done to thee?
Behold me here, a broken man,
For they have taken my hero, Jan,
Who should my feeble hands sustain,
And plant my name and race again!
Calamities have fallen before
Upon my house, but not another
Like unto this, and nevermore
Can this befall, for none remain;
For what is *she*, and what am *I?*
A weeping woman, not a mother,
And an old man, soon to die!"

The young child, Wratislaw, till now
Had kept his tears back, inly grieved
To see his father so bereaved;
But now they gushed, and his pale brow
Flushed for his brother's childless wife
Who by his father's taunt was stung,
And for himself, for he, though young,
Would not be blotted out of life,
Even by his father's evil tongue.
So with a hurt, proud look he said,
"O father! wherefore dost thou say
That thy great stem is broken—dead,
Because one branch is torn away?
True, Jan is gone, but Jan lives still,
And Wratislaw is still with thee;

It is his duty now to be
What the brave Jan was, and to fill,
Till he returns, his vacant place,
And so uphold the name and race."
Sir Berka answered not, but smiled,
A smile that was not good to see,
Then, turning to his daughter, he:
"The spirit of his ancestry
Flames up a moment in the child,
Crackles in words, but words are wild,
For deeds, not words, are wanted now.
To think this weakling sprung from me,
This slip from our ancestral tree!
He has his mother's eye and face,
And he repeats her saintly race,
Not mine, by Heaven! his woman's hand
Will never bear the battle brand,
It may the censer; he shall be
A servant in some pious place,
And pray for me with shaven brow;
And if I live—but I shall die,
He shall prepare me for the sky!"
The child a moment crouching low,
For every word had been a blow
That smote his heart, started at length,
And rose up in his boyish strength:
"My lord and father, we are taught,
By holy men in Holy Writ,
The boasted strength of man is naught,
Unless the Lord sustaineth it."
"Peace! I have heard the words before,
And I will hear the words no more;
They will not rescue my poor Jan
From the claw of Genghis Khan!"
Sadly, but proudly, Wratislaw,

Whose courage in his clear blue eye
Shot like a falcon through the sky,
Answered, but with a voice of awe,
"God's ways are not the ways of man,
For when He wills the weak are strong:
And, father, thou hast done me wrong;
But thou my face no more shall see,
For, though the sword I cannot draw,
I will go find my brother Jan.
Farewell; he will return with me."

Before Sir Berka could reply
The boy had gone, but none knew where,
Had vanished, like a flying hare
That in an instant flashes by.
They sought him here, they sought him there,
They rode, they ran, like hounds in cry,
But nowhere found a trace of him;
For how he vanished no man saw,
So swift the steed, and strong of limb—
If steed he saddled for the flight
That swept him from his father's sight.
Sir Berka was a woeful man;
Before he had but lost his Jan,
Now he had lost his Wratislaw!
He cursed his wild, unpitying mood,
He cursed his dark and savage heart
That now against itself took part,
Because too late it understood
How dear the boy was, and how good.
He loved him now, if not before,
But he had always loved him, yes,
And hungered for his fond caress,
And now he loved him more and more.

Sir Berka was an altered man,
Whether he sat within his hall,
Or wandered slowly round his lands;
His wrinkled features grew more wan,
More white his hair that used to fall
So darkly down his shoulders; all
The man was shaken, most his hands,
That scarce could carve his meat, and raise
The wine cup to his withered lips;
He had no hope of better days,
A strong soul setting in eclipse.
Darkly Sir Berka's days were spent,
Darkly the seasons came and went;
Whether the flowers of spring were growing,
Whether the summer fruits were glowing,
Whether the autumn winds were blowing,
Whether the winter sky was snowing,
He knew not, cared not; all he saw
Was nothing to this lonely man,
Since tidings there were none of Jan,
And none of Wratislaw!
He had but one strong hold of life,
That poor, weak, fading, childless wife,
Whose pardon twenty times a day
He begged, whose dear head he caressed,
And closely to his bosom pressed,
Lest she, too, should be torn away.

One day, as thus disconsolate
Sir Berka sat within his hall,
A stranger rode up to the wall,
And halted at the castle gate:
A stalwart figure came in sight,
Of whom, if one but marked his height,

The noble carriage of his head,
He would—he must at once have said,
The stranger is a valiant knight.
He looked at first a Christian man,
But one who journeyed from afar,
And Christian armor surely wore,
But closer like a Tartar khan,
For he was dark or tanned, and bore,
As the khans did, a scymetar.
He strode—he seemed to know the way—
Straight through the castle to the door
That opened in Sir Berka's hall;
He strode between him and the day
That smote his shadow on the floor,
Weaponed, and broad, and tall.
He kneeled down at the old man's chair,
And at his childless daughter's feet,
Whose startled heart did strangely beat,
As if a ghost were there!
"Who is this kneeling, silent man?"
"O father, it is Jan!"
Who will may paint this, or may try,
I will go on, and tell the rest;
The secrets of the human breast
Are not for every curious eye.
Pass over, then, the shock of meeting,
Sir Berka's and Ludmilla's greeting,
And see the son and husband seated
Between his father and his wife,
Holding a hand in each hard palm,
Erect, and resolute, and calm.
They asked the story of his life
Since that destructive, glorious hour
That broke the dreaded Tartar's power.
This is the story he repeated:

"You stood upon the battlement
That day and watched the way I went;
You saw a portion of the fight;
The Tartars fled, and we pursued
Pell-mell behind the multitude,
And harried their disastrous flight.
They fled like hares, in such dismay
That had we numbered man for man
There would not be a Tartar clan
Upon the earth to-day!
But one fled not, but stood at bay,
With ten or twelve brave fellows more,
All horsemen; by the garb he wore
He should have been a khan.
He rode at me, and I at him,
We fought like men who fight to die,
Not careless, though, of life or limb,
But with a wary eye.
I smote his helmet off, and might
Have cloven his Tartar skull in twain,
But when I saw his hair was white,
I could not strike him,—wrong, perchance,
But I would do the like again.
He smiled, and shot a lightning glance
Full in my face, but never stirred;
He waved his hand without a word,
And in an instant I was bound,
Tied hand and foot upon my horse,
And borne, as all were borne along,
For now the panic was so strong
That nothing could withstand its force.
It was not long before I found
That old, bare-headed, white-haired man
I *should* have slain was Genghis Khan!
At first I knew the way they fled,

The woods they pierced, the streams they crossed,
The mountain passes and defiles;
But when one flees a thousand miles,
And sees strange starlight overhead,
The knowledge of his path is lost.
I only knew, or cared to know,
That they were driven back, and back,
That they were harried on their track,
That thousands perished in the snow;
I thanked the Lord God it was so!
I suffered somewhat, but you see
It did not make an end of me,
For, father, here I am with thee,
With thee, Ludmilla." Neither spake,
For fear, perhaps, their tears would break,
Their full hearts overflow.
"At last we reached the Tartar land,
The kingdom that is Genghis Khan's,
The remnant of a thousand clans,
But still a mighty band.
Pass lightly over them and him,
For they were sullen, he was grim,
And had a hasty hand.
Pass lightly over what came next,
As over a dream that long perplexed
The short hours of the night, and fled,
And left the morning in its stead,
And me—not as it threatened, dead,
But living, as I am to-day.
For God the Lord is strong to save
The hearts that trust him; only say
That I was there a slave.
You know what that is, you have seen
Those who have Tartar captives been,
But never one, I think, like me;

Or so, at least, thought Genghis Khan.
Dark man! he knew enough of man
To know that I was free,
And would be, though in chains, until
Death or deliverance came; his will
Was met and matched by mine; so he—
He went his way, and I went mine.
He never saw me peak and pine,
Nor heard me sigh for rest.
I thought to fill a Tartar grave
Were better than to live—a slave,
But God knew better, He knew best.
I was not wholly downcast; I
Believed the day and hour would come
(May Heaven forgive me if I lie!)
When I should rise, and journey home
And be with you—I was in heart;
There was no day, there was no hour
But I was here; no earthly power
Could keep our souls apart!
I saw you as I see you now,
With fewer furrows on your brow,
Father; and you, Ludmilla, saw,
And my young brother, Wratislaw,
His frank blue eyes, his yellow hair,
There never was a child so fair!
I think we never understood
How brave he was, as brave as good."
Sir Berka groaned, Ludmilla sighed;
But Jan went on, with tender pride:
"I loved the boy; my own dear son—
If God had pleased to send me one—
Could not have dearer been than he,
The flower of all our family!
Night after night I dreamed of him,

Bright dreams that did till morning last;
At length they lessened and were dim,
At last they vanished in the past.
Then suddenly I was aware,
Still in my dreams that sadder grew,
That something, some one followed me,
Some one did day and night pursue;
It might be beast, it might be man,
The face, the form I could not see,
Nor knew I when it was, or where:
And once my name was shouted, '*Jan!*'
This happened many moons ago,
When mountain sides were white with snow,
And I was slave to Genghis Khan.
One day he summoned me; I went,
And found him in his battle tent,
Girt round by bowmen; there I saw—
Great God!—my brother Wratislaw!
The grim, old king looked up and smiled.
'Come here, my slave, beside this child;
Behold how pale he is, how weak,
His wasted form, his sunken cheek;
He says he is your brother, says
He comes to get your freedom,—*he*
Who sees the end of all his days
Is nigh, death waiting, comes to *me*,
Offers himself to be my slave,
If I will set you free.
Slavonian, speak, I know you brave.
Would you advise this less than man
(Support him, for he faints you see,)
To be the slave of Genghis Khan?'
My brother proudly raised his head,
And with a flashing eye he said,
'Look not upon my wasted frame,

For thine will one day be the same,
But think, remember how I came,
Over mountain, over plain,
Where thy flying clans were slain,
Where unburied they remain;
From far Morava to thy throne
I came, but did not come alone,
For God was with me, led my hand,
Guided the feet that bore me here,
Through Poland, Russia, Tartar land;
Six moons of travel for a man,
Through ways a man might fear.
Now listen, therefore, Genghis Khan,
For God speaks through me and to thee:
Thou art to set my brother free,
I am to be thy slave!
The youngest I, the oldest he;
A man with one foot in the grave
Our father, with no son but Jan,
My brother, who is wed to one
That loves him, but has borne no son;
He must return, and I remain.
But hear, O Genghis Khan, again,
If thou refuse, what will be done:
Thou hast seven sons, and all men say
That they are what thy sons should be;
But thou shalt see them fade away
In seven short months, and from to-day,
But not if Jan is free.'
Seven long, dark days of dread suspense,
Days, ages that would not depart,
Interminable and intense,
That almost broke my heart—
I could not suffer more—
Then I was summoned, as before,

By Genghis Khan, who thus began:
'Slavonian, I have sent for you,
For you have done what few have dared,
Fought hand to hand with Genghis Khan,
Who, when he sees him, knows a man,
And, fighting, knows if he is brave;
It was for this your life was spared,
And you were made a slave.
I have subdued, and can subdue.
It suits me now to set you free,
Not for yourself, but for your brother,
For I have never seen another
That was as brave as he.
I have seven brothers, but not one
Would do for me what he has done;
I have seven sons, but not a son
Would do the same for me:
I would not do it for any man,
And not for God—if God there be—
For I am Genghis Khan!
But for that boy, that tender bird
That from his nest should not have stirred,
Too stout of heart, too weak of wing,
Methinks I would do anything.
Take him, and go. Through all my land
I have sent word that you are free;
Return to peace and happiness;
Depart, and think no more of me!'
I knelt and kissed—I could no less—
His world-dividing hand."
"And Wratislaw?" "But you shall hear.
They brought me armor, *mine*, you see,
And that great helmet shagged with hair,
And from his own side Genghis Khan
Took off the scymetar I wear;

They girt it on me—I was free!
Two steeds were brought me to pursue
My long, long journey back to you.
I rode, for all the ways were clear,
I rode and rode, as if for life,
And here I am, the same old Jan."
"But Wratislaw?" He rose up then,
And led his father and his wife
Straight to the casement, whence they saw
In the court-yard two Tartar steeds,
And his squire holding them: like reeds
They trembled, for two serving-men
Bore something forward—Wratislaw?
No, no, it was not *he* they bore
With slow steps through the castle gate,
And up the stairs, and in the hall.
It was a strong box, that was all,
Studded with knobs and bands of gold;
And it was heavy, too, to hold,
The bearers drooped beneath the weight;
An oaken chest, wherein of old
Brave Genghis Khan his treasure stored,
The crowns he had conquered with his great sword,
A treasure chest, no more.
Jan put his hand within his breast,
And then took out a curious key,
And, kneeling down where they could see,
Unlocked the treasure chest.
Yes, it *was* Wratislaw! He died
The day he found his brother Jan,
Died then, and almost at his side.
Struck with his greatness, Genghis Khan,
Whose stormy soul for once was calmed,
Had the dear body then embalmed.
It was his body that they saw,

The treasure there was Wratislaw!
They stood and looked at one another,
Like men whose days are nearly done:
"I thank thee, God, for such a brother!"
"I thank thee, God, for such a son!"
How beautiful he was! The child
Was lovelier than in life: his face
Had caught a more than earthly grace;
It was as if an angel smiled,
But a strong angel, one whose might
Was manifested there in light,
To which the light of day was dim.
Yes, it was Wratislaw who slept
In the rich chest of Genghis Khan.
His promise had been kept,
For he had found his brother Jan,
And Jan had now returned with him.

THE DEAD MASTER.

It is appointed unto man to die.
Where Life is Death is, dominating Life,
Wresting the sceptre from its feeble grasp,
And trampling on its dust. From the first hour
When the first child upon its mother's breast
Lay heavily, with no breath on its cold lips,
To the last hour when the last man shall die,
And the race be extinct—Death never came,
Nor ever will come, without apprehension.
The dying may be ready to depart,
For sleep and death are one to them; but we

Who love them, and survive them—unto whom
The places they once filled are filled no more,
For whom a light has gone out of the sun,
A shadow fallen on noonday, unto us,
Who love our dead, Death always comes too soon,
A consternation, and a lamentation,
The sorrow of all sorrows, till in turn
We follow them, and others mourn for us.

This tragic lesson of mortality
The Master who hath left us learned in youth,
When the Muse found him wandering by the stream
That sparkled, singing, at his father's door—
The first Muse whom the New World, loving long,
Wooed in the depths of her old solitude.
The green, untrodden, world-wide wilderness
Surrendered to the soul of this young man
The secret of its silence. Centuries passed;
The red man chased the deer, and tracked the bear
To his high mountain den—but he came not.
The white man followed; the great woods were felled,
And in the clearings cottage smokes arose,
And fields were white with harvests: he came not.
The New World waited for him, and the words
Which should disburden the dumb mystery
That darkened its strange life, when summer days
Steeped the green boughs with light, and winter nights
Looked down like Death upon the dead, old world;
For what was Earth but the great tomb of man,
And suns and planets but sepulchral urns
Filled with the awful ashes of the Past?

Such was the first sad message to mankind
Of this young poet, who was never young,
So heavily the old burden of the Earth

Weighed on his soul from boyhood. Yet not less,
Not less, but more he loved her; for if she
Was sombre with her secret she was still
Beautiful as a goddess; and if he
Should one day look upon her face no more,
He would not cease to look till that day came:
For he for life was dedicate to her,
The inspiration of his earliest song,
The happy memory of his sterner years,
The consolation of his ripe, old age.
What she was to the eyes of lesser men,
Which only glance at the rough husk of things,
She never was to him;—but day and night
A loveliness, a might, a mystery,
A Presence never wholly understood,
The broken shadow of some unknown Power,
Which overflows all forms, but is not Form—
The inscrutable Spirit of the Universe!
High-priest whose temple was the woods, he felt
Their melancholy grandeur, and the awe
That ancientness and solitude beget,
Strange intimations of invisible things,
Which, while they seem to sadden, give delight,
And hurt not, but persuade the soul to prayer:
For, silent in the barren ways of men,
Under green roofs of overhanging boughs,
Where the Creator's hands are never stayed,
The soul recovers her forgotten speech,
The lost religion of her infancy.

Nature hath sacred seasons of her own,
And reverent poets to interpret them.
But she hath other singers, unto whom
The twinkle of a dew-drop in the grass,
The sudden singing of an unseen bird,

The pensive brightness of the evening star,
Are revelations of a loveliness
For which there is no language known to man,
Except the eloquent language of the eye,
Hushed with the fulness of her happiness.
What may be known of these recondite things
Our grave, sweet poet knew: for unto him
The Goddess of the Earth revealed herself
As to no other poet of the time,
Save only him who slumbers at Grasmere,
His Brother,—not his Master. From the hour
When first he wandered by his native stream
To crop the violets growing on its banks,
And list to the brown thrasher's vernal hymn,
To the last hour of his long, honored life,
He never faltered in his love of Nature.
Recluse with men, her dear society,
Welcome at all times, savored of content,
Brightened his happy moments, and consoled
His hours of gloom. A student of the woods
And of the fields, he was their calendar,
Knew when the first pale wind-flower would appear,
And when the last wild-fowl would take its flight;
Where the cunning squirrel had his granary,
And where the industrious bee had stored her sweets.
Go where he would, he was not solitary,
Flowers nodded gayly to him, wayside brooks
Slipped by him laughingly, while the emulous birds
Showered lyric raptures that provoked his own.
The winds were his companions on the hills—
The clouds, and thunders—and the glorious Sun,
Whose bright beneficence sustains the world,
A visible symbol of the Omnipotent,
Whom not to worship were to be more blind
Than those of old who worshipped stocks and stones.

Who loves and lives with Nature tolerates
Baseness in nothing; high and solemn thoughts
Are his, clean deeds and honorable life.
If he be poet, as our Master was,
His song will be a mighty argument,
Heroic in its structure to support
The weight of the world forever! All great things
Are native to it, as the Sun to Heaven.
Such was thy song, O Master! and such fame
As only the kings of thought receive, is thine;
Be happy with it in thy larger life
Where Time is not, and the sad word—Farewell!

——o——

HYMN TO THE SEA.

If there is nothing sure but the unsure,
Which is at once its cradle and its grave,
Creative and destructive, hand that molds,
And feet that trample, instruments of Change,
Which is itself the instrument of Power:
If these, our bodies, conscious of themselves,
And cognizable by others like themselves,
Waste and supply their forces day by day,
Till there is nothing left of what they were,
The whole man being re-made from head to foot;
How comes it then, I say, that standing here
Beside the waters of this quiet bay,
Which welter shoreward, roughened by the wind,
Twinkling in sunshine, I am the same man
Who gazed upon them thirty years ago,
Lulled by their placid motion, and the sense
Of something happy they begat in me?

I saunter by the shore and lose myself
In the blue waters, stretching on, and on,

Beyond the low-lying headland, dark with woods,
And on to the green waste of sea, content
To be alone—but I am not alone,
For solitude like this is populous,
And its abundant life of sky and sun,
High-floating clouds, low mists, and wheeling birds,
And waves that ripple shoreward all day long,
Whether the tide is setting in or out,
Forever rippling shoreward, dark and bright,
As lights and shadows and the shifting winds
Pursue each other in their endless play,
Is more than the companionship of man.

I know our inland landscapes, pleasant fields,
Where lazy cattle browse, and chew the cud;
The smooth declivities of quiet vales:
The swell of uplands, and the stretch of woods,
Within whose shady places Solitude
Holds her perpetual court. They touch me not,
Or only touch me in my shallowest moods,
And leave no recollection. They are naught.
But thou, O Sea, whose majesty and might
Are mild and beautiful in this still bay,
But terrible in the mid-ocean deeps,
I never see thee but my soul goes out
To thee, and is sustained and comforted;
For she discovers in herself, or thee,
A stern necessity for stronger life,
And strength to live it: she surrenders all
She had, and was, and is possessed of more,
With more to come—endurance, patience, peace.

I love thee, Ocean, and delight in thee,
Thy color, motion, vastness,—all the eye
Takes in from shore, and on the tossing waves;

Nothing escapes me, not the least of weeds
That shrivels and blackens on the barren sand.
I have been walking on the yellow sands,
Watching the long, white, ragged fringe of foam
The waves had washed up on the curves of beach,
The endless fluctuation of the waves,
The circuit of the sea-gulls, low, aloft,
Dipping their wings an instant in the brine,
And urging their swift flight to distant woods,
And round and over all the perfect sky,
Clear, cloudless, luminous in the summer noon.

I have been sitting on the stern, gray rocks,
That push their way up from the under-world,
And shoulder the waves aside, and musing there
The sea of Time has ebbed with me, and I,
Borne backward with it, have beheld the Past,
Times, places, generations, all that was
From the infancy of Earth. The primitive race,
That skulked in caves, and wore the skin of beasts:
Shepherds and herdsmen, whose nomadic tents
Were pitched by river-banks in pasture-lands,
Where no man was before them; husbandmen,
Who shaped out for themselves rude implements
Of tillage, and for whom the Earth brought forth
The first of harvests, happy when the sheaves
Were gathered in, for robber-bands were near—
Horsemen with spears, who seized their flocks and herds,
And led their wives and children captive—all
Save those who perished fighting sold as slaves!
Rapine and murder triumph. I behold
The shock of armies in forgotten fields,
The flight of arrows, aud the flash of swords,
Shields pierced, and helmets cloven, and hosts gone down
Behind the scythèd chariots: cities girt

By grim, beleaguering, formidable foes,
With battering-rams that breach the tottering walls,
And crush the gaunt defenders ; mailèd men
That ride against each other and are unhorsed
Where lances shiver and the dreadful sweep
Of the battle-ax makes havoc : thunderous guns
Belching destruction through the sulphurous cloud
That wraps the league-long lines of infantry ;
The charge of cavalry on hollow squares—
Sharp shots, and riderless horses! This is War,
And these are men—thy children, Earth! The Sea
Has never bred such monsters, though it swarms
With living things ; they have not overrun
Its spacious realms, and left them solitudes :
The desolation of the unfooted waves
Is not of their dark making, but of thine,
Inhospitable, barren, solemn Sea!

Thou wert before the Continents, before
The hollow heavens, which like another sea
Encircles them, and thee ; but whence thou wert,
And when thou wast created, is not known.
Antiquity was young when thou wast old.
There is no limit to thy strength, no end
To thy magnificence. Thou goest forth
On thy long journeys to remotest lands,
And comest back unwearied. Tropic isles,
Thick-set with pillared palms, delay thee not,
Nor Arctic icebergs hasten thy return.
Summer and winter are alike to thee,
The settled, sullen sorrow of the sky
Empty of light ; the laughter of the sun ;
The comfortable murmur of the wind
From peaceful countries, and the mad uproar
That storms let loose upon thee in the night

Which they create and quicken with sharp, white fire,
And crash of thunders! Thou art terrible
In thy tempestuous moods, when the loud winds
Precipitate their strength against the waves;
They rave, and grapple and wrestle, until at last,
Baffled by their own violence, they fall back,
And thou art calm again, no vestige left
Of the commotion, save the long, slow roll
In summer days on beaches far away.

The heavens look down and see themselves in thee,
And splendors, seen not elsewhere, that surround
The rising and the setting of the sun
Along thy vast and solitary realms.
The blue dominion of the air is thine,
And thine the pomps and pageants of the day,
The light, the glory, the magnificence,
The congregated masses of the clouds,
Islands, and mountains, and long promontories,
Floating at unaccessible heights whereto
Thy fathomless depths are shallow—all are thine.
And thine the silent, happy, awful night,
When over thee and thy charmed waves the moon
Rides high, and when the last of stars is gone,
And darkness covers all things with its pall—
Darkness that was before the worlds were made,
And will be after they are dead. But no,
There is no death—the thing that we call death
Is but another, sadder name for life,
Which is itself an insufficient name,
Faint recognition of that unknown Life—
That Power whose shadow is the Universe.

www.ingramcontent.com/pod-product-compliance
Lightning Source LLC
LaVergne TN
LVHW021317110826
845150LV00003B/601

* 9 7 8 1 4 2 5 5 5 7 2 1 8 *